Social Work
Theories and Methods

Mel Gray & Stephen A. Webb

SAGE

Los Angeles • London • New Delhi • Singapore • Washington DC

First published 2009

SAGE Publications Ltd
1 Oliver's Yard
55 City Road
London EC1Y 1SP

SAGE Publications Inc.
2455 Teller Road
Thousand Oaks, California 91320

SAGE Publications India Pvt Ltd
B 1/I 1 Mohan Cooperative Industrial Area
Mathura Road
New Delhi 110 044

SAGE Publications Asia-Pacific Pte Ltd
33 Pekin Street #02-01
Far East Square
Singapore 048763

Library of Congress Control Number: 2008925811

British Library Cataloguing in Publication data

A catalogue record for this book is available from
the British Library

ISBN 978-1-4129-4740-4
ISBN 978-1-4129-4741-1 (pbk)

Typeset by C&M Digitals (P) Ltd, Chennai, India
Printed in Great Britain by TJ International Ltd, Padstow, Cornwall
Printed on paper from sustainable resources

Mixed Sources
Product group from well-managed
forests and other controlled sources
www.fsc.org Cert no. SGS-COC-2482
© 1996 Forest Stewardship Council
FSC

To Penni and Dave for their patience and love

Contents

About the Editors and Contributors

The editors

Mel Gray is Professor of Social Work and Research Professor in the Centre for Social Well-being at the University of Newcastle, New South Wales, Australia. Her interests range from creativity, spirituality, values and ethics, and theory and philosophy in social work to international social work, social development and culturally relevant social work practice. This led to the edited collection (with John Coates and Michael Yellow Bird) *Indigenous Social Work around the World: Towards culturally relevant social work education and practice* (2008). She is currently working on books on social work as art, evidence-based practice and value perspectives in social work. Mel serves on the editorial board of several major social work journals including the Sage Journal of Social Work in the UK and Families in Society in the USA.

Stephen A. Webb is Professor of Human Sciences and Director of the Centre for Social Well-being at the University of Newcastle, Australia. He is author of *Social Work in a Risk Society: Social and political perspectives* (2006), which has been widely acclaimed by international commentators on social work. His early work on social work ethics was at the forefront in developing a critical perspective that challenged the narrow deontological Kantian ethics of the British Association of Social Workers' (BASW) code of practice. He is currently writing *Evidence-based Social Work: A Critical Stance* (with M. Gray) for Routledge; editing (with M. Gray) *Value Perspective in Social Work* for Palgrave and co-editor of the first collection of seminal social work texts for the four volumes *International Social Work* to be published by Sage.

The contributors (in chapter order)

Stan Houston worked as a social worker in Belfast as a practitioner, manager and trainer before taking up his current post at Queen's University Belfast in 1998. Most of his working life has been spent in child and family social work. He is interested in the application of critical social theory to social work and has concentrated on the works of Habermas, Bourdieu, Bhaskar and Honneth. More recently, he has attempted to link theoretical ideas with empirical research, particularly in relation to residential childcare.

Harry Ferguson is Professor of Social Work at the University of the West of England in Bristol, UK. He is a qualified social worker and completed his PhD in the Faculty of Social and Political Sciences at the University of Cambridge. Harry has taught, researched and published on social work and social theory, child abuse and protection, domestic violence, fatherhood, men and masculinities. His books include *Best Practice in Social Work: Critical perspectives* (with Karen Jones and Barry Cooper, 2008) and *Protecting Children in Time: Child abuse, child protection and the consequences of modernity* (2004).

Paul Michael Garrett works at the National University of Ireland in Galway, Republic of Ireland. He is the author of *Remaking Social Work with Children and Families* (2003a) and *Social Work and Irish People in Britain: Historical and contemporary responses to Irish children and families* (2004a). His work has also appeared in academic journals across a range of disciplines. For a number of years he has been a member of the editorial collective of *Critical Social Policy* (where he is Editor of the Reviews section). He is also a member of the editorial board of the *European Journal of Social Work* and is consulting editor for the US-based *Journal of Progressive Human Services*.

Allan Irving is Professor, School of Social Work, and Coordinator, Centre for Creativity at King's University College, University of Western Ontario, Canada. He teaches courses on the meanings of community, suffering, compassion and social justice and the arts and social work practice. He has published on the history of social work and social welfare in Canada, and on postmodernity and social work. With degrees in philosophy and social work, he is particularly interested in applying contemporary Continental philosophy to social work. His books include *Reading Foucault for Social Work* (co-edited with Adrienne Chambon and Laura Epstein, 1999) and *Brock Chisholm: Doctor to the world* (Fitzhenry and Whiteside, 1998).

Brid Featherstone is Professor of Social Work at the University of Bradford in the UK. She has worked as a social worker in the field of child welfare and has a particular interest in applying feminist theory to child welfare policies and practices. She is a founder member of the international network on gender and child welfare. Her publications include *Mothering and Ambivalence* (with Wendy Hollway (eds), 1997), *Practice and Research in Social Work: Postmodern feminist perspectives* (with Barbara Fawcett, Jan Fook and Amy Rossiter (eds), 2000) and *Working with Men in Health and Social Care* (with Mark Rivett and Jonathan Scourfield, 2007). She is currently writing a book on contemporary fathers.

Lorraine Green (PhD) is a researcher and lecturer in social work at the University of Manchester in the UK. Prior to this, she was a lecturer in sociology at Sheffield Hallam University. Lorraine's key research interests include gender, sexuality, child sexual and physical abuse, power, children, residential care and various combinations of these. She has recently co-written an article exploring the relationship between deaf children and resilience and another on bereavement and sexuality. She is currently working on a research project examining the support needs of groups subject to sexual and domestic violence who have hitherto been little researched, such as ethnic minorities, the lesbian gay, bisexual and trans gender (LGBT) community and heterosexual men.

Joan Orme is Professor of Social Work at the Glasgow University School of Social Work in Scotland. She has researched and written about social work practice from a number of perspectives and is co-author (with Veronica Coulshed) of *Social Work Practice* (2006), a textbook for social work. In all her work, she has explored the relationship between feminism and social work practice and research. A synthesis of this analysis, which informs her chapter in this text, can be found in *Gender and Community Care: Social work and social care perspectives* (2001).

Steven F. Hick, from the School of Social Work at Carleton University, Ottawa, Ontario, Canada, is a writer, teacher, human rights advocate and researcher. Throughout his career he has used a structural approach to social work to examine and inform his work in human rights, teaching, co-founding War Child Canada, offering mindfulness courses and doing policy and community work. Two of his books have become the standard for teaching introductory social work. His current research examines the impact, on practice, of cultivating mindfulness within social workers. He is widely published in peer-reviewed journals and books.

Kate Murray is a PhD candidate at the University of British Columbia, Vancouver, Canada. She holds an Honours Bachelor of Recreation and Leisure Studies (University of Waterloo) degree and a Masters of Social Work (Carleton University). Since 2002, Kate has undertaken research, evaluation, education and communications activities in a range of community, professional, political and academic settings. Her experience includes coordination of international, neighbourhood and community-based initiatives, as well as research on healthcare, eviction, homelessness and social services. She has developed materials for social welfare and social policy education and has critically examined structures for the inclusion of residents with low income in municipal policymaking.

Purnima Sundar is the Research and Kowledge Exchange Consultant at The Provincial Centre of Excellence for Child and Youth Mental Health at CHEO (Children's Hospital of Eastern Ontario). She has several years of experience doing academic research, program evaluation, and community-based, participatory action research in the areas of diversity/multiculturalism, youth and identity, and community mental health. Purnima also teaches courses on race and culture in the School of Social Work at Carleton University in Ottawa, Ontario, Canada.

Sue Penna is a senior lecturer in the Department of Applied Social Science at Lancaster University in the UK. She is a sociologist and qualified social worker with expertise in the role of policy in social development. She has published on various aspects of contemporary welfare reform as well as social welfare policy at the transnational level. She is currently working on the relationship between crime and welfare through the concept of 'social harm'.

Martin O'Brien is a sociologist and criminologist. He is a Reader in the Centre for Criminology and Criminal Justice at the University of Central Lancashire in the UK. He is the author (with Sue Penna) of *Theorising Welfare* (1998) and an editor (with Sue Penna and Colin Hay) of *Theorising Modernity* (1998). His most recent books include *A Crisis of Waste? Understanding the rubbish society* (2007) and (with Majid Yar) *Criminology: The key concepts* (2008). He is currently developing a research project on material culture in the criminal world.

Barbara Fawcett is Professor of Social Work and Policy Studies at the University of Sydney in Australia and Honorary Research Professor at the University of Bradford in the UK. Her recent books include *Addressing Violence, Abuse and Oppression: Debates and challenges* (with Fran Waugh (eds), 2007), *Contemporary Mental Health: Theory, policy and practice* (with Kate Karban, 2005), *Contemporary Child Care Policy and Practice* (with Brid Featherstone and Jim Goddard, 2004), *Practice and Research in Social Work* (with Brid Featherstone, Jan Fook and Amy Rossiter (eds), 2000), *Feminist Perspectives on Disability* (2000) and *Violence and Gender Relations: Theories and interventions* (with Brid Featherstone, Jeff Hearn and Chris Toft, 1996).

Deirdre M. Kirke is a senior lecturer in sociology at the National University of Ireland, Maynooth, County Kildare, Ireland. She formerly lectured at University College Dublin where she completed her B. Soc. Sc., M. Soc. Sc. and PhD. degrees. She is a member of the International Network for Social Network Analysis (INSNA), has applied a social network approach in her own research and taught social network courses at the National University of Ireland, Maynooth and University College Dublin. Her publications include her book *Teenagers and Substance Use: Social networks and peer influence* (2006) and papers in *Social Networks* and *Connections*. Her publications range across the disciplines of sociology, psychology, psychiatry and social work and one of her friendship networks is exhibited in the New York Hall of Science.

Gerald de Montigny is an Associate Professor of Social Work at Carleton University in Ottawa, Ontario, Canada. In his youth he read Karl Marx and Friedrich Engels' *The German Ideology*, which generated a preoccupation with socially organized practices. He entered social work fuelled by a desire to combine theory and practice in a politically informed praxis. He sees ethnomethodology as providing ways of working that place practice at the centre of everyday realities.

Jerry Floersch is Associate Professor at the Mandel School of Applied Social Sciences, Case Western Reserve University, Cleveland, Ohio. He is the author of *Meds, Money, and Manners: The case management of severe mental illness* (2002), where, utilizing ethnographic and sociohistorical methods, he examines the rise of community support services and the case manager and case management, and the limits of management models in providing effective services. He is currently studying the myriad ways youth make meaning of their medication treatment, including what he has called, the social and psychological side-effects of psychiatric medication (for more background, see: http://msass.case.edu/faculty/jfloersch/index.html).

Jeffrey Longhofer, PhD, LISW, is Associate Professor at the Mandel School of Applied Social Sciences in Cleveland, Ohio and Adjunct Associate Professor of Anthropology and Clinical Instructor in Psychiatry at Case Western Reserve University. He has worked as an academic and applied anthropologist in areas related to health and mental health practice and the cross-cultural study of mental illness. He has served as editor and associate editor of journals for the American Anthropological Association and the Society for Applied Anthropology. He has also served on the editorial board of the *International Journal of Psychoanalysis* (for more background, see: http://msass.case.edu/faculty/jlonghofer/index.html).

Megan Nordquest Schwallie is a graduate student in the AM/PhD combined programme at the School of Social Service Administration, University of Chicago, USA. Previously, she earned her masters degree in medical anthropology from Case Western Reserve University, Cleveland, Ohio. Her interests include community mental health and the use of ethnographic methods to investigate children and adolescents' experiences of health and illness, including their perceptions and methods of care and treatment.

Sue White is Professor of Social Work at Lancaster University in the UK. Her primary research interest is in ethnographic and discourse analytic studies of clinical and professional decision-making and, particularly, professional talk. She has recently completed an Economic and Social Research Council-funded ethnographic study of electronic information sharing in multidisciplinary child welfare practice and is Principal Investigator on a further ESRC Public Services Programme study of 'error and blame' in child welfare practice. This latest study focuses on the relationship between the performance management of public services responsible for safeguarding children and the impact of anticipated blame within the decision-making practices of those providing, supervising and managing these services.

Debbie Plath (BA, BSW, MSW, PhD) is a senior lecturer in social work at the University of Newcastle, New South Wales, Australia. She has been a social work educator at Newcastle since 1992 and has published on experience-based education in social work. Her interest in evidence-based practice stems from a commitment to engaging in research that is useful and relevant to social work practitioners. Her research spans a range of social work practice fields, including ageing, family violence and single session social work in hospitals.

Ian Shaw chairs the Graduate Board in the Department of Social Policy and Social Work at the University of York in the UK. His interests, research and writing are clustered around the borders of research, methodology and practice, in which he has published fairly extensively. He founded and co-edits the journal *Qualitative Social Work* and is currently co-editing the Sage *Handbook of Social Work Research*.

Acknowledgements

Like all books, this one would not have been possible without the support, inspiration and expertise of a great many people. We would like to thank them all warmly, but will name only those to whom were are particularly grateful. First and foremost we would like to thank all the chapter authors for their first rate contributions. It was a great pleasure working with such a stimulating and talented group of researchers. We are also grateful to the staff at Sage, Susannah Trefgarne, Anne Birtchell, Anna Luker, Zoe Elliott-Fawcett and Imogen Roome for their valuable support and encouragement throughout the project. And finally we want to acknowledge our deep gratitude to our partners; Stephen would like to thank Penni, and Mel, Dave. We are indebted to them for their continuing support, patience, kindness and love. Stephen would also like to thank the social work students at University of Sussex who worked as collaborators and constructive critics in the early formulation of the ideas behind the book.

Introduction

Mel Gray and Stephen A. Webb

Ways of thinking about social work

One can think about social work in a number of ways. The simplest way to think about it is as a group of practical interventions that try to improve situations in people's lives. In trying to help people improve their situations, social workers are often required to follow legal procedures or policy guidelines that prescribe what they should or should not do under certain circumstances. This way of thinking about social work is based on making positive changes in people's lives that are either prescribed or not. From this perspective, social work is 'the difference that makes a difference' for people.

A second way to think about social work is to consider what makes it necessary or important to have such a thing called 'social work' in modern societies. In important ways, social work draws a line between the needs of people that are made a matter of public concern and those that must be left for the private domain to satisfy. In some important ways, the role of social work is a response to attempts to reconcile individual freedoms with social solidarity. It is located as a *social* agency in which individuals are given what they need so that they are free to choose the 'good' for themselves. In modern social work parlance, this is often referred to as 'empowerment'.

Within modern liberal societies, social work as a welfare bureaucracy in the modern State administers a 'shared good' on behalf of citizens (Ignatieff, 1984). Yet, despite this attempt to balance freedoms with State intervention to satisfy the requirements of needs and protection, there remains a deeply felt need for a sense of belonging and solidarity in modern societies that is not satisfied. Loneliness, isolation, exclusion and depression may be by-products of this failure to satisfy the human need for belonging.

How might social work contribute to a deeper sense of fraternity in societies characterized by division and fragmentation? While individuals need freedom, liberty and justice, they also need social solidarity. This requires new ways of thinking about social work and even, perhaps, a new language. Some of the material in this book draws attention to problems of modern daily life, points to possible solutions and asks how we got ourselves into this situation in the first place. This way of thinking about social work requires an additional push by asking that social workers address the 'difference that makes us different *or* the same' in modern societies.

Another way of thinking about social work is to consider all the books or journal articles that have 'social work' in their titles or contents lists. These books are written by people who describe themselves as social work researchers – that is, are classified as researchers or practitioners who write about social work. Thinking about social work in this way – as a collection of books or authors – makes one think that social work is a body of knowledge that has accumulated over the many years it has been taught or practised. Knowledge that is accumulated over time is often referred to as a 'tradition of knowledge' and so we speak of a 'social work tradition' or 'traditional social work'. This book makes further contributions to this research tradition with its many strands of concepts, ideas and theories.

Social work has been around in most developed countries for over a hundred years, which suggests that it has a well-established tradition of knowledge. That persistence through time and advances that have been made along the way, which may or may not be a matter of accumulated knowledge, is what the research tradition concept highlights. A tradition includes a number of frameworks that consist of specific theories or theoretical models and perspectives. Their interpenetration with the practice of social work, in terms of conceptual schemes and problems investigated, is what has advanced over time. The integration of theoretical models as explication of and in relation to comprehensive theories is a primary mode of advance of a research tradition. However, such a tradition changes when newcomers arrive and present new ways of thinking about social work. New books are put on the library shelves, new journals appear and students' reading lists are updated.

So, social work knowledge is in a constant state of flux and might best be described as a continuing activity that is formed and re-formed over time. Old wisdom is constantly tested against new ideas and conceptual formulations. Nevertheless, there is a body of knowledge referred to in the literature as 'social work knowledge' that is based on an accumulation of concepts, methods and values. Indeed, social work is a field of scholarship with a long tradition of thought that has made a deep impact on the whole of modern thinking about the social dimension as it deals with issues central to people's everyday concerns. With this type of thinking, social work is 'the difference that is different' from other ways of thinking, such as those found in psychology, sociology, history or philosophy.

With regard to the first way of thinking about social work, it is not simply a way of intervening in people's lives – that is, of developing concrete tasks or even applying commonsense skills that help people improve their lives or trying to empower people to become independent. Social work is much more than this. It is different from common sense in the way that it goes about 'making sense' of human reality. Social work tries to understand and explain why this rather than that happened. Most importantly, it tries to explain why something happened in the context of wider events. That wider context is a social dimension which is broader and more complex than the immediate situation in which people find themselves. We speak a language we did not create, we use technology we did not invent and we claim rights we did not establish and so on. Even feelings that appear completely spontaneous, such as the anger expressed at certain types of crime, are, in reality, the product of a social context. All of this might explain why the adjective 'social' in social work is so important in highlighting the primacy of the *social* context as it extends into all aspects of human life.

The value of interpretation in social work

When thinking about social work practice, it is apparent that it tries to make sense of *human* situations – in their social context – by analysing commonsense claims and conflicts about them, while encouraging people to reassess and discover different or more nuanced ways of interpreting them. Interpretation is at the core of social work. The rights of custody over children require interpretation of the law. Communication with others rests on the assumption that social workers can grasp the intended meaning of their speech or writing and thus understand cultural contexts. Similarly, during times of crisis, social workers are often required to reinterpret previous situations or routines. Interpretation seeks to establish a way forward or a way to orientate ourselves within a difficult situation. A crisis that suddenly envelops us can put a question mark by all previous interpretations.

While many aspects of social life appear routine and lend themselves to commonsense understanding, others are more complex and require 'specialist' interpretations. A commonsense interpretation, by its very definition, means that the interpretation is common to most people, but social work interpretations are very often *not* of this nature.

Interpretation in social work requires the recovery of the meaning or intention of clients' actions. As a client may describe her action retrospectively in ways in which she did not, or could not, describe before it was completed, interpretation has a privileged position in social work. Thus, social work interpretations are often not based on common sense.

A commonsense approach focuses on 'doing the right thing', while an interpretive perspective concentrates on 'doing the thing right'. It is our view that, despite being overlooked in social work skills training, interpretation is constitutive of social work and may specify the distinctive way of *becoming human in our social world*. To understand diversely shaped cultures, experiences, actions and beliefs – and to make their significance apparent in spoken and written forms – is the core of interpretation and it is indispensable to social work. One of the things that this book tries to emphasize is the great importance of the skill of interpretation for social work.

As we have mentioned, for over a century, social work has developed a 'tradition of knowledge' based on enquiries into social and personal relationships, moral values, social structures, social justice and the problems of modern life. Social work thinking questions the conditions of social life and its values as well as the purpose of social and human action. An engagement with such areas of life is often more challenging, difficult and arduous than commonsense thinking suggests and requires more than administration and policy implementation or simply fulfilling a legal mandate. Throughout its history, social work has taken issue with so-called facts and laws and often challenged normative mandates of what is a right, conventional or proper way to live. For many students, that is what makes social work so engaging, compelling and distinctive.

All of the chapters in this book are, in their different ways, acts of interpretation. That means, rather cyclically, your reading and thinking about the material is an interpretation of an interpretation. We think that by reading these kinds of interpretations, your own interpretive skills will improve. To do so can be difficult because some of the ideas, concepts and methods are complex. Theorizing can be hard work and does not lend itself easily to the lazy mind. However, wrestling with these kinds of things means that you develop a sensibility for or an attunement to theoretical ideas and concepts. We also believe that it encourages critical scrutiny and promotes the habit of self-analysis and questioning views that claim to be certainties. In developing good skills of interpretation, what we thought we understood fully, based on routines and habit, is questioned once again, opening up a new set of possibilities such that prior conceptions are replaced by new understandings. While the process may never end, we think that it will enhance your judgements and help you feel more certain about where you stand on important issues in social work and society at large. It will also help you become more aware of the way in which you habitually approach situations. Theories that fit with how you usually look at things will excite you; those which present a very different perspective might annoy you. When thinking about social work, we challenge ourselves to open up to new interpretations and perspectives and embrace complexity.

Thinking critically in social work

Good research-minded intervention depends on critical thinking at least as much as on factual knowledge, laws, proof or evidence. Social work is no exception to that rule.

Critical thinking is defined as a type of thinking that is orientated towards changing society for the better. Yet, despite the importance of critical thinking, social work students are not always taught how to think critically about the theories, methods and concepts they must use. This often results in the uncritical acceptance of facts and theories about human behaviour and the social environment. This can lead to bias, distortion or unpredictability when dealing with the complexity of the social world. Even though students are taught social work skills on professional training courses, such as interviewing, listening and communication skills, they are rarely taught about what is a good or bad judgement when dealing with challenging situations or other people's values.

For us, skills in making good judgements or interpretations are at the heart of social work thinking and are based on the evaluative ability to think critically. Critical thinking is a skill that must be developed in order to interpret successfully – and simultaneously – information from a variety of sources, such as interpersonal relationships, family life, government policy and legislation and changes in society.

This book shows students and researchers how to think critically about key topics, such as the relationship between theory and practice, and the way in which theory – and theoretical perspectives – opens up possibilities for change. As one student explained to the editors, 'If social work didn't have theory – and a variety of theories and perspectives – we would only have dogma'.

A central feature of the critical thinking tradition in social work has focused on what is loosely referred to as the 'theory–practice' debate. In more recent times, the emergence of the 'what works' agenda has further highlighted the significance of critical thinking in challenging government policies that extol a narrow, rigid framework for social work interventions. The idea that useful theory is merely 'what works' – that is, it should be judged on its utility and how it can be applied or used in practice contexts – helps to demonstrate the paucity of hard and rigid distinctions between theory and practice.

Critical analysis has demonstrated that theory and practice cannot be separated in any obvious way – the two dimensions are interdependent. Thus, for example, abstract changes in concepts are always embodied in real and particular events. Similarly, every social work practice is the bearer and articulation of more or less theory-laden beliefs and concepts. Even those who try to refute the value of theory by claiming that social work is just 'good common sense' are, in fact, articulating a distilled version of philosophical theories about common sense that emerged in English Enlightenment thinking (see Himmelfarb, 2004). This book helps demonstrate the value of theory in terms of its explanatory power and the way that it deepens our understanding of social work.

Contestable thinking in social work

Collectively, the material included in this book constitutes distinctive modes of thinking about social work. A 'mode of thinking' means considering the domain of relevance that relates to the explanations, beliefs and interpretations suited to the work in which we are involved. A social worker relying on ethnomethodology, for example, would treat social work as an extension of interpersonal experience, while a social worker relying on social networks would organize his or her practice around a set of salient group dependencies and identifications. For a social worker who considers feminist explanations to be important, gender relationships between men and women are likely to have a significant place in the way he or she interprets and makes sense of any interventions and the workings of society at large. A social worker influenced by the writings of Foucault would view relations between people and organizations and their consequences as effects of power relationships, some of which result in forms of social domination and oppression.

Modes of thinking in social work are contestable, however. Just as in other social sciences it is very difficult to find agreement on certain key themes, concepts and methods, so it is in social work, especially in relation to evidence-based (see Chapters 16 and 17) and constructivist (see Chapters 11 and 15) views of social reality. In philosophy, for example, there are several theories about the nature of truth – empiricism or realism, rationalism, relativism, constructivism and so on – each of which is very different from the other and makes different claims. Similarly, in social work there are contestable and debatable phenomena.

One significant debate in social work over the past decade has been about what is called 'the toolkit approach'. By this is meant an approach that is selective in appropriating bits and pieces of knowledge for particular pieces of work. Here, practitioners who have developed a flexible range of theories or perspectives use the tools that best fit the problem that is presented.

What happens, though, if they try to combine bits of knowledge for intervention that come from two contestable or even contradictory perspectives? This has led some to criticize the toolkit approach as being incoherent and fundamentally contradictory or, at least, resting too heavily on individual opinions about what is useful and, therefore, usable. Like a plumber mending a broken pipe, it assumes that good social work simply has to fit the problem to the solution in order to make it work. It has an image of the world as unambiguous and straightforward and implies that every problem has a solution, but perhaps the world is inherently ambiguous and more fluid than the toolkit approach allows for and suggests. In reality, we have to live with the tensions of irreconcilable forces and insoluble problems. Hence, a crucial question remains for those committed to the toolkit approach: how do they know that their interpretation of the fit between the problem and the solution is a good one? How do they know this is the best, perhaps most effective and right way to go about solving the problem?

Those who are critical of the toolkit approach claim that it is important for social workers to develop what German sociology calls a *Weltanschauung*, or a worldview, based not only on theories but also on a coherent set of strong values. A worldview may be defined as a set of presuppositions associated with one or more frameworks that are built on through time. Having a worldview means taking sides and showing a commitment to a set of beliefs rather than merely regarding theories or perspectives as simply different. It requires us to accept that some types of thinking have more value than others or else have better explanatory force.

The value of theory for social work

In 1998, the Economic and Social Science Research Council in the UK funded a research seminar series called 'Theorising Social Work Research' that aimed to raise the profile of social work as a research discipline. It also aimed to identify the specific contributions theorizing in social work makes to the social sciences. In the same year, Sage published a book called *Theorising Welfare* (O'Brien and Penna, 1998) that examined seven theoretical perspectives related to social work. These represent two explicit attempts to bring theory to the fore in social work research. However, theory and theorizing have long made a significant contribution to social work. We can say that theories embody frameworks of knowledge that have been developed in social work and the theoretical world where researchers validate or refute old knowledge and engage in building new knowledge in the form of new theories and perspectives.

Some students and researchers shy away from theory. Indeed, there are people in social work who are downright averse to any kind of theorizing. As educators, we often wonder why this occurs. Clearly some students are more comfortable with theory and theorizing than others, so that is something worth exploring here. Some in social work believe that we are ill-served by theoreticians, that theory operates in a largely quasi-philosophical domain rather than an empirical one and that *doing* social work is more important than *thinking* about it. This view has been crystallized in recent moves to formalize evidence-based practice and 'what works' in social work by drawing only on scientific methods.

We may respond to this quickly by paraphrasing Bryant (1989) who notes that: (a) empirical data in the sciences are theoretically informed; (b) scientific findings are not based solely on empirical evidence; and (c) fundamental shifts in scientific knowledge occur when empirical changes are accompanied by the availability of convincing theoretical alternatives. As long ago as 1980, Hesse summarized this position when she wrote (p. 56):

> I take it that it has been sufficiently demonstrated that data are not detachable from theory, and that their expression is permeated by theoretical categories.

We take the view that it is impossible, and potentially dangerous, to force dichotomies between theory and practice, value and fact or evidence and interpretation in social work.

About this book

This edited volume of chapters from leading international authors aims to make explicit the extent to which social work turns on competing social science theories and philosophical commitments. Each chapter is a short interpretative analysis that outlines the contributions made to social work by contemporary theorists, theories or perspectives. The book outlines key theoretical and methodological ideas that have been formed within social work and shows how these have been adopted and critiqued by social workers. A select bibliography of each thinker or approach is provided at the end of each chapter as a learning aid for students. A glossary is also given at the end of each chapter that defines key concepts, with links to theorists and perspectives and a timeline of influential journal articles and books is also provided.

To 'think social work' is to engage with and against contemporary and past theorists and theoretical concepts. This volume sees theorizing as essential engagement, to counter the new state of pragmatics in a post-9/11 world that encourages a severing of thought from practice. To this end, the book reflects on ways in which major theorists, theories and perspectives in social work may be brought together to take social work beyond familiar domains and prevent slippage into pragmatic quiescence.

The joy of 'thinking social work' is in creating alternative modes of understanding through critical engagement with competing perspectives. Readers are encouraged to join in the volume's spirit of debate and be challenged into reflecting on their own commitments. The book explores two distinct dimensions of this theoretical re-engagement: first, the critical excavation of existing theory through recent social sciences as applied to social work and, second, the engagement in critical dialogues between contrasting theoretical positions to show the pleasure of an 'uncompromising dialogue' in thinking about social work.

Given its remit, this edited collection is designed to offer critical discussion of a selection of thinkers, theories and perspectives dominating debates about social work. Our selection will, no doubt, prove contentious, in that some readers might be surprised by some of the theorists and topics we have included and others we have left out, such as Alain Badiou, Gilles Deleuze, phenomenology, behaviourism, psychoanalysis and conservativism. This was due entirely to restrictions on the number of pages we were allowed.

The structure of this book

In compiling this collection, we have sought to highlight those who, in our opinion, have contributed significantly to *theoretical* discussions shaping social work in recent years. These include those working in established and fundamentally important intellectual traditions, such as feminism and multiculturalism, as well as those developing newer discourses that relate to social work as they engage with postmodernism, neoliberalism or the writing of Judith Butler and Jürgen Habermas. Indeed, one of our strategies of selection was to include thinkers and theories and perspectives advocating different conceptions and perspectives in order to highlight the diverse ways in which social work has been theorized.

The book is divided into three parts.

- *Part I: Theorists* This section explores, in a focused way, the relevance to social work of contemporary thinkers who have set out influential and distinctive frameworks for making sense of the complexities of the social, including Habermas, Giddens, Bourdieu, Foucault and Butler.
- *Part II: Theories* Here we focus on the major 'isms' continuing to shape sociopolitical and philosophical thought, including, inter alia, feminism, multiculturalism, postmodernism and neo-liberalism and particular social work theories, such as critical and structural social work.
- *Part III: Perspectives* This section focuses on the connection between social work and methodologically driven approaches, such as social network analysis. ethnomethodology and ethnography, discourse analysis and reflexivity and evidence-based practice. It ends with an overview of epistemology, or ways of knowing, in social work.

The book provides a context for identifying the key ideas of particular thinkers as they have developed into a 'body of knowledge' or 'ism' and that 'ism's potential application in practice. This kind of approach enables the reader to move across various contributions, either forwards or backwards in the text. For example, it is possible to trace reflexive practice as a perspective back to the ideas of thinkers such as Bourdieu and Giddens and, in so doing, draw out contrasts of relevance and emphasis. Alternatively, our undergraduate readers may thread key concepts from, say, social network analysis or discourse analysis. In this way, the book provides a framework for mapping a set of influences and trajectories, particularly in relation to concepts and perspectives, by running them between or across one another. This helps to establish key links and identify relationships in terms of being for or against different standpoints, such as neo-liberalism versus structural social work, and the way in which these have been translated into various fields of practice.

How to use this book

Given the range of material, themes and subject matter, this is a very user-friendly book that allows you to dip into and pick and mix the kinds of reading you prefer in a leisurely way. We have already indicated that thinking about social work is not always an easy task because not only does it require focus, concentration and rereading of the material it also creates tensions, dilemmas and struggles with key value issues. Approaching the kinds of material in this book may also provoke contradictions in the various positions adopted by authors. Some central claims made in one chapter may be contradicted by other claims made in another. This is partly an effect of what we referred to as the contestable nature of social work knowledge, but is also a feature of wider problems that are called 'epistemological' in the social sciences. This is a branch of knowledge that enquires into the nature and possibility of knowledge, dealing with its scope and limitations. Our knowledge of truths and our knowledge of practical things may be different. The fact that there may be no correspondence between different types of knowledge or even truth claims means that there are no watertight guarantees about what constitutes true thinking. This leads to a situation where different thinkers make different claims about what is true thinking; inevitably some will contradict each other. Therefore, thinking about social work must be regarded as an accomplishment, like learning to play a musical instrument. Thinking takes practice. As in music the keys must be mastered, in this case, difficult concepts and methods need to be understood in order to make use of them. You will need to remember what the main arguments of a certain thinker or theory are so that you can contrast them with others. An uneasy contradiction that emerges can make us forget what those arguments are.

That is why it might be best to regard this book as an exciting train ride, an adventure that offers many points of departure and a choice of stations at which to alight, rest and refresh yourself before resuming the journey. It will take you along familiar tracks and make you reflect anew on what you already know. It will give you pause to 'step back' and ask questions that 'provoke new ways of thinking'. As Heidegger notes (in Bernstein, 1991: 93):

> Our common ways of 'thinking' become so familiar and entrenched that they conceal what needs to be unconcealed. It is only by showing how the familiar and the correct appear strange and uncanny … that thinking can be called forth.

This book will open up new vistas as you think anew on the familiar and encounter the unfamiliar, enter foreign territory and cover new ground. You can backtrack or forge ahead, skip a few stations and return to some you particularly enjoyed. You will meet new people and be absorbed by their ideas. You might also find fellow passengers with whom to share your enthusiasm and doubts. A truly good journey is one that feeds our imaginations and expands our vision. As Alain de Botton (2002: 57) says in *The Art of Travel*:

> Journeys are the midwives of thought. Few places are more conducive to internal conversations than a moving plane, ship or train. There is an almost quaint correlation between what is in front of our eyes and the thoughts we are able to have in our heads: large thoughts at times requiring large views, new thoughts new places. Introspective reflections which are liable to stall are helped along by the flow of the landscape. The mind may be reluctant to think properly when thinking is all it is supposed to do …Of all modes of transport, the train is perhaps the best aid to thought.

Once we begin to enjoy such journeys, there is no telling where they might take us. Let us hope this one gives you an unquenchable thirst for the possibilities that new ideas open up. Ideas capture the imagination, the possibilities then become endless and the destinations uncertain.

Glossary

Epistemology or the 'theory of knowledge', comes from the Greek word *episteme*, meaning knowledge. It refers to the branch of philosophy that studies the nature, methods (of acquisition), limitations and validity of different knowledge and belief systems that are often referred to as 'ways of knowing' (see Chapter 17). It concerns the means by which knowledge is produced, the way in which different knowledge claims are made and how particular knowledge systems come to dominate our thinking. It attempts to answer the basic question of what distinguishes true from false knowledge. It addresses questions such as 'What is knowledge?', 'How is knowledge acquired?' and 'How do people come to know?'

Method Refers to the way in which we acquire knowledge. We can acquire knowledge by reading, talking to people, archival research, direct observation, experience and so on. In the scholarly tradition of theory development, rigour is highly valued, such that a method is a systematic approach to theory or knowledge development and testing.

Methodology Refers to a particular procedure or set of procedures used to acquire knowledge that, within particular disciplines, are based on a range of theories and concepts concerning the best way of going about analysing that knowledge. It is more than the articulation of methods because it includes the reason or rationale and epistemological assumptions that inform the process of enquiry.

Perspective A way of seeing the world that is influenced by one's angle or particular point of view. Often our perspectives are shaped by a variety of theories. In other words, we integrate a variety of understandings (theories) about reality – in the case of social work, about human behaviour and the social environment – that come to colour the way in which we see our world and view situations and events.

Theory A more or less well argued *explanation* of reality. Collectively, then, theories are explanations of reality – or human behaviour or particular social phenomena, depending on the theory's central focus – that lead to particular *interpretations* of that reality. In other words, theorists offer particular explanations of reality that influence the ways in which people interpret situations or events.

Part I
Theorists

1

Jürgen Habermas

Stan Houston

Some biographical details

Jürgen Habermas was born on 18 June 1929 in Dusseldorf, Germany. His father was an industrialist. As a teenager, Habermas joined the Hitler youth along with many of his peers. However, after the war ended he was shocked and appalled when he learned of the Nazi regime's barbarity. He was also frustrated by Germany's slow progress in moving towards a new, democratic state. That said, the intellectual climate of post-war Germany flourished. Against such a backdrop, Habermas read voraciously. His interests were wide ranging. Books and tracts on political philosophy, psychology and economics were widely available at the time and Habermas soon realized his appetite for discursive enquiry.

In 1949, he began to study philosophy, psychology and German literature in Gottingen, Zurich, and then in Bonn. Developing a taste, early on, for critique, he initiated an excoriating assault on the existentialist Martin Heidegger, whom he believed had given intellectual credence to the Nazi regime. This episode highlights Habermas's enduring concern that Germany has failed to take ownership of its past.

The year 1956 was to see a formative move in his fledgling academic career. By joining the prestigious Institute for Social Research – known colloquially as the 'Frankfurt School' – he came into contact with a number of illustrious social theorists, including Max Horkheimer, Theodor Adorno and Herbert Marcuse. However, Habermas subsequently left the school to develop his own ideas. He was particularly concerned about the school's drift into social pessimism and political scepticism following the onslaught of fascism, the debasement of Marxist ideas in Russia and the rampant success of capitalism in the West. Faced with an implacable instrumental rationality in the modern world, his mentors in the school had embraced the enfeebled idea that social redemption lay in the empowering mediums of art, literature and music. For Habermas, this descent into aesthetics would lead to a philosophical cul de sac. Specifically, the adoption of a limited, and ultimately negative, view of rationality and antidote to the ills of the time would fail to bring about the ideals of the Enlightenment – modernity's unfinished project. By way of contrast, a more developed notion of rationality was required to expose false ideologies in society. Moreover, he laid claim to the seminal idea that language provided the soil in which the seed of rationality could germinate. By recovering and developing this faculty, humankind could build a better world order, thus realizing Marx's vision of a society free from alienation and material inequities.

Key ideas

Habermas's ideas have developed over the course of a long, studious and perhaps febrile career. Yet, in spite of some astringent attacks from modish postmodernists, he has retained a firm belief in the power of reason to expose injustice and oppression and direct our thinking about alternative ways of living. In this chapter, we consider how this challenging, centripetal insight has shaped aspects of his early, middle and later work.

Ideas on language

Habermas, following the philosopher Wittgenstein's lead, has taken the 'linguistic turn'. By this I mean that he sees language as the key medium for constructing reality. From this standpoint, he has made a number of very important observations about the way we communicate with one another. Central, here, are speakers' attempts to *validate* what they say through reasoned argument.

Exploring this idea further, Habermas suggests that there are three kinds of validity claim in *normal* language (we will address Habermas's views on the abnormal form later on in the chapter). First of all, we can assert that something is the case based on our reading of the evidence. For example, we may say, with some conviction, that all spiders have eight legs because we have undertaken a study of arachnids. Here the speaker is attempting to validate what she is saying on the grounds that it is true.

Second, we can validate what we say by being sincere. If I say that I am fond of you and this remark is congruent with my non-verbal presentation and inner disposition, then the statement is likely to be accepted because it comes across as genuine to the hearer.

The final validity claim invokes moral appropriateness. If I make the claim that homophobia is wrong, I might do so on the grounds that discrimination against alternative sexual identities contradicts a fundamental right to self-determination. Thus, there is an ethical dimension to the statement that could be upheld on the basis of reasoned, principled argument.

Habermas believes that this inbuilt tendency to validate what has been said emanates from an ineluctable quest for understanding and agreement in social interaction; or, to put this in Habermasian speak, 'our first sentence expresses unequivocally the intention of universal and unconstrained consensus' (Habermas, 1968: 308). This ontological thrust for mutuality is the inherent telos of communication, its driving goal.

Habermas provides complex arguments to support his core thesis that speakers are fundamentally attuned to understanding and agreement. He draws on the work of the social behaviourist George Herbert Mead (1962), to substantiate his claims. For Mead, the human subject develops a capacity to 'role-take' with others. *Role-taking* is a technical term for the prosaic notion of putting ourselves into another's shoes, of seeing the world from his or her unique position. This takes us beyond emotional and social development into the domain of moral advancement. To endorse the point, Habermas additionally draws on Lawrence Kohlberg's (1981) theory of moral development and Robert L. Selman's (1980) theory of perspective-taking in social life. Within this body of work Habermas finds sustenance for his view that moral maturity is attained when norms are not just accepted but also scrutinized objectively, reflexively and linguistically.

These preliminary comments on validity claims and the reciprocity of perspectives form the supportive pillars for Habermas's chief construct – *communicative action*. Communicative action occurs when two or more individuals reach a consensual understanding on goals and actions. This form of speech acts as a coordinating mechanism facilitating the expression of all three validity claims and reasoned argument. Because the speakers sign up to the need for mutual understanding and agreement, they put the brakes on the temptation to engage in bumptious diatribe, point-scoring invective or clever sophistry. Quintessentially, communicative action denotes accountability – that is, it invokes my responsibility to you to make claims that are truthful, sincere and morally appropriate and your responsibility to me to do likewise. Importantly, when institutionalized, communicative action strengthens social integration and solidarity in social networks and society at large. For Habermas, social order could not exist without it.

When communicative action occurs in the context of:

- agreement that is forged on the force of the better argument;
- participants, who are capable of speech and action, being allowed to engage in the discussion;
- participants being allowed to call into question any proposal in the discussion;
- participants being allowed to introduce any proposal into the discussion;
- participants being allowed to express their attitudes;

then, according to Habermas, we have achieved the *ideal speech situation*. This is a normative situation and should be used to identify 'disorders of discourse', where speech has fallen short of the expressed criteria. Thus, it can be seen that there is a counter-factual dimension to the ideal speech situation. In other words, it can be used as a moral yardstick to signal unfair practices in all their guises and disguises.

The full significance of communicative action in social life, and its extension into the ideal speech situation, only becomes fully apparent when it is absent. Here, Habermas directs our attention to an aberrant derivate of communicative action called *strategic action*. Following John Austin (1962), the latter occurs when speakers move away from mutual understanding, consensus and agreement and become strategic – that is, out for their own desired ends. A goal arises and the strategic communicator is consumed by the most efficient way of realizing it.

Strategic action is commonplace in business and professional life. Here, it can be purely functional, in the sense that corporate objectives have to be met and business plans conceived to guide the employee's actions. However, strategic action can also take the form of one-upmanship, courting favour with the boss and creating alliances when rumours abound of takeover bids and so on – hence the ubiquity of the manufactured compliment or, perhaps, the sycophantic opening gesture or even the gratuitous retreat from praise in order to feign humility. By way of contrast, backstage behaviour happens when the actor is alone or with trusted companions. Here, cynicism is vented, anger expressed and inner ambivalence revealed.

Whatever form strategic action takes, it is to be viewed as a pathological departure from communicative action. This is not to say that there is no role for strategic action in today's complex world. Clearly, for Habermas, our modern way of life could not be sustained without a means–ends form of rationality. The administration of corporate areas of business, industry and social life would simply crumble without it. However, what worries Habermas is the scale and predominance of strategic action in the modern world. Critically, it has eclipsed its forerunner – communicative action.

Ideas on society

In his magnum opus – *The Theory of Communicative Action* (1987) – Habermas identifies two core spheres of social reproduction. In practice, these spheres are joined together, but they are analysed separately by Habermas so that he can identify their discrete effects on social life.

The first sphere is termed the *lifeworld*. Borrowing from Alfred Schütz, it refers to the subterranean or background reservoir of shared, and often taken for granted, meanings that, through language, shape our personalities and group identities. It is here that we find daily incidents of communicative action. Hence, people meet and interact on the basis of shared definitions of tasks, duties and expectations. Most of these encounters are unproblematic and approached without conscious deliberation. Family reunions, for example, often start with shared rituals. Greetings may be intimate and conversations might start with a review of what has occurred since the last meeting and so on. Other cultures might follow different scripts, but, whatever happens, events are likely to be predictable for the actors concerned.

The other sphere – the *system* – by way of contrast, refers to areas of life that are organized and controlled by the State. Formative here are the political and economic subsystems that govern important aspects of our lives. Whereas the lifeworld is concerned with cultural integration and socialization, the system focuses on material reproduction. Consequently, it is dominated by power, money and strategic action. Take the day-to-day activities of a stock market. Here, the pursuit of money and power reaches its apogee as harassed, but ambitious, traders ply their trade. These incumbents revel in strategic action. Making expeditious decisions, outwitting the opposition, beating the market at its own game – all these things add to the allure of this cut and thrust role. This is not to say that communicative action is obliterated in this environment as traders must communicate and understand each other if they are to perform their tasks effectively, but the scales will clearly tip towards strategic action.

As capitalism developed, both the lifeworld and system became progressively differentiated and rationalized in markedly different ways. Habermas sees this as a necessary step from an evolutionary point of view. Nevertheless, there was a downside to the progression because the two spheres developed out of kilter.

Let us examine more closely Habermas's ideas on the rationalization of both spheres. As the lifeworld became more evolved, traditional customs and practices that had been inherited from the past began to recede and lose their influence – particularly when they could not be defended on rational grounds. For example, whereas in the past religion shaped morality, in the modern, pluralistic world, people increasingly have to resort to reason to resolve ethical dilemmas. This presents opportunities for existential growth, but also leads to existential uncertainty. Habermas also sees the formerly homogeneous lifeworld developing into a number of distinct subspheres incorporating aesthetics, ethics and science (the beautiful, the good and the true). Each of these subspheres rests increasingly on communicative action to sustain its validity. No longer at the behest of tradition, they advance through increasing secularization, reflexivity and social criticism.

As to the system's rationalization, it is important to point out, first and foremost, that it emerged from the lifeworld in much earlier times. As society evolved, though, it became more autonomous from its progenitor. Put another way, the system *uncoupled* from the lifeworld. In doing so, it spawned three distinct subsystems: the economy, political administration and the judiciary.

Habermas then takes us to a critical stage in society's development. Having uncoupled from the lifeworld, the all-powerful system re-enters it, this time to colonize its functions. This means that instrumentality, rationality, money, bureaucracy and power – the trappings of the system – usurp communicative action as the chief means for resolving issues and problems in the lifeworld. As a consequence, social life becomes increasingly monetarized, commodified and bureaucratized. In short, entropy sets in. An example of colonization is the bureaucratization of schools, where league tables and other performance criteria undermine the practice of education as a communicational discipline.

Habermas makes similar points in relation to the welfare state. By offering mainly bureaucratized interventions to those who are in need, it erodes earlier traditions of care, such as are found in neighbourhoods and social networks, and also undermines the informal, communicational mechanisms that coordinate them. More than this, the system uses social welfare as a protective mechanism to ward off discontent in the lifeworld. This occurs mainly when there are legitimation crises in the economy and the disparities between rich and poor become most acute. To offset the crisis, and mollify discontent, the welfare state provides social assistance and other benefits.

Habermas (1987: 355) goes on to suggest that it is important to protect the autonomy of the lifeworld: 'It is a question of building up restraining barriers for the exchanges between lifeworld and system and of building sensors for the exchanges between lifeworld and system'.

In each of these examples of colonization, we can find experts or professionals who are trained to carry out the system's functions. Imbued with technocratic consciousness, these representatives of the State find solace in convening meetings, applying procedures, following checklists, adhering to performance indicators and implementing eligibility criteria.

Rather than approaching issues from the standpoint of communicative action – the domain of the face-to-face interchange – they favour instrumentalism.

To conclude, what Habermas envisages is not an all out war between lifeworld and system. Rather, he wants to restore some kind of balance between the two spheres so that they become mutually enriching and enhancing. In restoring the balance, the lifeworld needs to play a more active role in challenging the system. Pivotal here are the new social movements. Social protest, as activated by gay, green and feminist campaigners, is to be encouraged. What interests Habermas is the organization of these movements. Critically, they arise from the lifeworld and base their activities on communicative action. Habermas sees hope in these forms of protest because they re-create an active public sphere – a part of the lifeworld that operated in the nineteenth century as a critical voice against the State.

Main contribution

Much like the way iron fillings are inextricably drawn towards the poles of a magnet, so critique has attached itself to Habermas's ideas. Let us start with Habermas's pivotal notion of communicative action. If this is found to be wanting then, to a large extent, his wider project will be compromised. To put it bluntly, do people communicate essentially on the basis of validity claims, reasoned argument, understanding and agreement or is it the case that communication often leads nowhere and sometimes ends in disagreement? It could be argued that many people do not yield to the better argument (Layder, 1995). Indeed, some theorists (for example, Turner, 1988) see all communication as distorted. In an abusive talk show, it is argued, we might see a distilled form of modern communication.

Moreover, even if people do strive to understand one another, it is a non sequitur to assume that agreement will arise in every case or that liberating actions will necessarily follow agreement. Leading on from this, first, are the public really interested in deliberating (as per communicative action) on legal and other matters to shape public law and policy and, second, are they sufficiently well informed to carry out this task? Many citizens are not even sufficiently motivated to carry out the simple act of voting every five years, let alone engage in concentrated, rational debate on public issues of importance.

Against these critiques, though, there is still something compelling about the idea of communicative action, particularly when we consider how social order arises and is sustained. For most of us, life is predictable and orderly. Social routines happen more or less within expected parameters. People relate to one another on the basis of organized turn-taking. Ordinary conduct in everyday life proceeds from commonsense, tacit knowledge that is shared. Language appears to be the medium through which this stability is created. Fundamentally, how could we maintain this order without some inherent understanding and agreement in everyday conversation? Social life would simply fall apart, without it resulting in a Hobbesian war of all against all.

However, this critique has not gone away. For some, Habermas's 'talking cure' for the ills of the modern age appears naïve, superficial and irredeemably idealistic. On the geopolitical stage, America and Iraq never came anywhere near communicative action. Other examples from history abound. In fact, it seems that conflict, power and the threat of nuclear retaliation are the real stabilizing forces in the modern world.

Habermas's enduring response to this nagging polemic goes as follows: if we believe in the importance of the universal need to communicate, we have to believe in reason; and, in according reason such a prominent place in daily living, we can be moderately optimistic that, in the final analysis, sanity will prevail.

Perhaps a more damaging critique comes from feminism (see Fraser, 1989). Here, it is argued that Habermas concentrates inordinately on the masculine notion of reason without giving due attention to emotion and the unconscious. People are not purely rational subjects, so the argument goes; they have feelings, desires, intuitions and impulses. A satisfactory theory of social action would have to account for these aspects of our being.

Any review of Habermas's work would not be complete without examining the Marxist critique. It is important here to reflect on why Habermas departed from Marx. Essentially, it was because Marx had not, in his opinion, addressed social interaction and language sufficiently, preferring to concentrate on labour. Many Marxists, however, may dispute this assertion, arguing that the intersubjective realm was central in many of his ideas, particularly in his early writings on class consciousness. Clearly, for these apologists and Marx himself, it is men – and, we must quickly add, women, too – who make history (by interacting), but not, it seems, in circumstances of their own choosing.

A more stringent Marxist critique centres on Habermas's idealism. Marx had departed from Hegelian idealism early on. What concerned him, first and foremost, was the material realm. Remember, materialism argues that matter is primary and thought, consciousness and ideation secondary. Habermas, in concentrating on how ideas are expressed through language, does not give sufficient attention to this material world. Consequently, his view that change will arise from communicative action may at best be a placebo.

Moreover, what has incensed many Marxists is Habermas's apparent turn in his later work towards social democracy, demonstrating a discernable shift to the centre ground in politics. Here, the system is no longer typified as a colonial master rapaciously subduing a forlorn lifeworld. In fact, his later work seems to exonerate the system to some extent, while suggesting that impediments to critical debate lie within the lifeworld itself. Furthermore, adding insult to injury, he admits to wanting 'to tame the capitalist economic system' (Habermas, 1996: 410) rather than cage it.

Introducing Habermas's ideas to social work

There is a growing interest in Habermas's ideas in Western social work. For some commentators, his work provides a viable alternative to postmodernism, which, because of its perceived, inherent relativism, fails to offer the required justification for ethical practice (see Donovan, 2003; Gray and Lovat, 2006).

Other writers view his analysis of contemporary society as explaining, in a most apposite way, the structural constraints facing the profession, particularly its entanglement with bureaucratic procedures and elephantine, organizational cultures (Blaug, 1995; Houston, 2003). Some find Habermas's stress on ethical discourse as restating the sine qua non of social work (Willumsen and Skivenes, 2005).

Let us review some of this work in more detail. Kam-shing Yip (2006), Mary Henkel (1995) and Debbie Skerrett (2000) have applied Habermas's early thinking on epistemology (see Chapter 17) to different dimensions of social work.

Yip analyses levels of reflectivity in students' social work practice with clients with mental illness, drawing on Habermas's critical and emancipatory ideas on knowledge. For him, developing students' practical reflectivity requires multifaceted strategies of learning and development. Much of this is congruent with Habermas's plea for enhanced moral awareness of the dynamic interface between the 'self' and the 'other'.

Henkel (1995), charting a different course, applies Habermas's ideas to critique what she sees as an atomistic scientism in social work education and practice. The hermeneutic approach outlined by Hans-Georg Gadamer and developed by Habermas, with its stress on meaning, language and interpretation, provides, for Henkel, a means of understanding the 'multiple marginalities' and 'ambivalences' facing social work. That said, she sees Habermas's stress on consensus as opening up the potential for a new totalitarianism because of its neglect of difference. This critique is perhaps consonant with Seyla Benhabib's (1986) insistence that egalitarian and democratic discourse must take account of a situated, concrete and different 'other'.

In a parallel paper, Skerrett (2000) critiques the prevailing model of care management in social work, with its emphasis on performance indicators, budgets, care plans and a 'tick box' approach to assessment. She locates this model within Habermas's first category of knowledge: the empirical–analytical sciences that have a technical interest at their heart. For Skerrett, though, it is the critical–emancipatory sciences that should provide the foundation for ethical social work practice.

Various contributors have sought to apply Habermas's ideas on society and its differentiated systems to social work practice in the (late)modern world. For example, Stan Houston (2002b) critiques the theory base underpinning the Department of Health's (England and Wales) guidance for child protection social workers. He sees it as problematic because it fails to explain how power operates at the systemic level. Habermas's critical systems theory is then explored as a way of remedying the deficit.

Staying with Habermas's systemic analysis, Trevor Spratt and Stan Houston (1999) react against the preponderance of instrumentalist ideologies in the child protection system. Tom Sinclair (2005), in a similar vein, explores how ideology impinges on child protection practice, leading to distorted communication. Such themes resonate with Samantha Ashenden's (2004) conclusion that the system colonizes the private lifeworld of family relations in relation to the management of child sexual abuse. However, for her, we need to problematize the system–lifeworld distinction as power lies in both domains.

To conclude this section, it is important to review some of the academy's interest in Habermas's ideas on ethical communication. In this connection, Vishanthie Sewpaul (2004) applies his theory of communicative action and discourse ethics to issues such as HIV and AIDS, class, race and gender while Houston (2002b) develops and extends Habermas's discourse ethics to decisionmaking in fostering and adoption.

Another connection is made by Mary Donovan (2003). In discussing the ethical orientation of contemporary family therapy practice, she suggests that there has been a worrying marginalization of ethics in this field, brought about by the influence of postmodernism and hermeneutics. For her, Habermas's ideas provide a route to re-establishing ethical communication and reflective processes within systemic therapies.

Many of these ideas are encapsulated in Ricordo Blaug's pioneering (1995) reflection on Habermas's contribution to social work (his paper is a 'moral must' that never ceases to inspire). He concludes that the:

> solutions being offered to the profession by social policy and management initiatives are based on an overly instrumental conception of human reason. This results in a colonization of our communicative practices and a distortion of the face-to-face interaction which lies at the heart of human caring. (1995: 429)

Blaug (1995) concludes that Habermas's critical theory, with its emphasis on communicative action, provides the antidote to these tendencies. He further opines that practices such as increasing user involvement, networking, action learning and peer supervision, are just some of the ways in which communicative action can be embedded within social work. In the next section, this theme is explored more fully.

Significance for social work practice

There is one aspect of social work practice that is ubiquitous: communication. No matter what the setting or who is involved, social work encounters depend on a clear interchange between the parties involved. For many social workers, communication is about a set of skills. We need to be proficient in asking open questions, clarifying, reflecting what has been said and so on. This is surely right, but to what extent have social workers considered communication as a moral enterprise (as captured in the notion of communicative action), one that is fundamental to human development, regardless of culture? More specifically, have we stopped to think deeply about the goal of daily exchanges between ourselves and welfare recipients?

If we were to take Habermas's lead idea of communicative action seriously, then communication would become the focal point of all social work activity. Let me unpack this by taking a Socratic turn and asking some awkward questions. Do we consciously strive to validate our statements according to reason alone? When justifying our ideas and actions, is our speech always truthful, sincere and morally appropriate? Do we continuously strive to understand another person's perspective, difficult as that may be? Do we build on that understanding to achieve consensus with points of view that differ from our own?

In considering these questions, we must also query our propensity to engage in strategic action. Again, more questions need to be asked here. To what extent do we enter exchanges with others with prefigured ends in mind? Are these 'ends' necessarily ones that service users would accept? Do we ever deceive ourselves that we are being cooperative when, with the benefit of hindsight, we realize that we have been self-interested all along? Do we consciously manipulate conversations to achieve our own ends?

Painful as the foregoing questions may be, they are crucial because, as Habermas reminds us, it is through communication that we construct reality. In a world where instrumentalism rages much like a behemoth, social work must stand firm as an ethical leviathan by committing fully to communicational practices that are egalitarian, participative and democratic. It must battle against the hegemony of technical rationality to continuously reaffirm Habermas's leading idea of the primacy of the face to face, for it is here that human identity flourishes.

Study questions

1. Think of an important meeting you attended recently involving a service user. Use the criteria established within the ideal speech situation as a yardstick to assess the content and form of the discussion. Note any breaches of the criteria and consider how the meeting could have been planned and executed more fairly.
2. Examine the extent of strategic action in your place of work. How might communicative action be strengthened with colleagues and service users?
3. Habermas's theory rests on the communicative competence of participants in dialogue. How might the perspectives of those lacking in such competence (such as young children) be taken into account to ensure fairness and equality?

Glossary

Colonization This refers to the social process whereby the system intrudes into the lifeworld so that everyday consciousness is tainted and fragmented by expert subcultures and strategic action.

Communicative action This occurs when people communicate together using reasoned arguments to support the validity of what they are saying to reach mutual understanding, agreement and consensus.

Ideal speech situation This sets the conditions for moral decisionmaking, in so far as all the affected parties are allowed to speak, listened to and allowed to question others.

Lifeworld This is the everyday context or repository of common, shared meanings in which validity claims are put forward to coordinate action.

Strategic action This occurs when people communicate on the basis of wanting to achieve particular ends for themselves. This form of action is shaped by the use of influence, force, sanctions or money.

System This is the part of society comprising the legal, political and economic domains. Here, the 'steering mechanisms' of money, administration and power operate achieve desired ends.

Select bibliography

As well as entries for Habermas's work in the References section at the end of the book, his major works include:

(1976, 1973) *Legitimation Crisis*. London: Heinemann.
(1984, 1981) *The Theory of Communicative Action* Volume 1. Cambridge: Polity Press.
(1988, 1963) *Theory and Practice*. London: Heinemann; Cambridge: Polity Press.
(1989, 1962) *The Structural Transformation of the Public Sphere: Inquiry into a category of bourgeois society*. Cambridge, MA: MIT Press.
(1990, 1983) *Moral Consciousness and Communicative Action*. Cambridge: Polity Press.
(2003, 1999) *Truth and Justification: Philosophical essays*. Cambridge: Polity Press.

Anthony Giddens

2

Harry Ferguson

Some biographical details

Anthony Giddens was born into a lower-middle-class family in north London in 1938. Following his education at a local grammar school, he studied sociology and psychology at Hull, graduating in 1959. He was the first in his family to attend university. He completed an MA in sociology at the London School of Economics (LSE) and began lecturing at Leicester University in 1961 – then a leading intellectual seedbed of British sociology. In 1969, he moved to a lectureship and a fellowship at King's College, Cambridge, where he was promoted to Chair in Sociology and Head of the Faculty of Social and Political Sciences in 1986. In 1996, challenged by the desire to make the social sciences more relevant to policy and public life, Giddens became the Director of the London School of Economics. Up until then, he'd been purely a social theorist whose politics were little known, but he now began taking his ideas about the nature of modern societies and the renewal of social democracy beyond academia to a wider audience through the media. His BBC Radio 4 Reith Lectures entitled *Runaway World* (Giddens, 1999) effectively cast him as a public intellectual – a move that, as we shall see, literally embodied key components of his sociological perspective.

From the outset, Giddens was a gifted, charismatic teacher and remained committed to engaging with students until his retirement in 2003. At the LSE he initiated a weekly 'Director's Lecture', which was attended by up to a thousand people. When working towards my own PhD in Giddens's faculty between 1987 and 1990, I experienced first hand his passion for developing a sociology fit to do justice to the complexity of personal and global life in the advanced modern world, his enormous work rate and productivity, his accessibility and his remarkable capacity to teach complex social theory and hold an audience's attention without ever using a note (never mind PowerPoint). Following his retirement, he was given a life peerage in June 2004 – Baron Giddens of Southgate in the London Borough of Enfield – and sits in the House of Lords for Labour. He continues to write books and is very active as a public intellectual, increasingly, in politics.

Giddens's major publications

Giddens has had a massive influence on social science and public life in Britain and throughout the Western world. He has written at least 34 books, well over 200 articles and reviews and has been published in some 40 languages. He is co-founder and director of one of the most successful social science publishing houses in the world – Polity Press – and has, since the late 1990s, been a key intellectual mentor for Western governments, being an advisor for, among others, Bill Clinton and Tony Blair.

Giddens established himself as a scholar of significance with his first major book, *Capitalism and Modern Social Theory* (1971), in which he outlined and critically appraised the work of classical sociologists Karl Marx, Max Weber and Emile Durkheim. It continues to be a core text on social theory courses and alone has sold well over 100,000 copies.

From the mid-1970s, he began to rework the classical tradition and fashion his own social theory for the modern age, especially in *New Rules of Sociological Method* (1976) and *Central Problems in Social Theory* (1979). This momentum culminated in the publication in 1984 of *The Constitution of Society*, in which he outlined his famous *theory of structuration* – an ambitious attempt to revise how sociology can explain human action, social systems and society.

The Consequences of Modernity (1990) continued to deal with some of the core concerns of structuration theory, but marked the beginning of an important new phase in his work. He moved into a concern with not just local but also global processes. Thus, for example, he continued to think through issues to do with the capacities of human beings to act and reflect on their lives and social structures and to influence the shape of both – what he called 'reflexivity'. Thus, he showed how personal lives and institutions were shaped by globalization and changing environments of trust and risk in social relationships.

He developed and deepened this work on personal lives and what he called 'reflexive modernization' in *Modernity and Self-identity: Self and society in the late modern age* (1991), *The Transformation of Intimacy* (1992), *Beyond Left and Right: The future of radical politics* (1994a) and 'living in a post-traditional society' in *Reflexive Modernization* (1994b), co-authored with Ulrich Beck and Scott Lash. The hallmarks of this phase of his work were a concern with emotions, democratic relationships, expertise and how personal lives and institutions are changing through knowledge being 'reflexively' ploughed back into how people and organizations define themselves and act in what he now called 'high' or 'late modernity'.

In what began in the 1970s and 1980s as a project that was related to but separate from the development of structuration theory, Giddens was concerned with developing an historical and sociological theory of the nature of the State and welfare. His initial focus was on a reappraisal of Marxism in *A Contemporary Critique of Historical Materialsm,* volume 1 (1981), moving to a broader scholarly analysis of power, citizenship and the welfare/nation state in *The Nation State and Violence: Volume 2 of a contemporary critique of historical materialism* (1985). This theoretical project culminated in *Beyond Left and Right: The future of radical politics* (1994a). I emphasize 'theoretical' because, while essentially a book on theory, *Beyond Left and Right* contained, for the first time, some indication of what would become for Giddens a political stance.

This ideology 'beyond' the politics of Left and Right became known as *The Third Way* and, in 1998, Giddens published a book with that title, subtitled *The renewal of social democracy.* It was the political project of the Third Way that was, to some degree, taken up by Bill Clinton in the USA and Tony Blair in Britain. Giddens was now an avowed social democrat, making sophisticated (but, for politicians, accessible) arguments about key contemporary issues, such as individualism, risk and its management, and the role of the State in advanced capitalism.

Giddens's intellectual ideas have had many supporters and a huge impact, but there have been many critics, whom Giddens replied to in *The Third Way and its Critics* (2000; see also Giddens, 2001). He has been developing his views on social democracy and good government ever since (Giddens, 2003, 2005, 2007a). In 2007, for instance, one of the (two) books he published, *Over to You Mr Brown: How Labour can win again* (2007b), was launched to coincide with Gordon Brown succeeding Tony Blair as Prime Minister and leader of the Labour Party, setting out what he believed Brown needed to do to renew a weary Labour Government and social democracy. Giddens is both a critic and loyal supporter of New Labour.

As Giddens chose in the 2000s to devote much of his energies to politics (as a member of the House of Lords), political science and being a public intellectual, he published less and less sociology. The notable exception is the work he continues to update – namely, his classic academic textbook, *Sociology.* First published in 1993 and now in its fifth edition, it is recognized across the Western world as the standard introductory textbook on the subject.

Key ideas

With a career spanning almost 40 years and a publishing output of almost as many books, Giddens's work defies easy summation. Yet, as I have begun to indicate above, his theoretical work can be summarized into three broad phases, which approximate to key themes:

- his reworking of classical sociology and the development of what he called 'structuration theory';
- globalization, risk, the reflexive self and intimacy in late modernity;
- Giddens the public intellectual, political scientist and social democrat.

While I shall have something to say on the last of these themes, my main focus here will be on the first two themes, given that they cover his theoretical work and are most relevant to social work.

Structuration theory

At the centre of Giddens's work in the 1970s and 1980s and his notion of *structuration theory* was an attempt to overcome the classic problem in sociology of the relationship between social structures and individuals in shaping institutions and everyday life. Giddens argued that social science had created a false 'dualism' of 'structure' and human 'agency' in which they had been split off from one another. He was particularly concerned about how sociology had created a view of human beings as always being constrained by social structures (Giddens, 1984). It is necessary, he suggests, to examine what these so-called 'structures' are and how they are made up. Social structures are not something that simply bear down on individuals in menacing, controlling ways, but are themselves made up of human actions, within which people draw on what Giddens calls 'rules' and 'resources'. This notion and how it has been applied in sociological research can perhaps best be illustrated with an example from health and social care.

Antonia Beringer, Margaret Fletcher and Ann Taket (2006) apply this theoretical framework to nursing and show how the practices that shape interprofessional work in hospitals are governed by certain rules and resources, but they only come to have meaning in how practice itself and the service delivered to patients have to be recreated every moment in every day. The 'structure', therefore, is not simply pregiven and constraining, but comprises the actions of professionals and patients that go into making nursing what it is.

Through this kind of thinking, Giddens (1984) argued that the traditional dualism – the split between structure and agency – needs to be recast as 'the duality of structure'. Crucially for Giddens, 'structures' are both enabling and constraining. They make actions possible as well as stopping or controlling them. The same, as I shall show below, can be said about social work.

The reflexive self, globalization and the transformation of intimacy

Giddens placed the capacities of human beings to reflect on their lives and adjust their actions accordingly – what he called the 'reflexive monitoring' of conduct – at the heart of structuration theory. In the 1990s, he took this further in his theory of *reflexive modernization* and the *reflexive project of the self*.

The Consequences of Modernity (1990) is a brilliant analysis of the trials and tribulations of what happens to expert knowledge in conditions where the trustworthiness of professionals is routinely questioned by laypeople, the media and other experts.

Along with Ulrich Beck, Giddens helped to place risk on the sociological agenda, introducing the concept of 'manufactured uncertainty', which refers to the way in which risks are, today, created by expert systems themselves. As I have shown elsewhere, social work and child protection fit Giddens's analysis very well as, following the disclosure that children have died in cases where social workers were involved, attempt after attempt has been made to make the system safer and less risky (Ferguson, 1997, 2004). A key dimension of this concerns changes in the nature of risk, which mean that professionals have to live with the knowledge that, despite itself, no expert system can guarantee safety and that it won't fail to protect children and adults (Giddens, 1990).

Risk in late modernity is about 'colonizing the future' (Giddens, 1991) and, since the 1970s, welfare states have attempted to manage manufactured risk through the development of new procedures and rules that professionals are expected to implement in their practice to address the emergence of 'knowledge gaps' shown up by inquiries into how they have failed (Ferguson, 1997).

Giddens refers to this process of constant reflection on, and change of, institutional structures and rules as 'reflexive modernization'. It is the dynamic nature of the experiences of security and danger, chaos and control that reflexive modernization introduces that creates a dynamic, anxious, risk-laden sensibility in modern citizens where it feels like we all must ride the juggernaut of late modernity (Giddens, 1990).

Reflexive modernization, Giddens argues, is accompanied by the increasing ability of people to reflect on structures and the rules that govern their lives and everyday practices. This creates new obligations and opportunities for people to choose which rules to follow and which to change and what kinds of lives they wish to lead. The self becomes what Giddens (1991, 1992) calls 'a reflexive project'. People are now compelled to plan their own lives, which faces them with new choices about how to be and how to live (Giddens, 1992). Helping professionals, such as psychotherapists, are increasingly drawn on to provide 'methodologies of life-planning' (Giddens, 1992: 180).

Giddens (1991) refers to this new domain of choice and personhood as 'life politics'. As I have shown elsewhere, social workers are increasingly involved in working with the 'life politics' of service users (Ferguson, 2001, 2003b). They are being used even by the most marginal members of society to assist them with their 'life-planning', particularly in situations where abused and vulnerable children and adults have acquired new rights to protection and healing from the trauma of violence (Ferguson, 2003a, 2004, 2008; Ferguson, Cooper and Jones 2008).

Social work steps in when what Giddens (1991) calls 'fateful moments' occur in people's lives, such as when older people become vulnerable in their own homes, children need to be accommodated in care and intimate abuse has to be stopped. Social workers help people with their life-planning and the decisions that have to be made as well as the courses of action that have to be initiated (Webb, 2006).

The net result is what Giddens (1992) calls the 'transformation of intimacy'. While homophobia remains a painful reality, individuals still have new freedoms to choose their sexuality. In heterosexual or family relationships, men and women no longer crudely tied to traditional assumptions about gender roles are required to negotiate about whether or not to live together, have children, stay together and who will mind the children, do the housework, be the breadwinner and so on. Also, as they get older, their children enter these negotiations, too.

Giddens (1998) argues that this change in intimate relationships has given rise to what he calls the 'democratic family'. He does not mean by this that equality is practised in all families, but that a key shift has occurred in the way personal lives are lived. Relationships based on trust, openness and negotiation cannot survive today without there being a 'discursive space' at their core. If relationships no longer bring satisfaction, they now can, and regularly do, end.

This is quite an optimistic view of the impact of change on social life. For Giddens, in conditions of reflexive modernity, trust, risk and expertise have become radicalized in ways that do not lead to a uniformly pessimistic scenario for the future – unlike that painted by some theorists of (post)modernity (see Chapter 11). The same individuals who are increasingly subject to, and the subjects of, globalization and social regulation have simultaneously become increasingly critical and *reflexive* with reference to them (see Deacon and Mann, 1999; Lash and Urry, 1994).

Considerable debate surrounds all Giddens's ideas. For instance, the degree to which democratic relations within families are becoming the societal norm is disputed. Lynn Jamieson (1998) suggests that empirical evidence for such a change is weak, while Carol Smart (2007) draws on a wealth of research to show that negotiation is a core value and practice in personal relationships today. These debates have also moved to the centre of social work theorizing.

Introducing Giddens's ideas to social work

Despite the enormity of his profile and influence on the social sciences over almost four decades, explicit use of Giddens's work in social work has, until recently, been remarkably limited. There are no books explicitly dedicated to applying his ideas to social work, as there are for other leading social theorists – notably Michel Foucault. However, some social work theorists have drawn heavily on his ideas (Featherstone, 2004; Ferguson, 2001, 2004; Smith, 2001; Webb, 2006), while others have rejected them (Garrett, 2003b, 2004a, 2008b) and a growing interest in and debate about the relevance of his work to social work is occurring (Ferguson, 2003b; Garrett, 2004a; Gray, 2008; Houston, 2004; Smith and White, 1997; Webb, 2006).

A full 'structurationist' approach to social work remains to be written. While Giddens does not give an example drawn from social work, his work has sensitized research to examine how 'structures', in the sense of rules and resources, enable social work to go on. In a study of social work and child protection in an environment that had become increasingly structured and bureaucratized in response to system failures to protect children, I found that social workers were broadly in favour of the increasing rules and procedures that governed their practices because they lent some predictability to work pervaded by uncertainty. How those rules and procedures were interpreted and put into practice by individuals and teams varied considerably. The structures both enabled the work to go on in ways that were regarded as good practice and were often brought into being differently from case to case, worker to worker and team to team (Ferguson and O'Reilly, 2001). One can, following Giddens, say that this is the 'duality of structure' in social work in action. What constituted the social work was a product of the relationship between the structures and the actions taken by professionals and service users.

Giddens's work provides resources for the study of the ways in which professionals work knowledgeably with and within structures to carve out actions that make a (positive) difference to service users and their lives. That does not mean simply accepting structures for what they are, but having an understanding of them as providing rules and resources that are given meaning through human action and how they are mobilized by the creative practices of laypeople, service users and professionals who, together, co-construct what social work is (Ferguson, 2008).

Giddens had many things to say about the role of the welfare state and expertise in people's everyday lives that are deeply relevant to social work. Indirectly, Giddens's work has contributed greatly by helping to create the conditions within which reflexivity and critical reflection are now central to the social sciences and social work (see D'Cruz, Gillingham and Melendez, 2007; Fook, 2002, 2004; Taylor and White, 2000). Carole Smith (2001), Stephen Webb (2006) and Harry Ferguson (2004) have drawn on Giddens in developing understandings of the nature of trust and risk in late modern social work, as has Mel Gray (2008) with respect to spirituality.

Giddens's work has been subject to a huge amount of commentary and critique. Structuration theory has been and continues to be both developed (Stones, 2005) and rejected as a basis for sociology. Many critics have pointed out that the notion of 'structuration' is problematic in that it implies an equal relationship of power and influence between social structures and actors. Thinking of social work, just what scope is there today for service users to create their own lives and, indeed, for social workers to create their own practice?

A number of critics of how social work has developed over the past 20 years argue that the discretion social workers once had has diminished because of the rise of bureaucracy, managerialism and targets. Thus, Webb (2006) is critical of Giddens because he gives too much scope to individuals to create their own lives and simplifies notions of power and social regulation. This is a common criticism of the theory of reflexive modernization, that its model of the self-reflexive individual relates primarily to people who are socially and economically privileged, those who have the cultural and material resources to engage in self-inspection (Lash, 1994).

Another strand of criticism comes from those influenced by psychoanalysis and psycho-social studies who suggest that Giddens is too optimistic in his view of the positive capacity of individuals to understand their lives and always know why they act as they do. This is because Giddens's view undermines the impact of the unconscious and people's capacity for sabotaging themselves and others – something that is familiar to a lot of social workers (Hoggett, 2001).

There is some substance to these criticisms. Because of how he tried to reorient sociology away from its pervasive 'structure as constraint' position, Giddens's work tends to point to the enabling, creative features of human beings and systems and underplays the significance of constraints on how people can live. However, what these critics overlook is how social work goes on not only in circumstances of struggle where there is poverty but also where there are problems such as abuse, addiction and trauma. Help with life-planning is a crucial dimension of what people need and desire from social workers and other professionals (Ferguson, 2004).

It is in the area of intimacy and personal life that Giddens's ideas are having the most impact and prompting debate in social work. Paul Garrett (2003b, 2004a) rejects Giddens's (1991, 1994a) notion of 'life politics' and its application to social work (Ferguson, 2001) and argues that the evidence for more democratic relationships both within families and between service users and social workers does not exist. The dominant pattern, he suggests, is for mothers to continue to be oppressed by social workers who regulate them according to traditional expectations of motherhood so they continue to carry an unequal share of domestic responsibilities (a broadly similar view of the 'social control' role of social work is taken by Scourfield and Welsh, 2003). Like Webb (2006), this leaves underanalysed just what social workers actually do do in their practices.

Giddens's work forces us to examine the creative ways in which social workers use knowledge and create their own practice and the possibilities for them to help to shape and change the systems in which they work.

Brid Featherstone (2004), drawing on feminist perspectives and a range of research, shows how the aim of trying to make families more democratic is hugely relevant as a goal in social work and family support work. Crucial to this, she argues, is the need to disaggregate the 'family' in terms of power, gender and age relations if the meanings of child welfare interventions and the possibilities for promoting democratic relationships in households are to be understood (Featherstone, 2004; see also, Smart and Neale, 1999; Smart and Shipman, 2004). This requires recognition of the diversity of 'family' forms that typify social work and family support work and the importance of using power constructively to work with such fluid relationships in creative, skilful ways (see also, Gordon, 1989, and Chapter 6).

Sally Holland, Jonathan Scourfield, Sean O'Neill and Andrew Pithouse (2005) skilfully test the validity of Giddens's notion of democratic families through a qualitative study of family group conferences (FGCs). These are large group meetings at which the family (defined widely in terms of any relatives and significant others they wish to include) and professionals discuss and assess family problems and negotiate ways forward. Conscious efforts are made to give the family time to decide what their difficulties are and what they need.

Holland et al's (2005) careful analysis of how all family members experienced FGCs shows that such interventions can enable children and all adults and other significant people in the family's life to be heard and for negotiation around rights and needs to occur. In following up the research subjects six months after the conference, they found that significant changes had occurred for many children and family members (see also, Dalrymple and Horan's sensitive (2007) analysis of the use of advocacy at FGCs and case conferences).

Yet, for Holland et al. (2005) (and, to a much larger extent, Garrett, 2003a, 2004a, b, c and d and Scourfield and Welsh, 2003), where child welfare and issues of State power are at stake, promoting democracy in any absolute sense is difficult. That is because what they call 'imposed empowerment' – the imposition of power in telling parents and carers and sometimes children what to do, irrespective of what they wish and say – is so central to the work.

Harry Ferguson (2001, 2003a, 2004, 2008) argues that community-based child protection and family support interventions can and do promote democratic families. Even statutory social workers can use their powers to enable all family members to have the kinds of relationships within which children, women and men can live safe, satisfying lives, enabling people to shape a 'life of their own' (Beck and Beck-Gernshiem, 2002).

A Giddensian perspective helps us appreciate how this means enabling service users to practise the 'new intimacy' in terms of emotional communication and negotiation in the context of equal relationships (Giddens, 1992). This involves assisting people to move beyond traditional hierarchical forms of patriarchal relationships and towards the creation of 'democratic' forms of relationships that promote equality for all in terms of the distinct needs and life plans of women, men and children, where the children are heard as well as seen and feel safe; women as well as men are treated with respect and given rights to protection and an identity; and men as well as women are enabled to have expressive emotional lives and relationships (Featherstone, 2004; Ferguson, 2008).

Research into work that goes on when engaging with fathers also shows that such interventions focus on improving men's parenting skills and their emotional capacities and ability to communicate and be in equal relationships with their loved ones (Ferguson and Hogan,

2004). This is precisely what 'democracy of the emotions' is, enabling men as well as women to become 'good enough carers' (Giddens, 1992).

Jane Donoghue (2008) uses Giddensian theories of reflexive modernization and life politics to argue that the social control orientation that dominates the theorizing of youth justice work and ASBOs is one-dimensional as it fails to analyse how service users and professionals can work together creatively to achieve greater self-actualization and life-planning for vulnerable people.

Significance for social work practice

I have sought to set out Giddens's ideas and establish their relevance to social work practice. It is vital in doing this to distinguish Giddens's role as a public intellectual and the impact of his thinking on political philosophies and practices from his theories and concepts (Deacon and Mann, 1999; Mouzelis, 2001). Giddens's concepts and rich theoretical work have a real relevance to social work practice, irrespective of the political position he has increasingly adopted in his career. Social workers need to assess the extent to which they assist in making sense of societies and people's experiences. The role of sociology in Giddens's hands is to increase understandings of society, not to – in any ideologically driven way – change it. He does, however, have real faith in the capacity of human beings to be moral agents and critically reflect on and change their lives and society in democratically advantageous ways. People will obviously accept or reject his more political later work on the basis of their own politics, but this should not be the basis for rejecting the validity of his concepts. When this distinction is made, what becomes evident is the absence by his critics in social work of any real interrogation of the lived experiences of service users and the meanings of social work practices in the reflexive conditions of late modernity.

Giddens's ideas enable us to see that, in a context where we all have new choices about how to live and who to be, 'helping' practices like social work play an increasingly important role in enabling vulnerable people to choose well and gain control of their lives, which involves learning about and changing the self and one's emotional life. Promoting life-planning and 'mastery' for service users is central to best practice in late modern social work. That does not mean there are no limits and controls on what people can do and be. Poverty, racism, sexism, 'disablism' and other social divisions continue to create inequalities that severely limit people's life chances. Yet, Giddens's ideas do have much in common with critical social work's traditional concern with issues of equality and the development of democratic relations with service users. It provides the basis for developing critical social work to include significant areas that it has tended to ignore, including the 'self', life-planning, the emotions and democratic relations and families.

Study questions

1. What does Giddens mean by 'structuration' in accounting for the nature of the individual and society?
2. According to Giddens, a 'transformation of intimacy' has occurred and personal relationships and families have become more 'democratic'. What does this mean and how does it apply to social work?
3. How can social workers help people with their 'life-planning'?

Glossary

Democratic family A household in which relationships between adults and between adults and children are based on values and practices of equality, negotiation and shared decision-making.

Duality of structure Refers to the way in which the structural properties of social life and systems are not separate from the actions of human beings, but inherently linked – what people do in their day-to-day lives produces and reproduces what social structures are.

Fateful moments These occur when consequential events happen in people's lives and decisions have to be made or courses of action initiated. Social work often intervenes in such moments, such as when older people become vulnerable in their own homes, children need to be accommodated in care and abusive relationships have to end.

Late (or high) modernity The current phase of development of modern institutions, marked by the globalizing and radicalizing of the basic traits of modernity.

Life-planning The process in which individuals engage when faced with choices about how to live and who to be. It is also the work that professionals such as social workers engage in with service users in helping or directing them to make (healthy) decisions.

Life politics is the politics of choice in a late modern context where people have new choices to make about how to make the most of their life chances. Life-planning is the practical application of life politics and is how social workers enable service users to reflect critically on their choices, emotions and change.

Reflexive modernization The routine incorporation of new knowledge or information into cultures, organizations and individual's actions that reconstitutes what those cultures, organizations and lives are.

Reflexive project of the self The process whereby self-identity is constituted and reconstituted by people reflecting on their lives and the rules they live by, which leads to them changing their lives and, in some instances, the rules.

Structuration The structuring of social relations through the interaction between powerful institutions – such as the State – and the actions of human beings. It refers to how social structures are made up of rules and resources that enable as well as constrain what people can do and how they act.

Select bibliography

Probably the best place to begin when reading Giddens is *The Consequences of Modernity* (1990) and his essay 'Living in a post-traditional society' (1994b), both of which provide accessible overviews of many of his key ideas. The best overview of the development of Giddens' work, critiques and key debates it has provoked is by Bryant and Jary (2001).

In social work, the most rigorous application of Giddens's ideas is to be found in Ferguson's (2004) *Protecting Children in Time: Child abuse, Child protection and the consequences of modernity* and Webb's (2006) *Social Work in a Risk Society*. For an introduction to Giddens's ideas for social work, see Ferguson (2001) and for a debate about the value of Giddens's ideas for social work see Ferguson (2003b), Garrett (2003b, 2004a, 2008b) and Houston (2004).

3

Pierre Bourdieu

Paul Michael Garrett[1]

Some biographical details

Pierre Bourdieu, 'a philosopher turned anthropologist (and, later, sociologist)', was born the 'son of a postman in a remote peasant village in southern France' (Callinicos, 1999: 288; Noble and Watkins, 2003: 521). He was drafted in 1955 and sent to Algeria where he served as a conscript during the Algerian war of independence that had begun the previous year. He remained in Algeria, as the war continued, working at Algiers University and carrying out the fieldwork he was to constantly draw on throughout the rest of his career. On his return to France, he went on to occupy a prestigious position within the higher education field, as Chair at the Collège de France, and wrote more than 40 books and over 400 articles. For Bridget Fowler (2003: 486) his 'magnum opus' was *Distinction* (Bourdieu, 2004), originally published in 1979 – the same year that Jean-François Lyotard's immensely influential *The Postmodern Condition* (1994) appeared in France. Bourdieu's book, *The Weight of the World: Social suffering in contemporary society* (Bourdieu, Accardo, Balazas, Beaud et al., 2002), a collaborative work with more than 20 sociologists, had an impact unmatched by any social science book in recent

---

[1] This chapter draws on prior work (see Garrett, 2007a and b).

memory in France: it sold over a hundred thousand copies in three months and remained at the top of the bestseller list for months. The book was also extensively discussed in political circles and popular magazines, even going on to be adapted for the stage (see Wacquant, 1998).

Key ideas

Bourdieu's 'leading theoretical claim is that his work transcends the dualism between explanations that attribute social change and social reproduction to certain overarching structures and theorizations that privilege individual subjective intentions or experience' (Bridge, 2004: 59). Similarly, his closest academic colleague has argued that Bourdieu's thought and work lies at the 'confluence of intellectual streams and academic traditions that have typically [been] construed as discordant or incompatible' (Wacqaunt, 1998: 218). Moreover, Bourdieu 'forges an original conceptual arsenal' (218) anchored by the notions of *habitus, field* and *capital*.

Habitus, therefore, as 'social life incorporated, and thus individuated', was meant to 'transcend' the opposition between the individual and society that has tended to dominate social theory (Bourdieu, 1994). It is the 'constraint of social conditions and conditionings, *right in the very heart* of the "subject"' (Bourdieu, 1994: 15, emphasis added). According to Bourdieu, it is a person's 'whole manner of being' (in Bourdieu et al., 2002: 510; see also Bourdieu, 1994; 2002a; 2002b).

The fullest characterization of habitus is found in *Outline of a Theory of Practice*, published in 1977 (Bourdieu, 2003a). This book draws on his fieldwork in Algeria and – in what Charles Lemert (2000: 101) describes as 'one of the most beautifully composed passages in the whole of sociological literature' – Bourdieu states that habitus is a 'system of durable, transposable *dispositions*, structured structures predisposed to function as structuring structures'.

In truth, Bourdieu was, perhaps, seeking to reformulate an idea that already had currency within philosophical and sociological literature and discourse. Roy Nash (1999: 180), for example, maintains that habitus 'derives from *habere*, to have, which was the Latin translation given to the Greek *hexis*'. Jeremy Lane (2000) also draws attention to the writings of Saint Thomas Aquinas and his use of habitus. Similarly, Loïc Wacquant (1998: 322) acknowledges that habitus is 'an old philosophical concept, used intermittently by Aristotle (under the term *hexis*), Hegel, Weber, Durkheim, Mauss and Husserl, among others'.

For Bourdieu (1994: 10) none of this is to be disputed. The key point is that he 'completely rethought' the concept, which 'can be understood as a way of escaping from the choice between a structuralism without subject and the philosophy of the subject'. Indeed, as Jim Wolfreys (2000) argues, in a sense, the whole of Bourdieu's sociology was constructed as a reaction to the two major intellectual currents of this period (the 1960s and 1970s), existentialism and structuralism. His intellectual project, therefore, was to overcome the opposition between the subjectivist emphasis on individual consciousness and the objectivist preoccupation with social structures.

Bourdieu (1994: 4–5) saw structuralism, and the 'structuralist generation', as a response to the 'need to react against what existentialism had represented for them: the flabby "humanism" that was in the air, the complacent appeal to "lived experience"'. His habitus formulation, therefore, while being equally opposed to existentialism and other subjectivist visions, was seeking to 'reintroduce agents that Levi-Strauss and the structuralists, among others Althusser, tended to abolish, making them into simple epiphenomena of structure ... Social agents, in archaic societies as well as in ours, are not automata regulated like clocks, in accordance with laws which they do not understand' (Bourdieu, 1994: 9). The problem, as he saw it, was that structuralists, such as Louis Althusser, were producing a 'grand theory without agents', without ever seeing 'a worker, or a peasant, or anything' (Bourdieu, in Karakayli, 2004: 359). In short, they left 'no scope for human agency' (Bourdieu, in Ovenden, 2000).

Perhaps unsurprisingly, given his theorization, childhood is particularly important. That is because habitus is 'laid down in each agent' in their 'earliest upbringing' and from then on it continues to reverberate throughout a person's lifetime (Bourdieu, 2003a: 81). Moreover, Bourdieu was to maintain an interest in the function and role of education, in its broadest sense, but also specifically within the institutionalized domain, or field, of education with a capital 'E'. Indeed, despite their different theoretical orientations, for both Althusser and Bourdieu, school was 'the major modern ideological base' (Fowler, 1997: 22).

Indeed, in the conversations reported in *The Weight of the World: Social suffering in contemporary society,* school was frequently at the 'core of the suffering of the interviewees' (Bourdieu, in Bourdieu et al., 2002: 507). Also relevant in this context, for Bourdieu, is how 'materially secure children' with their 'casual ease' within Education are able to glide through this particular field, whereas working-class children and children of the unemployed are likely to encounter obstacles and difficulties (Fowler, 1997). This is not to dismiss those miraculous exceptions – *des miracules* – the educationally highly successful children of the working class and unemployed who 'make it', thus allowing us to 'believe that the system is egalitarian and meritocratic after all' (Moi, 1991: 1026). It is, however, to recognize, along with Bourdieu, that 'the education system is one of the principal agents of *symbolic violence* in modern democracies' (Moi, 1991: 1023, emphasis added): that is to say, it is a form of ideological violence that is apt to stigmatize or devalue, but is apt to be viewed as legitimate by those subjected to it because of previous patterns of socialization.

According to Bourdieu, the relationship between habitus and what he terms *fields* is also crucial, with neither the former nor the latter having the 'capacity to determine social action' (Wacquant, 1998: 222). In brief terms, a field is 'a structured social space, a field of forces' (Bourdieu, 1998: 40) with agents and groups of agents being defined by their relative positions in that space.

Fields can be interpreted as having at least three key characteristics that are important within Bourdieu's conceptual paradigm. First, the field (or particular fields) is crucial in terms of the evolution of the habitus of those located or positioned there. Second, a field seeks to maintain its autonomy. So, crucially for Bourdieu, maintaining the autonomy of the fields of cultural and scientific production becomes increasingly important, indeed urgent, as the forces of neoliberalism attempt to penetrate them, undermining this (relative) autonomy. Related to this is a third characteristic of fields, which is the competition that takes place within them. As Bourdieu states, in 'most fields, we may observe what we characterize as competition for accumulation of different forms of *capital*' (Bourdieu, in Bourdieu and Eagleton, 1994: 271). In a lecture in 1989 (Bourdieu, 2002a: 233–4) he maintained:

According to my empirical investigations [there is] economic capital (in its different forms), cultural capital, social capital, and symbolic capital ... Thus agents are distributed in the overall social space, in the first dimension, according to the overall volume of capital they possess and, in the second dimension, according to the structure of their capital, that is the relative weight of the different species of capital, economic and cultural, in the total volume of their assets.

Main contribution

Aside from seeking to evolve and promote a conceptual paradigm pivoting on the interplay of habitus, field(s) and capital(s), Bourdieu's intellectual project is also significant on account of his preoccupation with the role of intellectuals during a period of neoliberal incursion into *all* areas of life (see Penna and O'Brien, 2006, and Chapter 10). This chapter, therefore, now turns to briefly examine this dimension.

In comments made with reference to France, but equally applicable elsewhere, Bourdieu (in Bourdieu, et al., 2002: 182–3) was scathing about the role that some notable intellectuals fulfilled in promoting a so-called 'modernization':

[B]y associating efficiency and modernity with private enterprise, and archaism and inefficiency with the public sector, they seek to substitute the relationship with the customer, supposedly more egalitarian and more effective, for the relation to the user; finally, they identify 'modernization' with the transfer into the private sector of the public services with the profit potential and with eliminating or bringing into line subordinate staff in the public services, held responsible for inefficiency and every 'rigidity'.

It is probably comments such as this that have led a number of writers to argue that in Bourdieu's later contributions there is something of a 'political turn'. Wolfreys (2000, 2002), for example, appears to think that there was such a 'turn' with the abandonment of reformism by French social democracy, leading Bourdieu to adopt a more radical stance. This interpretation is reflected by a number of other commentators who, similarly, detect a 'refocusing' in Bourdieu's later work. However, Willem Schinkel (2003: 69) is more likely to be correct in concluding that there is 'no real "turn" of this kind in his work'. Indeed, some of Bourdieu's earliest contributions – a number of which are, unfortunately, unavailable in English – were already critical and political pieces (see Lane, 2000). Perhaps what 'changed in the later years was the directness with which the critique was put forward' (Schinkel, 2003: 69).

Which particular social and politics issues and causes, therefore, did Bourdieu support? Not surprisingly, given his remarks above, the key struggle was to be waged against the 'scourge of neoliberalism', which has come to 'be seen as an inevitability' (Bourdieu, 2001: vii, 30). On occasions, because of political 'spin', the true intent of the neoliberal project was disguised, perhaps even appearing, 'new', 'modern' and 'radical' (Bourdieu, 2001: 35, original emphasis):

It is characteristic of *conservative revolutions* ... that they present restorations as revolutions ... [This new form of conservative revolution] ratifies and glorifies the reign of what are called the financial markets, in other words the return of the kind of radical capitalism, with no other law than the return of maximum profit, an unfettered capitalism without any disguise, but rationalized, pushed to the limits of its economic efficacy.

Given this was so what was to be done? Essentially, Bourdieu called for a return to a more 'Keynesian state-regulated market' (Schinkel, 2003: 71). Important, in this context, was the need to restore a human dimension to economic planning (Bourdieu, 2001: 39):

> All the critical forces in society need to insist on the inclusion of the social costs of economic deci-sions in economic calculations. What will this or that policy cost in the long term in lost jobs, suf-fering, sickness, suicide, alcoholism, drug addiction, domestic violence, etc. all things which cost a great deal, in money, but also in misery?

Moreover, we are now witnessing the 'destruction of the economic and social bases of the most precious gains of humanity' (Bourdieu, 2001: 37). It is vital, therefore, that the 'critical efforts of intellectuals [and] trade unions … should be applied as a matter of priority against the with-ering away of the State' (Bourdieu, 2001: 40). Unlike voguish social theorists, such as Ulrich Beck (2000), for whom trade unions are to be derided and ridiculed as 'zombie categories', Bourdieu recognized the vital role that they fulfil within social democracies. Furthermore, during the wave of public-sector strikes that took place in France in December 1995, Bourdieu intervened in various ways and spoke, for example, at a meeting of striking railway workers (Wolfreys, 2000). More broadly, Wolfreys (2000: 13) argues that Bourdieu presents a 'vigorous optimistic antidote to the pessimism which has gripped sections of the Left'. Indeed, shortly before his death in early 2002, Bourdieu claimed that he was 'more optimistic about the future than at any time in the last three decades, despite the seeming triumph of global capital' (in Stabile and Morooka, 2003: 338).

Indeed, he viewed it as crucial to combat the 'myth of globalization' (see, particularly, Bourdieu, 2001: 28–9) – a 'myth' that is, of course, central to the faltering New Labour 'project' in the UK. A further dimension relating to Bourdieu's role as a critical intellectual pivots on his analysis and critique of the 'cultural imperialism' of the United States. For Bourdieu and Wacquant (1998: 41; see also Garrett, 2007a) this:

> rests on the power to universalize particularisms linked to a singular historical tradition by caus-ing them to be recognized as such … [T]oday numerous topics directly issuing from the intellec-tual confrontations relating to the social particularity of the American society and its universities have been imposed, in apparently de-historicized form, upon the whole planet.

This process – often masquerading within the social sciences as benign and simply indicative of 'policy transfer' (Dolowitz with Hulme, Nellis and O'Neill, 2000) – could, however, be viewed as a form of 'symbolic violence'. In this context, one of the key points Bourdieu was alert to – indeed, horrified by – in his later work was the way in which capitalism is continu-ing to transform the United States and he was fearful that Europe risked being transformed in a similar way. This specifically relates to his, and Wacquant's, concern with the impact of neoliberalism on those in contact with social workers – the social and economically marginal-ized. The ghettos of the USA he saw as 'abandoned sites that are fundamentally defined by an absence – basically that of the state and of everything that comes with it, police, schools, health-care institutions, associations, etc.' (Bourdieu, in Bourdieu et al., 2002: 123). Indeed, in some cities in the USA 'public authority has turned into a war machine against the poor', with social workers only able to see 'clients' in their offices (Wacquant, in Bourdieu et al., 2002: 137–8).

There remain, however, major conceptual problems with some of Bourdieu's formulations. For example, it can be suggested that his lack of engagement, even flawed contributions, relating to issues pivoting on multiculturalism, race and ethnicity is important. Furthermore, Bourdieu's 'conceptual arsenal' (Wacquant, 1998: 220) possibly lays too great an emphasis on the dulled passivity of social actors, particularly the working class and the dominated. Perhaps his ideas on the function of the State can also be viewed as problematic. These are substantial areas that lie outside the scope of this short chapter to explore (see, however, Garrett, 2007a and b).

Initially more irritating for readers new to Bourdieu will be an assortment of obstacles that can 'get in the way' of comprehending him. Here we might, for example, include his prose style, the sheer scale of his 'output' and related matters, the fact that most readers (perhaps especially those situated outside the French intellectual field and its associated cultural milieu) might fail to recognize key contextual factors only hinted at in his work and, the misleading labels frequently attached to Bourdieu, such as 'Marxist' or 'postmodernist' (see Garrett, 2007a).

Introducing Bourdieu's ideas to social work

At the heart of this chapter is the understanding that Bourdieu is of significance for social work theory and practice, irrespective of his neglect in these spheres (see also Garrett, 2007a). Indeed, beyond France, and specifically in terms of social work, Bourdieu's theorizing and his critical engagement with key contemporary political issues have been insufficiently recognized with, for example, Lena Dominelli's (1997a) *Sociology for Social Work* failing to even find a place for him in the index to the volume. However, and perhaps paradoxically, Bourdieu frequently revealed his interest in social work and attempted to comprehend the situation of social workers confronted by the impact of neoliberalism (see particularly, Bourdieu et al., 2002: 181–255). This concern with the trajectory of social work is unusual in a high-profile social theorist, with only Zygmunt Bauman (2000) – a sociologist of a very different theoretical orientation – appearing to have a similar interest.

Related to his conceptualization of the State, Bourdieu viewed social workers as 'agents of the state' who are 'shot through with the contradictions of the state' (Bourdieu, in Bourdieu et al., 2002: 184). There are, moreover, a number of examples, particularly in *The Weight of the World*, of his trying to highlight the 'real institutional dilemmas haunting "street-level" bureaucrats' (Stabile and Morooka, 2003: 337). He also recognized the fact that many social workers, and those undertaking similar work, should 'feel abandoned, if not disowned outright, in their efforts to deal with the material and moral suffering that is the only certain consequence' (Bourdieu, in Bourdieu et al., 2002: 183) of rampant neoliberalism. One of the chief problems is that social workers (Bourdieu et al., 2002: 190):

> must unceasingly fight on two fronts: against those they want to help and who are often too demoralized to take a hand in their own interests, let alone the interests of the collectivity; on the other hand, against administrations and bureaucrats divided and enclosed in separate universes.

Indeed, it can be argued that there is a need, if not for a Bourdieusian social work, then for a social work *informed* by Bourdieu's theoretical insights and his opposition to neoliberalism. Indeed, the definition of social work appears to orientate the profession in the direction of Bourdieu. More specifically, the International Federation of Social Workers' definition of social work connects to a range of Bourdieu's preoccupations (Hare, 2004). Thus, the references to the relation between people and their environments and more expansive ideas associated with the championing of liberation, human rights and social justice are all *core* themes for Bourdieu. Furthermore, there are at least two significant ways in which he might aid in the construction of a reconfigured critical and 'radical' social work in the early twenty-first century.

First, Bourdieu's theorization – what has been described as his 'conceptual arsenal' – might assist social workers in evolving better forms of practice. In the welfare field, the concept of habitus becomes particularly relevant at the point of contact between the social professions and the users of services. His theoretical contribution might, in this context, enable social workers working with children and families to gain greater insight into doxic ideas on 'good enough parenting' (Polansky, Ammons, and Weathersby, 1983). What, moreover, might be the forms of capital deployed in the formulation and promotion of constructs such as that preoccupied with the 'social presentation' of young people in public care (Garrett, 2003a)? Furthermore, how is capital being implicitly marshalled in the context of child adoption? More specifically, how might the differential access to capital(s) impact on, and help determine, the outcomes for the 'birth parents' and those seeking to adopt children? Are the differing positions that they frequently occupy in social space a crucial and insufficiently examined factor?

Specifically in terms of social work activity, an awareness of habitus, fields and capital(s) might, for example, enrich social work assessments. Indeed, it might be argued that a more Bourdieusian reading of the Laming Report (which investigated the circumstances related to the death of Victoria Climbié and was subsequently to influence the Children Act 2004) is a potentially rich area for future investigation given the 'complex field of differentiated economic and social statuses, ethnicities, identities, rights and entitlements' in which Victoria and her aunt moved (see also Lewis and Neal, 2005: 426). The pair covered a range of physical sites (inter-country, intra-country, inter-city, intra-city, etc.), but they also moved through social space. Indeed, key Bourdieusian concepts, such as habitus, capital and fields, could be deployed to try and better comprehend how these two black African females – one a child and the other an adult – were perceived and engaged with in their many encounters with child welfare professionals in France and England.

Clearly social workers themselves operate 'in a field with a political capital, and the exercise of their power' can produce 'stigma, negative symbolic capital for their clients' (Peillon, 1998: 223). However, Bourdieu's work can also serve to emphasize the profession's more benign characteristics and help map its future direction.

Important in this respect is Bourdieu's recognition of the centrality of 'talk' for social work (see also Parton and O'Byrne, 2000). Thus, his theorizing might assist in combating the damage rendered to the 'work' in social work on account of the increasing use of centrally devised schedules, tick lists and electronic templates that have been introduced into practice since the 1990s (see also Garrett, 2005).

In contrast to this development, Bourdieu's approach is pluralistic and open to hearing many 'voices'. As he states, following the lead of novelists such as James Joyce, 'we must relinquish the single, central, dominant, in a word, quasi-divine, point of view ... We must work instead with the multiple perspectives that correspond to the multiplicity of coexisting, and sometimes directly competing points of view' (in Bourdieu et al., 2002: 3). These and many similar remarks are connected to the process of research in the social sciences, but they could have a resonance for social workers and others in the welfare field.

Related to this is his commitment to 'active and methodical listening', as opposed to 'half-understanding' based on a 'distracted and routinized attention' (in Bourdieu et al., 2002: 609, 614). Furthermore, this notion (perhaps formerly so central to social work and reflecting 'traditional' values rooted, in part, in 'respect for persons') is oddly subversive when social workers are now increasingly subjected to a new 'time discipline' (Garrett, 2005) and, along with others in the public sector, are working under pressure inside of nervous and edgy neoliberal regimes that demand fast thinking and tangible outcomes (Bourdieu, 1998: 28–30: see also Harvey, 2005).

Second, Bourdieu's work could help social work to reflexively *fold inwards,* with social workers and 'social work academics' scrutinizing their own personal and collective habitus. Certainly there is an urgent requirement to interrogate more closely these destabilized and evolving professional fields. More fundamentally, of course, this could relate to an aspiration to be 'critical intellectuals' (Garrett, forthcoming). For example, how might a critical orientation interpret the changing habitus of social workers (Garrett, 2005, 2008 a and b)?

Still connected to social workers' need to interrogate their habitus and the field(s) they occupy, Bourdieu encourages us, of course, to see the social totality, the 'bigger picture' (see also Bourdieu, 2003b). Importantly in this regard, for him (and, perhaps, for social work), 'the main issue ... is neoliberalism and ... the retreat of the State' (in Ovenden, 2000: 1). Bourdieu emphasizes how this is a more than abstract consideration because, on a daily basis, neoliberalism *bites into* practice in social work and related fields (see also Harlow, 2004). It is, therefore, particularly important in this context for social workers to defend the autonomy of the field and champion a form of democratic professionalism (see also Davis and Garrett, 2004). As Mary Pileggi and Cindy Patton (2003: 318) maintain, when working in a neoliberal context, 'practitioners of a field become liable to two masters: the practices and norms of the discipline and the practices and norms of the market'. Given this tension, individual workers are, therefore, confronted with a choice as to which 'master' to follow.

Significance for social work practice

Bourdieu's disruptive, insistent interrogation of established 'truths' and his 'refusal to compromise with institutions' (Bourdieu, 1994: 4) that are increasingly steered, directed and shaped by the needs and demands of economic capital can serve as a guiding light for a renewed 'radical' social work practice as it attempts to 'pick up the pieces' in the early twenty-first century. His work frustrates, confuses, annoys and enlightens. Like the best of social theorists he *unsettles.* Moreover, he compels his readers to return, to read him again and again, and take away different or refined understandings of his mammoth contribution. Most importantly, Bourdieu's theorization and his nagging insistence on the relevance – and sheer *stickiness* – of social structure provide a useful counterweight, within the discourse of social work, to those contributions, often somewhat shallow and lacking in substance, that are apt to unduly inflate the role of individual agency within neoliberal modernity (Garrett, 2003b).

When Bourdieu died in January 2002, the world lost one of that rare and 'perhaps most endangered species: a prominent university intellectual who was also ... coolly and passionately and scientifically and politically engaged with the world around him' (Stabile and Morooka, 2003: 326). Bourdieu's early work 'focused on how class is *lived*, on how social differences inhabit the grain of everyday life' (Callinicos, 2000: 118–19), making him 'especially sensitive to the scale of socially unnecessary suffering – what he ... called *la misère du monde*'. Indeed, by the time of his death, Bourdieu had come to be seen as arguably 'the unofficial ideologue of the anti-globalization movement(s)' (Schinkel, 2003: 81).

Study questions

1. Why is Bourdieu mostly absent from the social work literature?
2. How can his writings and political activism aid social workers' understanding of neoliberalism?
3. What might be some of the problems with Bourdieu's theorization?

Glossary

Capital Different 'kinds of capital, like trumps in a game of cards, are powers which define the chances of profit in a given field' (Bourdieu, 1991: 230). Bourdieu refers to three main forms of capital:

Field A 'structured social space, a field of forces' (Bourdieu, 1998: 40), with agents and groups of agents being defined by their relative positions in this space. In 'most fields, we may observe what we characterize as competition for accumulation of different forms of capital' (Bourdieu, in Bourdieu and Eagleton, 1994: 271).

Habitus A 'system of durable, transposable *dispositions*, structured structures predisposed to function as structuring structures, that is as principles of the generation and structuring of practices and representations which can be objectively "regulated" and "regular" without in any way being the product of obedience to rules ... collectively orchestrated without being the product of the orchestrating action of a conductor' (Bourdieu, 2003a: 72).

- *economic* capital, which refers to material and financial assets, ownership of stocks and shares and so on;
- *cultural* capital, which can be viewed as 'scarce symbolic goods, skills and titles' (Wacquant, 1998: 221);
- *social* capital, which can be understood as resources or contacts 'accrued by virtue of membership of a particular group' (Wacquant, 1998: 221) or network.

Symbolic capital is best viewed as different from the three other forms of capital in so far as it can be *any* of these forms. As expressed by Bourdieu (1991: 230), 'symbolic capital, commonly called prestige, reputation, fame, etc, ... is the form assumed by these different kinds of capital when they are perceived and recognized as legitimate'. In the 'symbolic struggle for the production of common sense or, more precisely, for the monopoly of legitimate naming as the official – i.e. explicit and public – imposition of the legitimate vision of the social world, agents bring into play' symbolic capital (Bourdieu, 1991: 239).

Symbolic violence A form of ideological violence that is apt to stigmatize or devalue, but is also apt to be viewed as legitimate by those subjected to it because of previous patterns of socialization.

Select bibliography

For readers new to the work of Bourdieu, the best starting point is probably his overtly political journalism (Bourdieu, 2001, 2003b; see also Bourdieu, 1998). The mammoth *The Weight of the World: Social suffering in contemporary society* (Bourdieu et al., 2002) is also easy to read, dip into and may particularly interest social workers. His, and Wacqaunt's, polemical and controversial work on the 'cultural imperialism' of the United States can also be read by those with little acquaintance with French social theory (Bourdieu and Wacquant, 1999, 2001).

Bourdieu's more challenging sociological work is most accessible in the interviews that he gave and some of these are collected in Bourdieu (1994). His exchanges with Eagleton, Grass and Wacquant are also interesting, with his core sociological and political preoccupations being lucidly presented (Bourdieu and Eagleton, 1994; Grass and Bourdieu, 2002; Bourdieu and Wacquant, 2004). Bourdieu's formulation of habitus and related concepts is outlined in the volume edited by Hillier and Rooksby (Bourdieu, 2002b). A more detailed mapping of his conceptual arsenal features in *Outline of a Theory of Practice* (Bourdieu, 2003a; see also Bourdieu, 2004). *Pascalian Meditations*, one of Bourdieu's later works, is difficult, but will, perhaps, come to be regarded as one of his most substantial and rewarding books (Bourdieu, 2003c).

Illuminating articles on Bourdieu's work are, of course, available (see, for example, Garrett, 2007a, 2007c; Houston, 2002a; Moi, 1991; Wacquant, 1998). However, the best introduction to his life and work remains Jeremy Lane's lively and informative *Pierre Bourdieu: A critical introduction* (2000).

Michel Foucault

(4)

Allan Irving

Some biographical details

Michel Foucault (1926–1984) was a French philosopher whose work overturned many of the certainties of the eighteenth-century Enlightenment. There is an unmistakable shadow theme of darkness, transgression and disruption that inhabits all Foucault's work. The following five intellectual influences shed some light on this.

Five intellectual influences

What is it about Don Francisco Goya, the Marquis de Sade and Martin Heidegger that so captivated the young Foucault when he studied at the Ecole Normale Supérieure? The answer to that question furnishes a key to much of his subsequent thought. All three sparked Foucault's intellectual leave-taking from the thought of French philosopher René Descartes (1596–1650).

Descartes was committed to rational thought and explanation and, through the rational methods he set out in his *Discourse on Method* (1637), he believed it was possible to establish the truth – a complete, rational understanding of everything (Stone, 2006: Preface).

Foucault's *The Archaeology of Knowledge* (1972) is a brilliant parody of Descartes' work and a derisive dismissal of the notion of the truth, objective knowing and the belief that the world could be subjected to a rational ordering (Megill, 1985).

1. Don Francisco Goya

Foucault was always invigorated by the work of artists, particularly those who created dark, disturbing visions of death, secrecy and madness. His early attraction to Don Francisco Goya (1746–1828) ensured that his writing would never be tepid or without intensity.

Goya's 'Black Paintings' capture the artist's tortured soul. In one of these paintings, the *Witches' Sabbath,* the steely reason of the Enlightenment has disappeared (Tomlinson, 1992). Goya's 80 aquatint etchings, released in 1799 and known as *Los Caprichos* (The Caprices), form a series with which Foucault was thoroughly acquainted. They portray dreams, nocturnal scenes, the intricate play of light and darkness, ambiguous spaces, owls, bats, witches, grotesque figures, phantoms and monsters – all of which challenge rational, ordered Enlightenment thought (Schulz, 2005).

Recent scholarship suggests that *Los Caprichos* present us with two types of vision: observation and fantasy. It is worth noting that Foucault's work is replete with both types. Artistic creativity and creating the self as a work of art, which Foucault espoused in his later work, is closely associated with the fantastic and visionary in Goya's Work.

2. The Marquis de Sade

The Marquis de Sade (1740–1814) may well be troubling for social work, but to ignore de Sade's bearing on Foucault's thought would be to miss one of his central projects: creating and recreating the self as a work of art. This does have widespread implications for social work practice.

For Foucault, de Sade is a decisive thinker in the history of philosophy and it is evident in his work and experiences that he very much aspired to linking his voice to that of de Sade (LaCapra, 2000). Among the many aspects of de Sade that appealed to Foucault are de Sade's relentless pursuit of sexual transgression, his subversive iconoclasm, his reputation as a life-long rebel and his disdain for conventional authority and morality (Phillips, 2005; Schaeffer, 1999). Foucault was undoubtedly attracted by de Sade's view that the truth about the human condition was located in the sexual body and not in some notion of a mind, soul or spirit.

De Sade was an author on whom Foucault relied to reaffirm his continuous opposition to a normalizing rationality and sexuality; a writer and practitioner who understood the profound and shattering truths running through rivers of madness and 'directly recapture[d] the uncontaminated experience of madness'. As well, Foucault admired and paid tribute to de Sade for keeping alive dialogues with unreason (Whitebook, 2005). In *Madness and Civilization* Foucault (1988: 210, 285) wrote:

> Sadism is not a name finally given to a practice as old as Eros; it is a massive cultural fact which appeared precisely at the end of the eighteenth century, and which constitutes one of the greatest conversions of Western imagination; unreason transformed into a delirium of the heart, madness of desire, the insane dialogue of love and death in the limitless presumption of appetite … For Sade as for Goya, unreason continues to watch by night; but in this vigil it joins with fresh powers. The non-being it once was now becomes the power to annihilate. Through Sade and Goya, the Western world received the possibility of transcending its reason in violence, and of recovering tragic experience … After Sade and Goya unreason has belonged to whatever is decisive for the modern world.

It was from de Sade (and others) that Foucault derived the notion of what he called *limit experiences* – experiences that were wellsprings of surging creative energy and thought with the accompanying desire for transgression (Foucault, 1977). In order to enter places and spaces of limit experiences, it was necessary, thought Foucault, to embrace maladaptation, failure and pain (Miller, 1993). In the autumn of 1983, less than a year before he died, Foucault reputedly told friends that in the bathhouses of San Francisco 'he joined again in the agonies of torture, "trembling with the most exquisite agonies" voluntarily effacing himself, exploding the limits of consciousness, letting real, corporeal pain insensibly melt into pleasure through the alchemy of eroticism' (Miller, 1993: 28).

3. Martin Heidegger

On several occasions, Foucault spoke of his intellectual debt to the philosopher Martin Heidegger (1889–1976). In his final interview, just before his death in 1984, Foucault said that 'for me Heidegger has always been the essential philosopher ... my entire philosophical development was determined by my reading of Heidegger' (Foucault, 1990: 250; Martin, 1988: 12–13).

Much of Foucault's originality drew from Heidegger's intention to think the 'unthought' and Foucault discusses his own version at some length in *The Order of Things* (1970). One of Foucault's biographers writes that Foucault thought anyone prepared to 'descend into what Heidegger called the "unthought" must be prepared to probe beyond the limits of reason and to think without statute or rule, structure or order' (Miller, 1993: 49–50). Two recent books discuss in great detail and considerable originality the Heidegger/Foucault connection: Stuart Elden's (2001) *Mapping the Present: Heidegger, Foucault and the project of a spatial history* and Alan Milchman and Alan Rosenberg's edited (2003) collection, *Foucault and Heidegger: Critical encounters*.

Certainly Foucault noted Heidegger's emphasis on the importance of language, absorbing his characterization of language as 'the house of being'. He also enthusiastically pursued Heidegger's arguments that concepts, such as truth, knowledge and objectivity, were historically and culturally determined, not timeless, lying beyond time and chance (Sluga, 2005).

4. Samuel Beckett

In the early winter of 1953, Foucault saw Samuel Beckett's *Waiting for Godot*. The play was an epiphany for him. He often mentioned later that Beckett (1906–1989) was a radical departure from most prevailing schools of thought in the 1950s. Shortly before his death, he remarked (Begam, 1996: 185):

> I belong to that generation who, as students, had before their eyes, and were limited by, a horizon consisting of Marxism, phenomenology, and existentialism. Interesting and stimulating as these might be, naturally they produced in the students completely immersed in them a feeling of being stifled, and the urge to look elsewhere. I was like all other students of philosophy at that time, and for me the break was first Beckett's *Waiting for Godot*.

Both Beckett and Foucault rejected the postmedieval tradition of humanism, which developed through the Renaissance into the full-blown rationality of the Enlightenment. Closely associated with this tradition is the belief in the ability of humanity to know the universe and to understand our place in it. This is the empirical world of the schoolroom, the laboratory, science, mathematics, proportion, the world of the *pensum* (the mind, cogito).

For Beckett's characters, the *punctum* (the body), the lived, feeling experience of existence, punctures the known world of the mind. Offsetting the certain world of the mind – and this undoubtedly appealed to Foucault – is the dark, mysterious, inexplicable, chthonic (the underworld) of the punctum (Gontarski, 1995).

Beckett's novel *Murphy* (1938) does not find rationalism and the stability and certainty of the Enlightenment at the centre of the mind but unreason – a region that Foucault subsequently brilliantly explored in *Madness and Civilization* (1988). There are many examples in Foucault that show conclusively the enormous influence of Beckett. When he gave his inaugural lecture, 'Discourse on Language', at the Collège de France, he quoted one of his favourite passages from Beckett's novel, *The Unnamable* (Foucault, 1972: 215):

> I can't go on, you must go on, I'll go on, you must say words, as long as there are any, until they find me, until they say me – heavy burden, heavy sin; I must go on; maybe it's been done already; maybe they've already said me; maybe they've already borne me to the threshold of my story, right to the door opening onto my story; I'd be surprised if it opened.

5. Friedrich Nietzsche

With Goya, de Sade, Heidegger, Beckett and the anti-Enlightenment aesthetic they represent firmly in his mind, Foucault was now ready to absorb the work of the philosopher Friedrich Nietzsche (1844–1900).

In 1984, he said in an interview, 'I am simply a Nietzschean, and try as far as possible, on a certain number of issues, to see with the help of Nietzsche's texts' (cited in Sluga, 2005: 210). Nietzsche appears throughout Foucault's *Madness and Civilization* (1988: 289) and the book concludes by invoking him: 'the world that thought to measure and justify madness through psychology must justify itself before madness, since in its struggles and agonies it measures itself by the excess of works like Nietzsche'. Foucault is often viewed as the most iconoclastic of the postwar Nietzscheans.

After reading Nietzsche's *Untimely Meditations* (1997, 1876), a collection of four essays, in the summer of 1953, Foucault declared that, henceforth, he would carry out all his intellectual enquiries 'under the sun of the great Nietzschean quest' (Miller, 1993: 67).

Untimely Meditations was Nietzsche's attempt to sort out some purpose and direction for himself. He searched, as did Foucault later, for a realization of how one becomes what one is. Foucault was especially taken with one of Nietzsche's aphorisms: 'The enigma which man is to resolve he can resolve only in being, in being thus and not otherwise, in the imperishable … Be yourself! All you are now doing, thinking, desiring, is not you yourself' (Nietzsche, 1997, 1876: 127, 155).

Foucault, following Nietzsche, dismisses the notion that the self is simply given. Truth, and this includes the truth about one's self, 'is not something there, that might be found or discovered … but that must be created' (Nietzsche, 1968: 298). Reading Nietzsche convinced Foucault that even to begin to approach the truth means tearing oneself out of the routines and habits of everyday life. Those concerned with finding their own truth must descend,

Nietzsche writes in *Untimely Meditations* (1997, 1876: 154), 'into the depths of existence, with a string of curious questions: why do I live? What lesson have I to learn from life? How have I become what I am and why do I suffer from being what I am?'

Nietzsche's profound message, which completely changed Foucault's outlook, is that there are no enduring truths beyond time and chance. Rather than a futile search for eternal unchanging truth and meaning, Nietzsche urges the creation of new meaning out of the contingencies of one's existence. Life is something to be fashioned in the process of becoming who one is, an artistic creation (Nehamas, 1985; Rorty, 1989). 'We possess *art*,' Nietzsche wrote (1968: 435, emphasis in the original), '*lest we perish of the truth*'. Towards the end of his life, Foucault, picking up on Nietzsche's sentiments, often wrote and talked about creating ourselves as works of art.

Throughout his life, Foucault drew intellectual sustenance and courage from Nietzsche's thought and, in a 1971, lecture, 'The Will to Knowledge', he set out Nietzsche's depiction of knowledge and how it is created. By 1971, Nietzsche's point of view about knowledge and how it is created was also Foucault's (1997).

- Knowledge is an 'invention' behind which there is something quite distinct from it: an interplay of instincts, impulses, desires, fear, will to appropriation. Knowledge comes into being where these things clash.
- It arises not as an effect of their harmony or successful equilibrium, but of their hatred, their dubious, provisional compromise. It is not a permanent faculty; it is an event or at least a series of events.
- It is always servile, dependent, alert to advantages (not to its own, but to what might interest the instinct or instincts that dominate it).
- If it professes to be a knowledge of the truth, this is because it produces the truth through the action of a primordial and renewed falsification that establishes the distinction between the true and the untrue.

It is clear that Foucault derived his all-important power/knowledge connection from Nietzsche.

Key ideas

Foucault's work is often divided into three periods, or analytic shifts. The first is the archaeology of knowledge period of 1961–1969, in which he produced four major publications: *Madness and Civilization, The Birth of the Clinic, The Order of Things* and *The Archaeology of Knowledge*. In these books, Foucault depicted the birth of the modern social and human sciences, including social work, as being the result of a new humanist 'regime of truth'. Foucault characterized these as 'disciplines of knowledge', which he then analysed in terms of their 'discourses' (language practices), and what he called 'epistemes' – that is, the scientific conceptual frameworks that were used to create moral–legal norms – normalization – and establish regulatory practices of control and subjugation (Gabardi, 2001).

The second phase is the genealogy of power period of 1971–1976 and the major works he wrote during that time are his crucial essay 'Nietzsche, genealogy, history' and three books, *Discipline and Punish, The History of Sexuality, Volume I: An introduction* and *Power/Knowledge: Selected interviews and other writings, 1972–1977*. In these works, Foucault, borrowing from Nietzsche, develops a genealogical approach to history that holds out the potential for unveiling knowledge that has been subjugated and suppressed by power as it created 'true' and acceptable knowledge.

He views history as a dark chasm into which we descend looking for anomalies – a task he described as 'grey, meticulous, and patiently documentary' (Foucault, 1977: 139). Also, rather than starting in the past and working forwards to the present, as did traditional historians, Foucault started with the present and worked back, calling his approach a 'history of the present'.

For Foucault, Nietzsche 'is the philosopher of power' and he aspired to be Nietzsche's heir in his philosophical work during this period (Foucault, 1980b). His genealogical explorations of the emergence of Western morality, rationality and the autonomous individual are informed by his view that human values, identities and general outlooks on the world are all formed within specific historical frameworks and regimes of power – hence his anti-Enlightenment stance that there is no universal morality or rationality that can be applied to everyone.

Gabardi (2001), in *Negotiating Postmodernism*, suggests that these first two periods of Foucault's work can be defined by six themes:

- his archaeological and genealogical methodological creativity;
- his conception of discourse;
- his critical assessment of Enlightenment rationality;
- the notion of disciplinary power;
- the power/knowledge connection;
- the actual topics of his histories: madness, clinical medicine, the human and social sciences, prisons and sexuality.

Foucault's third stage – from 1980 to 1984 – can be portrayed as the aesthetic, ethical, subjectivity period of work, during which two important and final books were produced: *The History of Sexuality, Volume 2: The use of pleasure* and *The History of Sexuality, Volume 3: The care of the self*. Both explored 'practices of the self', where ethical practices of self-transformation are employed by the self on the self. Foucault probed Greek and Roman techniques of self-cultivation, by which means individuals worked to transform themselves to attain states of happiness, purity, wisdom, perfection or immortality.

In this last phase, Foucault was primarily interested in the 'arts of existence'. In an interview he gave in 1983, he remarked that 'we have to create ourselves as a work of art … couldn't everyone's life become a work of art' (Foucault, 1997: 261–2). Greco-Roman cultures saw desire and sexual practices as ethical or moral issues but not in the repressed or shameful way that Christianity was to later view them. Foucault's aim in his two final books was to show how sexual activity and sexual pleasure were problematized in classical antiquity through practices of the self, using the criterion of an 'aesthetics of existence' (Foucault, 1985: 12).

Introducing Foucault's ideas to social work

Foucault wrote in *Discipline and Punish* (1979: 29), 'The soul is the prison of the body'. Of special importance for social work is Foucault's lifelong concern with how our disciplinary practices, enforcing normalization, constrain human possibilities. He wrote (1983: 208):

> what has been the goal of my work during the last twenty years ... has not been to analyse the phenomenon of power ... my objective instead has been to create a history of the different modes by which, in our culture, human beings are made subjects.

Two aspects of Foucault's thinking about subjectivity are important for social work:

- to be aware of the multitude of ways discourses, including the discourses of social work, create particular subjects;
- the ways in which subjects can pursue the 'arts of existence in their lives'.

An in-depth understanding of Foucault can help social workers gain a more penetrating grasp of the transition from modernity to postmodernity – a transition that is often described as one of ever-increasing complexity, creating – in unsettling ways – social and personal worlds of greater contingency. It has been suggested that Foucault's work evokes an interplay between complexity and contingency, surging through our pluralized social spaces with their 'intersecting and overlapping flows and networks of power, knowledge, desire, and identity' (Gabardi, 2001: 65).

All Foucault's work revolves around the conviction that Enlightenment reason is historically contingent and all concepts of justice are not timeless and universal, but simply the outcome of particular historical power conflicts and temporary resolutions.

Social work could well benefit from an awareness that Foucault's works are a rich array of different and competing narratives, and are exercises in splitting apart our usual and standard ways of understanding things (Loesberg, 2005). Foucault's intellectual output is a beautiful example of a postmodern philosopher and writer at work: his creations taken as a totality abandon all grand narratives for sprawling, spider-like webs of texts in which everything weaves itself into everything else.

Foucault's archaeological and genealogical approaches have been a significant stimulus in taking us away from the notion that there is only one legitimate knowledge – scientific knowledge. Instead, he urges us to develop the capacity to unearth buried, suppressed and neglected knowledge that, historically, has been marginalized because of particular discursive power formations. If we allow ourselves to follow Foucault, it will give us the diversity we so desperately seek.

An example for social work is to understand how indigenous knowledge has been suppressed and subjugated in favour of 'scientific' knowledge. A fine example is Ken Moffatt's book, *A Poetics of Social Work* (2001), which is a genealogy of suppressed knowledge and practice in Canadian social work from 1920 to 1939. In speaking about subjugated knowledge, Foucault (2003: 8) refers to knowledge that is 'local, regional, or differential, incapable of unanimity ... different from all the knowledges that surround it, it is the reappearance of what people know at the local level' (see also Gray, Coates and Yellow Bird, 2008).

There is a strong social activism inherent in this approach as, once the repressed knowledge has been reclaimed, it is in a position to oppose and struggle against 'the coercion of a unitary, formal, and scientific theoretical discourse'. For Foucault (2003: 10), the archaeological/genealogical approach promotes the 'insurrection of knowledges' and, hence, promotes diversity. Foucault (1998: 359) also saw categories as blocking the expression of difference: 'the most tenacious subjectivation of difference is undoubtedly that maintained by categories ... they suppress anarchic difference, difference can only be liberated through the invention of acategorical thought'.

Foucault viewed the welfare state as the reinvention of earlier Christian pastoral power as secular experts – in the form of social workers, psychologists, welfare workers and healthcare professionals – made it their task to guide and enforce rules, procedures and regulations and control populations (Gabardi, 2001). What Foucault (1979: 304) calls a 'normalizing judgment' comes to prevail. In *Discipline and Punish* (p. 304). Foucault cogently observes the 'judges of normality are present everywhere', including 'the social worker-judge'. Another important dimension of Foucault's thought for social work and social work education and research is found in the following comment he made (2003: 287–8):

> I do not have a methodology that I apply in the same way to different domains. On the contrary, I would say that I try to isolate a single field of objects, a domain of objects, by using the instruments I can find or that I can forge as I am actually doing my research, but without privileging the problem of methodology in any way.

As Foucault sees it, the weather is always closing in: judgments rendered, surveillance practised, normalization coerced, control and discipline exercised, differences homogenized, transgressions prohibited and self-creation stifled. Foucault looks for openings, for transformations in our discontinuous moments. As a philosopher of dispersions, Foucault sought freedom – an imperative in all his work – and he believed that we could create alternative discourses that would shift us away from Enlightenment restrictions on what might be possible (2000: 273): 'Couldn't it be concluded that the Enlightenment's promise of attaining freedom through the exercise of reason has been turned upside down, resulting in a domination by reason itself, which increasingly usurps the place of freedom?'

Throughout his life, Foucault relentlessly applied his formidable intellectual powers to the problems and dilemmas of human life and existence. It is not hard to imagine, though, that he appreciated the comment of the protagonist in Beckett's novel *Molloy* (1965: 169) who, on an arduous winter journey home, is comforted and made happy by the thought of the complexity of the dance of his bees, saying to himself, 'here is something I can study all my life, and never understand'.

Significance for social work practice

Foucault's significance for social work practice lies in the fact that he overturned two pivotal ideas for evidence-based practice and the centrality of the individual in social work thinking and, in so doing, disrupted two kinds of certainties: the idea of an external objective empirical reality to be perceived, measured and counted; and an internal solid subjectivity. He showed how freedom in every moment of our lives, in its fluctuating intensities, needs to be reinvented. Foucault whispers to us across the years of multiplicity, power and resistance, transgression, endless decentrings, descent, excess, absence, humanity scarred and wounded, dotted with points of pain.

When he died in June 1984, Michel Foucault was unquestionably the world's best-known and most controversial intellectual (Miller, 1993). Spreading through the complexities of his thought and animating it is the hope 'that something new is about to begin, something we glimpse only as a thin line of light low on the horizon' (Foucault, 1973: 384).

Reason and scientific objectivity – as they had been constructed by the eighteenth-century Enlightenment – are viewed by Foucault, as they were by Nietzsche, as just intricate metaphors, forms of a culture of modernity now coming to a close. He intimated that, in the distance, we could perhaps faintly perceive other metaphors for a different kind of culture approaching 'in the dim light of dawn, in the brilliance of noon, or in the dissension of the falling day' (Foucault, 1973: 384–5). In the 'night of truth', there are no overarching truths that are universal and apply throughout history beyond time and chance (Foucault, 1987).

Study questions

In what ways do the following have relevance for social work practice?

1. What do you think Foucault meant when he told an interviewer, 'I am fully aware that I have never written anything other than fictions'?
2. For Foucault, the present historical moment is like any other present in the past in being problematic, but different always, too, in that it involves different problems. Foucault's genealogical method is, therefore, the investigation of a unique and problematic present.
3. Are there ways to offer resistance in Foucault's sense to our disciplinary and controlling society? Can resistance be positive and create new experiments in living?

Glossary

Archaeology The 'method' Foucault employs in *The Order of Things* and *The Archaeology of Knowledge* whereby, through a process of historical unearthing, it is possible to find the discursive formations that, in any historical period, determine what it is possible to say, think and even experience. It is a form of enquiry the aim of which is to rediscover on what basis knowledge and theory became possible.

Episteme The conditions of possibility for a particular discourse (such as the discourse of social work) in a given historical period.

Genealogy The 'method' Foucault began developing from 1971 on and employed in *Discipline and Punish*. Genealogy is an alternative way of doing history that introduces Foucault's understanding of power. Genealogy does not start with the past and work forwards in an inevitable linear progression to the present, as does conventional history. Instead, it works by a method of descent from the present to the past, finding, in the process, not historical inevitability, but historical emergence that is brought into existence by particular formations of power, which are always attempting to impose their own systems of domination, definitions of the truth and what counts as knowledge.

Governmentality and the Panopticon Governmentality for Foucault is both what we do to ourselves and what is done to us through all the techniques of bio-power. What he called 'normalizing judgment' by experts, such as social workers, is done through dividing practices and binary division all under the universal management of the normal: normal/not normal, sexually deviant/sexually normal, mad/not mad, and offenders/conformers. In *Discipline and Punish*, Foucault discussed at length how the management of normality is implemented by constant surveillance. Here, he made creative use of philosopher Jeremy Bentham's architectural plan for the ideal prison as a metaphor for how our society induces self-surveillance and compliance with normalization. Bentham called his model the Panopticon, where prison cells are arranged around a central observation tower so that inmates can always be observed by guards in the tower, but the tower watchers are not visible to the inmates. This arrangement puts the inmates in a position of not knowing if they are actually being watched at any given moment, so the effect is the same as constant surveillance and, hence, conformity and compliance with norms soon become internally habitual. Foucault argues that our entire society now practises constant surveillance in various ways, including social workers with their clients.

Problematization In his third and last period, Foucault immersed himself in what he called *problematizations* and, in his (1985: 10) *The use of pleasure*, he describes his work as trying to understand 'the conditions in which human beings "problematize" what they are, what they do, and the world in which they live'.

Power, bio-power, power/knowledge, resistance Power, for Foucault, in his post-1971 work, was not a form of sinister repression of one group or class by another. Instead, he (1980a: 93) saw power 'as something which circulates … and is exercised through a net-like organization … it is produced from one moment to the next … power is everywhere because it comes from everywhere'. Power is diffuse, unstable, local, fluid and embedded in our everyday practices, working in and flowing through the micropractices of institutions. Individuals both undergo and exercise power. Power is productive and produces different truths (never universal truths) and different knowledge in different historical periods and different cultural arrangements. Knowledge and truths are inventions, fictions behind which there is a complex playing out of forces and arrangements of power creating and recreating 'regimes of truth'. Bio-power is disciplinary power and creates 'docile bodies' through practices of surveillance and normalization acting on the body. However, Foucault suggested that where there is power there is always the possibility of resistance.

Select bibliography

As well as his own works there is an immense number of scholarly publications on and about Foucault. Besides Miller (1993), there are two excellent biographies that are a good place to start for those unfamiliar with his life and work:

Eribon, D. (1991) *Michel Foucault* (translated by Betsy Wing). Cambridge, MA.: Harvard University Press.
Macey, D. (1994) *The Lives of Michel Foucault*. New York: Pantheon.
Burchell et al. (1991) and Dreyfus and Rabinow (1982) are also worth looking at, as well as Deleuze (1988).
Besides Margolin (1997), Chambon, Irving and Epstein (1999) deal specifically with Foucault and social work.

Judith Butler

Brid Featherstone and Lorraine Green

Some biographical details

Judith Butler is Maxine Elliot Professor in Rhetoric, Comparative Literature and Women's Studies at the University of California, Berkeley. She received her PhD in philosophy from Yale in 1984 and her dissertation was subsequently published as *Subjects of Desire: Hegelian reflections in twentieth-century France* (1987), but her second book, published in 1990 and entitled *Gender Trouble: Feminism and the subversion of identity*, was to make her the most cited feminist academic of the 1990s. The book sold over 100,000 copies internationally and even inspired an intellectual fanzine, 'Judy'. Since 1990, she has written a range of influential books (see the References section at the end of the book). *The Judith Butler Reader* (Salih with Butler, 2004) gives an overview of key themes from all but her most recent works.

While it is the early challenging analyses of work on sex, gender and sexuality for which she is most well known, her later work continues to develop such analyses, but has seen her take on broader ethical and political questions, partly in response to developments such as 9/11, American military interventions in Afghanistan and Iraq and Israeli policies towards the Palestinians. She contributes to the fields of philosophy, ethics, humanities, gender and sexuality studies, and queer theory. It is important to note, however, that she consistently interrogates disciplinary boundaries, including those within which she has been placed herself.

Politically, Butler has always expressed an allegiance to feminism, while interrogating many feminist claims. As indicated, she has taken public stances in relation to contemporary political issues. A key theme is her concern with how processes of recognition and silencing contribute to make certain lives not only unliveable but also ungrievable. Her own battle to adopt a son challenged the Californian courts' categorization of a 'parent' and she has been active around AIDS.

As a girl of 14 experiencing same-sex desires, she became aware of what could and could not be publicly acknowledged. Her work is, however, deconstructive of identities or categories and challenges 'the frames of reference within which people speak, think, and live subject categories' (Salih, 2004: 2). Thus, there is no recourse to a straightforward occupation of categories, such as 'woman' or 'lesbian'. Indeed, she asks, 'What is a human?' in order to disrupt and critique the currently constituted social world, where she considers responses to such a question are given too straightforwardly and constituted through the violence of exclusion. Committed to 'radical democratic' practices, she asks her readers to engage in 'rumination' and critique in order to challenge the most basic of issues, such as who is recognized as human.

Butler cautions against expecting 'radical accessibility' from her work as it sets itself 'the difficult task of rethinking and reconfiguring the possible within political theorizing' (Salih, 2004: 2). Her work is often criticized for its inaccessibility and her philosophy background means that it can be difficult for those without such a background to engage with her work. However, she does return to key themes, allowing readers the chance to revisit key ideas. Moreover, we suggest that her most recent work – particularly that inspired by specific political developments – seems more accessible.

Key ideas

We explore Butler's work in relation to themes that are integrally linked but, for the sake of clarity, dealt with discretely. These are the deconstruction of sex, gender and sexuality; and recognition and 'the human'.

Sex, gender and sexuality

Gender Trouble (1990) deals with the interconnections between sex, gender and sexuality, tracing how hegemonic heterosexuality is created through the simultaneous, yet fictitious, but fused co-construction of binary sex and gender within a heterosexual matrix.

To contextualize this work, prior to the 1970s, the assumption that one's gender identity could be read from one's biology was dominant in both academic and wider discourses. However, the emergence of 'second-wave' feminism, within the context of the rise of many civil rights (identity) movements, was to challenge such an assumption. A flowering of feminist scholarship ensued, documenting women's disadvantage and inequalities.

Anne Oakley (1972) theorized a clear division between *sex* – the biological positioning of one as male or female – and *gender* – the social construction of femininity and masculinity. Although Simone de Beauvoir's earlier book *The Second Sex* (1993) established important groundwork, a key aspect of the context in which Oakley's claims were being made was that of the emergence of a wider feminist movement. The emergence of a movement, challenging accepted ideas about sexuality, was also germane here. Therefore, between the 1970s and early 1990s, there was recognition of the socially constructed nature of gendered and sexual identities. Postmodernist and some psychoanalytic writers did contribute to a questioning of the binary distinction between sex and gender, implied in analyses such as Oakley's (see, for example, Flax, 1990). The connection between sex, gender and the compulsory nature of heterosexuality was also made.

While the publication of *Gender Trouble* by Butler in 1990 must be seen within such contexts, it was to take matters much further and provide a theoretical, troubling and impassioned critique that was to prove controversial and highly influential.

Butler's *Gender Trouble* is a theoretical bricolage that weaves together ideas from philosophy, psychoanalysis and history. A key argument is that we have so much difficulty subdividing sex and gender because they are one and the same thing (Butler, 1990: 7)

> If the immutable character of sex is contested, then perhaps this construct called 'sex' is as culturally constructed as gender, indeed perhaps it was already gender, with the consequence that the distinction between sex and gender turns out to be no distinction at all.

According to Butler, we cannot think about or even conceive of the body prior to gender because there is no sexed body or 'I' prior to gender and to discourse. The ontological 'truth' of gender is achieved through performative iterations that become inscribed on the body and the mind. It is repeated and often painful and involuntary performativity that simultaneously creates and constitutes our understandings of a 'natural', sexed, gendered and heterosexual body and mind.

Butler invokes the notion of male drag and its performed exaggerations to show that there is no natural origin of gender. She argues that an analysis of drag exposes gender's artificiality and constructs gender as always a chimera – 'copy to copy' rather than 'copy to original'. White's excellent (2003) analysis of how the blind were gendered and heterosexualized through blind-specific sex education in the 1970s and 1980s also reinforces Butler's claims.

Butler uses de Beauvoir's claim that one is not born a woman but becomes one as her starting point, but also draws from Foucauldian poststructuralist theory (see Chapter 4 on Foucault for a more detailed analysis) and Sigmund Freud, Jacques Lacan, Jacques Derrida and Monique Wittig, among others. Like Foucault, she is anti-foundationalist conceptually in that she attributes the body with no original desires or expressions. Butler takes up Foucault's notion of discourse (a regime of assumed and hegemonic 'truth' constructed through a multiplicity of practices, law, ideology, language, beliefs and behaviour) to explain how binary positions in the context of heterosexuality are produced as 'natural'. Butler (1990) sees the subject and subjectivity as constituted by and within discourse – in this case, the discourse of hegemonic heterosexuality, within which stabilized gender identity is created and sustained.

Butler explains how the fictitious co-construction of sex and gender within a rigidly hetero-sexual matrix produces anomalous and unintelligible positions. These are nonetheless inhabited but are frequently derided and marginalized because they are seen as unintelligible – incomprehensible and outside 'normal' consciousness – and abject. One example might be a biological man who does not want 'gender reassignment' surgery – that is, he does not identify as a transsexual (a woman trapped in a man's body). However, he may want to identify as both a man and a woman without surgery or as possessing multiple genders or a third gender, neither male nor female.

Butler's theorizing is complex and multilayered, acting at both the surface and depth levels. Borrowing from Lacan, it explores the power of the symbolic and the phallic signifier in language. It incorporates the corporeal, exploring how the surface of the body is engraved upon and disciplined by performativity. It also brings in the psychic, drawing on both Freud and Lacan to explore the interiorization of gender in our psyche through bodily inscription and iterative repetitions.

Butler's radical exposé and deconstruction of gender and sexuality in *Gender Trouble* was inspirational but also troubling as it profoundly threatened the validity of identity politics, such as traditional feminism or traditional gay politics, by destabilizing the categories they represent. She saw identity politics as unnecessarily homogenizing, monolithic and restrictive, as not recognizing differences within one group and multiple oppressions, as well as being a potential instrument of manipulation by oppressive regimes. Her alternative suggestion for challenging naturalized gender and associated and linked hegemonic heterosexuality is to create 'gender trouble' through subversive acts of gender and sexuality that involve parody. This point is returned to again below.

In *Bodies that Matter* (1993), Butler extends her analysis out from gender to all those she sees as 'violently excluded'. She pays much more attention to the corporeality of the body and its sexed materialization. She also places more emphasis on the 'iterative' nature of performativity to dispel criticisms of *Gender Trouble*, which saw her as arguing that gender is a voluntary performance (that is, something which can be done or not done as one wishes). She uses Derrida's notion of iterability to reinforce how gender is sedimented through ritualistic and repeated reiterations that discipline and are inscribed on the body. She argues against the conflation of 'performance' and 'performativity'. *Performativity* is a term drawn from John Austin (1962) and means that the performance or speech can create what it names by its very naming. Gender is not a freely chosen dramaturgical presentation – particularly as the subject is constituted within discourses.

In *The Psychic Life of Power* (1997b), Butler, returns to an issue touched on in *Gender Trouble* and *Bodies That Matter*: the taboo on homosexuality. This, she argues, lies below Freud's incest taboo. She claims that the price of a stable heterosexual gender identity is the prohibition of the enactment or admission of desire for anyone of the same sex. She explores how power is psychically incorporated in subject formation, particularly in relation to 'melancholy'. This is a state of loss that, in the taboo, cannot be mourned or grieved for openly because it involves the desire for that which, at a deep psychic level, is illegitimate, abject, taboo and foreclosed (Butler, see Bell, 1999: 170, emphasis in original):

> There are certain kinds of love that are held not to be love, loss that is not held to be loss, that remain in this kind of unthinkable domain or in an ontological shadowy domain; it's not real, it's not real love, it's not real loss ... that can be linked with some of the work I have done on the *unthinkability* or *ungrievability* of homosexual attachment.

Butler also sees melancholy as strongly indicated in the history of miscegenation and the way that cross-racial sexual relations have been both prohibited and foreclosed. In this book and others, such as *Antigone's Claim*, as well as articles, Butler (2000, 2002) also looks at kinship and lesbian and gay marriage and civil partnerships. She argues that the potentially subversive nature of gay and lesbian relationships is diluted by the State's acceptance of their validity only if they mimic heterosexual models. However, even then there are limits. For example, she notes (2002: 23; see also Rasmussen, 2006) that civil solidarity pacts in France and Germany for gay partners were only given legal recognition as long as gay couples were proscribed from adopting children and accessing reproductive technology: 'For understanding this debate, it is important to recognise how ... the child of non-heterosexual parents becomes a cathected site for anxieties about cultural purity and cultural transmission'. Butler also notes, critically, the influence of Lacanian psychoanalysis on such developments, in that it lends itself to prescriptive notions of what children require psychically, and she critically aligns herself with feminist psychoanalysts who are rethinking notions such as the Oedipal complex in the light of the diversity of parenting and familial arrangements in contemporary society.

Butler's *Undoing Gender* (2004b) reflects on gender and sexuality, focusing on new kinship, psychoanalysis and the incest taboo, transgender and intersex diagnostic categories, social violence and the task of social transformation. While there is much here that links strongly with themes developed more fully in our next section on recognition and the human, this section focuses on sex, gender and sexuality. She reconsiders her earlier views in *Gender Trouble* with the focus more on the 'undoing' rather than the 'doing' of gender. She argues that she had two aims at the time of writing *Gender Trouble*: to expose the pervasive heterosexism within feminist theory and to try to imagine a world in which those who live at some distance from gender norms might still understand themselves and consider themselves worthy of recognition (Butler, 2004b). She argues that gender is not clearcut or univocal but has been constituted variously as both by different feminisms, despite also being challenged as such by some of those same feminisms. She worries that the frameworks we commit ourselves to, because they have strong explanatory power, may recommit us to seeing sexual difference as inevitable or, indeed, primary, as, she would suggest, feminist Lacanians do.

Butler addresses some key criticisms that have been made of her work in relation to agency. Being constituted by and within discourse does not necessarily coincide with being determined or trapped immovably within or by discourse. She sees normative and hegemonic sexual and gender positioning being potentially 'undone' in contexts where psychological survival is at stake in relation to seeing oneself as possessing a valued identity. She also returns to a critique of her work which suggests that in engaging with drag, she reduced politics to parody. She suggests that this was, in part, a way to think not only about how gender is performed, but also is resignified through collective terms. Drag artists tend to live in communities where recognition becomes possible and this can work to ward off violence, racism, homophobia and so on. Drag does not exhaust the realm of political possibilities, but it returns us to questions about what is considered 'real' and what can be questioned and rethought.

Recognition and 'the human'

The notion of 'recognition' runs throughout Butler's work. She argues in *Undoing Gender* (2004b) that the Hegelian tradition links desire with recognition and that it is only through the experience of recognition that any of us become constituted as socially viable beings. However, while recognizing the importance of the Hegelian tradition, she (2004a: 2) also suggests that important points have been missed:

> The terms by which we are recognized as human are socially articulated and changeable. And sometimes the very terms that confer 'humanness' on some individuals are those that deprive certain other individuals of the possibility of achieving that status, producing a differential between the human and the less-than-human.

While this has clear implications for engaging with how the norms that structure intelligible gendered 'positions' and sexualities work, Butler extends out to consider wider questions in terms of who is able to be heard, whose lives can be grieved for and so on.

In *Excitable Speech* (1997a), she examines the power of 'hate speech' to name, subordinate and wound individuals in bodily and psychic ways, thus refusing recognition to persons. She also interrogates the political strategies that can be employed to make subordinated or hitherto unrecognized persons 'heard'. She explores the famous case of Rosa Parks who, in refusing to give up her seat on a segregated bus to a white person, was commonly seen as playing a pivotal role in the civil rights movement. However, Rosa was carefully chosen by the civil rights movement as a woman of the 'utmost respectability' who could challenge the Establishment while not straying beyond the conventions of femininity (Disch, 1999; Lovell, 2003).

Butler is against State censorship or regulation of speech. She argues it is the social context – how language is intended, received and responded to – that is important, not the actual words themselves. One also has to recognize oneself in the naming – a process that draws on the Althusserian notion of hailing or 'interpellation'. Butler criticizes the feminist Catherine MacKinnon for conflating pornographic speech with violent pornography and demanding censorship of such language. Butler gives the example of when 'abortion' was seen to constitute an obscene word and was bleeped out and censored from a radio broadcast. This is a clear example of the need for caution about censorship and who it might benefit.

Butler distinguishes between illocutionary speech – that which performs an actual act, such as a judge sentencing someone – and perlocutionary speech – speech that may have less definite effects. She suggests that insurrectionary counterspeech (insubordinate use of a derogatory or authoritarian term) should be used to defuse, subvert and challenge the latter. She suggests that subjects should call for justice in the very terms that have been used to disenfranchise them. However, sometimes there is no 'room' for apparent positive resignification, as Anita Hill found in the famous case in the USA that dealt with her claims of sexual harassment by Clarence Thomas. By recounting assertively his sexualized words and intimations in court, she was seen to be a woman standing outside the conventions of femininity and, therefore, not deserving of belief or protection. However, had she taken on the montage of passive victimized femininity, she would have been unable to 'speak' his offensive actions and words and would, therefore, have been equally ineffectual in gaining justice.

In *Precarious Life: The powers of mourning and violence* (2004a), Butler returned to the question of what and whose is a life worth living and defending, but this time in the context of the destruction of the World Trade Centre in New York in 2001. She locates this in the context of global US military, imperial violence, where the lives of those brutalized – for example, in Afghanistan, Palestine and Iraq – are glossed over by Western consciousness. Butler asks herself and us to look at questions of humanness and recognize how some lives are mourned and glorified whereas others are rendered invisible. Butler posits an ethics of non-violence and hopefulness through an examination of Emmanuel Lévinas's face of the 'Other'. She advocates a new moralism that is not based on fear, but on a recognition of our own and others' vulnerability and interdependence.

Butler is clearly critical of new forms of governmentality in the USA, whereby public fear is politically mobilized to foreclose resistance to US violence and due process in law is evaded, as exemplified by the indefinite detention of people suspected of terrorism in Guantanamo Bay. In her work on Israel and Palestine (i.e., in *Precarious Life* and various articles such as Butler, 2003), she also shows how the label 'anti-Semitic' impedes discussion about and potential criticism of the USA and Israel. Reflecting on Israeli government policies, she highlights how the positioning of victim is shifting and ambivalent – one can be an oppressor in one sense at one particular moment in time and/or a victim in another. As Angela McRobbie (2006: 73) contends, this overt stance is not just a theoretical exposé but also a passionate and brave position to take:

> In a situation in the US academy, where to engage critically with US support for Israel is to put oneself in some position of vulnerability, if not danger, we might suggest that Butler here is (not cynically, indeed passionately) utilizing a strategy which permits the possibility of critical intervention.

Butler's most recent book, *Giving an Account of Oneself* (2005), examines what it means to lead an ethical life under problematic social and linguistic conditions and she offers an outline for ethical practice, although it is important to note her consistent refusal (and her explicit allegiance to Foucault in this regard) to offer prescriptive political programmes. She argues that when one gives an account of oneself, one is not merely relaying information through an indifferent medium. In arguments, which have resonance with currents within sociological thought that have influenced social work (see Chapter 15), she emphasizes (2005: 130) that the 'account is an act – situated within a larger practice of acts – that one performs for, to, even *on* an other, an allocutory deed, an acting for, and in the face of, the other and sometimes by virtue of the language provided by the other'. The 'I' giving the account has no story of its own that is not also the story of a relation or set of relations to a set of norms. She refutes fears that this means there is no concept of the subject that can serve as the ground for moral agency and accountability. If the 'I' is not at one with moral norms, for example, a process of ethical deliberation finds itself embroiled in the task of critique.

Butler also suggests that one gives an account of oneself to an other and every accounting takes place within a scene of address. The scene of address, or what might be called the 'rhetorical conditions for responsibility', means that the question is not restricted to whether or not my account of myself is adequate, but rather whether or not I establish a relationship with the one to whom my account is addressed and whether or not both parties are sustained and altered by the scene of address.

The 'You' who is addressed by 'I' is variable and imaginary at the same time as it is bounded and stubbornly there. She questions whether or not there can be telling without 'transference' in the psychoanalytic sense. I tell a story to you and we consider the story together, but I am doing something with this telling, acting on you, and this telling is also doing something to me, acting on me in ways that I may well not understand. The latter point is key to this book: one can never be known fully by oneself and, in asking the other 'Who are you?', the other will not be captured by any answer that is given. We will not achieve closure in relation to self-knowledge or knowledge of the other. The notion of responsibility, therefore, has to be rethought – it cannot be tied to the conceit of a fully transparent self. To take responsibility for oneself is to avow the limits of any self-understanding. As Patrick White (2003) suggests in his endorsement of the book, the height of self-knowledge may consist of the realization that, in matters of the self, insight is perilous, perception flawed and judgement weak. Moreover, it cautions against the conceit of ever fully knowing (and, therefore, perhaps being able to sum up or dismiss) the other.

Drawing particularly from the work of Lévinas, Butler argues that we need to rethink our concept of responsibility in relation to acts by another. We do not take responsibility for their acts as if we authored their acts, but we do affirm the unfreedom at the heart of our relations (Butler, 2005: 91):

> I cannot disavow my relation to the Other regardless of what the Other does, regardless of what I might will. Indeed, responsibility is not a matter of cultivating a will, but of making use of an unwilled susceptibility as a resource for becoming responsive to the Other. Whatever the Other has done, the Other still makes an ethical demand upon me, has a '"face" to which I am obliged to respond – meaning that I am, as it were, precluded from revenge by virtue of a relation I never chose'.

None of us is fully bounded, utterly separate, but, rather, in situations that we did not choose, *given over* to each other. While this can be intolerable, it is a reminder of our common vulnerability.

Introducing Butler's ideas to social work

The space available here precludes a consideration of the multiple critiques that have been made of Butler's work in terms of its theoretical premises and political effects (see, for example, Benhabib, Butler, Cornell and Fraser, 1995, in relation to her early work). It is important to note that, within her own work, as it has developed, she has thoughtfully engaged with critics over the years.

We think that Butler's work carries important possibilities for social work, although we also see some limitations. Such a radically deconstructive thinker clearly poses great difficulties if one wants to advance political claims on the basis of stable categories, such as women, lesbians and so on. Her reluctance to foreclose categories, but, instead, to keep them open to resignification and contestations (for example, the category of woman or gay), is welcome and problematic – advancing category claims is necessary in terms of specific issues, as she would recognize. Moreover, while she gives visibility to those often excluded from progressive campaigns – such as transsexual and transgender people – she does not devote attention, in the main, to the lack of recognition suffered by those who are economically vulnerable and the 'mundane' everyday pain of many of those who come to the doors of social work. This is linked to the abstract nature of many of her analyses – the everyday world does not appear much in terms of exploring domestic violence, poverty and so on.

This does not mean that her mode of analysis, albeit often critical and partial, cannot be applied by others in order to understand these issues. Butler's theories of sex and gender, performativity and melancholy have, for example, been used to try and understand certain aspects and representations of disability (Shildrick and Price, 1996; Stocker, 2001), teen motherhood (Lessa, 2006) and the complexities of love and attachment within violent, but enduring relationships (Narayan, 2005). However, Butler's abstractness can be rather frustrating, particularly for those looking for readymade analyses and solutions to the ephemerally complex and multifaceted problems social workers routinely experience.

We find Butler's emphasis on loose coalitions of people – for example, women temporarily joining collectives for particular purposes – opens up possibilities for drawing more people into particular battles rather than signing up to universalist programmes. This is not unique to her, though, as it has been advocated by other feminists over the years. Moreover, her attempt to 'jam' the theoretical machinery is highly persuasive, especially in the sterile intellectual context of social work where dogma has often ruled in relation to anti-oppressive practice. For those of us who find ourselves caught between the Scylla of moral certainty, which often seems to characterize analyses promoting anti-oppressive social work, and the Charybdis of government-sponsored sanitized rational technicality within social work, Butler opens up possibilities for other kinds of conversations.

Giving an Account of Oneself attempts to think about what we can do within the limitations of self-knowledge and a knowledge of others and, moreover, to think about such limitations as holding important possibilities in terms of recognizing our vulnerability. *Precarious Life*, too, is premised on a recognition of others' and one's own interdependency and vulnerability.

A difficulty with these works, however, is that, despite her interest in psychoanalytic theory, she rarely engages with concrete concerns about whether or not there are particular kinds of care practices that can facilitate the construction of those who use their shared vulnerability to build connections rather than destroy the 'other' (see, for example, Hollway, 2006). This is a serious omission for social work practitioners, who often engage with unloved and unrecognized people who, in turn, behave in damaging and destructive ways towards others.

Significance for social work practice

We would suggest that the greatest significance of Butler's work for social work practice lies in the asking of important questions. Thus, we can engage with and recognize the experience of those who are marginalized and excluded and expand the categories beyond what is usually included in social work. In particular, Butler supports those who wish to challenge heteronormativity and validate the lives and loves of gay, lesbian and intersex people.

Butler returns us to a tradition in social work that asserts our common humanity, but, at the very same time when we recognize our humanness, she asks us to question the grounds on which we have constructed what it is to be human. She challenges us to recognize our strangeness to ourselves and our familiarity to others as well as our strangeness to others and our familiarity to ourselves. Thus, we see her as opening up and supporting possibilities for the kinds of critical humane practices advocated by others in this book.

Study questions

1. How can Judith Butler's work help to 'shake up' the pervasive heterosexism of much social work theory?
2. Recognition is an important concept in helping to move beyond the dogma and certainties of anti-oppressive theory as it is currently used in much of the social work literature. Discuss.
3. Who can be heard and who can be grieved for? Where are the silences in Butler's own work and how can the everyday practices of social work enrich her analyses?

Glossary

Compulsory heterosexuality requires and regulates gender as a binary relation in which the masculine term is differentiated from the feminine term. The 'unity' of gender is the effect of a regulatory practice that seeks to make identity uniform through a compulsory heterosexuality.

Performativity does not equate with performance – a point that Butler has consistently argued when responding to critics. Gender is a doing, not an essence, and there is no gender identity behind the expressions of gender. The identity is constituted by the very expressions that are said to be its results.

Recognition It is only through the experience of recognition by others that we become constituted as socially viable beings. However, the terms by which we are recognized as human are socially articulated and changeable.

Select bibliography

Salih, S., with Butler, J. (eds) (2004). *The Judith Butler Reader*. Oxford: Blackwell.

Part II
Theories

Feminist Social Work

Joan Orme

Introducing feminist social work

There are multiple feminist perspectives that draw on, critique and spawn further theoretical approaches. This is not to suggest that feminism plagiarizes other theories or is a disordered 'eclective', adopting an 'anything goes approach'. The shared aim of diverse feminist perspectives is to develop a theoretical understanding of the position of women and frameworks for action to improve this.

Feminist theorizing is developmental – not in a chronological sense, but in an iterative and reflective way, such that emerging positions raise questions about the nature of theory and its relation to practice. Feminism, like social work, draws on diverse theoretical perspectives, but is more than the mere application of these. Feminist theorists reflect on mainstream theories and test their implications for meanings related to the construction of the category 'women' and the conditions of women (Orme, 2002a). As Sheila Rowbotham (1992, 1973: 45) notes, 'the bizarre complexities and combinations of women's lives' require theory. However, there has been resistance to pure 'theorizing'. Liz Stanley and Sue Wise (2000) express concern about 'deontological feminism', arguing that reifying theory leads to prescriptive actions and practices.

That feminism does not provide a single, coherent and unified way of analysing and conceptualizing the world is part of its complexity and maturity, but this creates problems for practitioners looking for codified practice – that is, prescriptions for how to act. In this context, this chapter begins with an overview of a range of feminist perspectives and identifies significant concepts and debates that have implications for social work theory and practice. It then analyses the influence and impact of feminist theories on social work.

Feminist theory

For feminists, classification is an artificial process associated with rational, male ways of organizing knowledge. Feminism comprises fluid, interlocking ways of thinking (Bryson, 1999), 'takes its meaning from the moment' (Mitchell and Oakley, 1986: 4) and reflects on the interrelationship between theory and experience – in so doing, developing new perspectives and understandings. Though resistant to classification, feminists realize that it is sometimes necessary to create order, if only to disrupt it by highlighting the paradoxes and contradictions in the way in which the world and women's place in it is explained and understood.

The most frequent distinction drawn is between *liberal* (conservative) feminism – associated with epistemological developments (that is, theory building and research – see Harding, 1987) – and *Marxist* (socialist, radical) feminism – associated with its political project or praxis (Stanley and Wise, 1990). However, neither category is totally distinct or all-embracing and each has differing theories within it.

Liberal feminism

Historically, feminism was linked to liberal democratic theories of rights. Mary Wollstonecraft's (1975, 1792) text on the rights of women is often seen as stimulating 'first wave' feminism – the suffragette movement – and the beginnings of 'second wave' feminism. The principles of equal rights, equal treatment and access to, for example, the vote, work and owning property were based on liberal notions of citizenship: if women could participate, they would achieve the same position(s) as men.

Liberal feminists reflected the concerns of white, educated, middle-class women who worked within the State apparatus and political system to ensure the universal and consistent application of rights (Bryson, 1999). Their approach was individualistic and overlooked the meritocratic nature of liberal systems wherein citizenship involved male participation in the public domain. Consequently, they did not see private, familial and personal relationships as a site of male domination and oppression that created barriers to women's participation.

Regardless of their weaknesses, Imelda Whelehan (1995) notes that subsequent feminist positions derived their impetus and inspiration from early feminists, such as Betty Friedan (1986), who echoed de Beauvoir (1972) in exploring the 'nature' of femininity. They created precedents for debates about nature and nurture that still exercise feminists, and others, in the twenty-first century.

Marxist feminism

Marxist feminists addressed the lack of attention to class differences in liberal constructions of equality. They drew on 'classic' Marxism where class is seen as the ultimate determinant of oppression. They argued that inequality related to power and its distribution. This resonated with women's experience (McKinnon, 1992). They saw collective interests, based on socio-economic groupings, rather than personal equality as an important and effective means of liberating oppressed groups. Collective interests provided the power of the 'standpoint' (see Glossary at end of this chapter) for understanding the world from a particular perspective.

The writings of Marx – and their manifestations in political activism – however, did not recognize particular conditions for women. In fact, Marxism often placed women as subordinate to the politically, materially and ideologically dominant man (Whelehan, 1995). Nevertheless, Marxist feminism can provide a useful guard against the individualism and elitism that arise when collective inequalities and strategies based on, for example, class and race are ignored (Bryson, 1999).

Socialist feminism

Although liberal and Marxist feminism share a belief that women's oppression is caused by sexism, racism and class divisions produced by a patriarchal society (Payne, 2005), socialist feminism is based on mainstream political thinking that focuses on individual rights and opportunities and champions the collective interests of working-class people as a group; socialism stresses economic and social rights (Bryson, 1999). It argues that the divisions created by patriarchy permeate private – and interpersonal – relationships and this supports capitalist arrangements of production. For socialist feminists, patriarchy is fundamental because the oppression of women pre-dates capitalism (Rowbotham, 1992, 1973).

Though not of concern to Marxism per se, matters of sexuality and identity became the focus of socialist feminism: 'even the loosest analysis of Marxism suggests class and capitalism is more fundamental than gender and patriarchy' (Bryson, 1999: 20). Feminism applied the Marxist concept of consciousnessraising to reflect on women's social situation, which Marxism ignored. The feminist mantra 'the personal is political' identified that the subordination of women in their everyday lives had to be the focus of political action at all levels. It counteracted the individualism of liberalism, took strength from the notion of the collective – which was more in tune with women's ways of taking action – and, while focusing on women's position, did not ignore or eradicate men but sought to dialogue with them (Segal, 1987).

Radical feminism

All approaches based on mainstream political positions and strategies were seen by some feminists to be limited inevitably by their masculinist assumptions (Bryson, 1999). Taking 'the personal is political' to new territory and recognizing that oppression permeated all aspects of human relationships, radical feminism saw the means of reproduction as key.

Among the first to use 'patriarchy' (see Glossary) as shorthand for the multiple ways in which women were oppressed (Whelehan, 1995), radical feminists eschewed political structures and male-orientated philosophies where patriarchy was omnipresent, claiming that they had to be rejected, dismantled and overthrown. There was no single philosophical doctrine other than the negation of 'phallocentric political hegemony' (Whelehan, 1995: 68).

This led, inter alia, to a new theory of politics (Mitchell, 1974) in which women were a class in their own right with men as the antagonists (Firestone, 1971). It led to separate women's structures within and women only organizations. Heterosexuality in all its forms was an abuse of women (Daly, 1990; Dworkin, 1981).

Post(modern) feminism

If radical feminism demanded a new theory of politics, postmodern feminism questioned the project of theorizing or, at least, producing monolithic, all-encompassing grand theories. This was problematic for feminist theory because it challenged the hegemony of certain theoretical positions and the means by which these positions had been reached.

Although he did not address the position of women directly, and has been misquoted on notions of discourse (Sawyer, 2002), the work of Foucault became influential (see McNay, 1992). With reference to his work, the role of language and discourse was said to provide the means for women's voices to be heard and enable the creation of new meanings and possibilities for understanding and action (Healy, 2000).

Feminists embraced postmodernism to disturb the roots of patriarchy and modernism (Rossiter, 2000) but also disturbed feminism. Black women (hooks, 1984), women with disabilities (Morris, 1993) and older women questioned postmodern feminism defined by white, able-bodied, young, middle-class, educated women who had divested it of its political force. This led to explorations of diversity and difference (see Glossary).

The multiplicity, plurality, contradiction and conflict in contemporary feminist thinking require a conceptualization that neither collapses the categories of 'personal' and 'political' nor presents them as binaries (Braithwaite, 2002). The rejection of 'the personal is political' mantra is sometimes associated with postfeminism (see Glossary), suggesting that there is no need for feminism. However, feminist theory remains relevant in social work.

Feminist social work practice

Social work is a profession mainly providing services for women by women (Balloch, 1997; Howe, 1986). While the 'feminization' of the profession has had implications for women (Harlow, 2004) and men (Christie, 2006), it is not necessarily a fertile area for feminist theory and practice.

Early feminists were critical of social work as a profession and of women working in it, arguing that, at best, it ignored women and, at worst, held women responsible for social problems. It kept them under surveillance, constrained them to subjugated roles or victimized them.

Arguing from a Marxist critique of the State, Elizabeth Wilson (1977) suggested that women's needs would be better met by providing services outside of State-organized systems.

Thirty years on, Payne (2005) suggests that the contribution of feminism to social work practice has been recognized but is resisted – that, while it provides prescriptions for working with women, it offers no extensive account of how theory is applied to generalist social work practice. It could be argued that the prescription and codification of social work practice are together an example of rational–technical approaches resonant with masculinist, logocentric thinking, but also reflect resistance to practice theory within social work and feminism (Featherstone and Fawcett, 1995a; Healy, 2000) and misrepresent the feminist contribution as atheoretical (Orme, 2003).

Nevertheless, it is possible to discern three strands of feminist social work that are informed by and responsive to developments in feminist thinking:

- synergies between feminism and social work based on shared values (Collins, 1986);
- prescriptions for practice with women (Dominelli, 2002b; Dominelli and McCleod, 1989; Hanmer and Statham, 1988) and men (Cavanagh and Cree, 1996);
- use of feminist perspectives to understand the gender dimensions of social work practice (Orme, 2002a).

Synergies between feminism and social work

Early writers elaborating on the relevance of feminism to social work (Collins, 1986; Wearing, 1986) drew heavily on socialist feminism as representing mainstream feminist thought. The critique of male dominance as part of the economic foundation of society and the subjugation of women through a multitude of State, institutional and interpersonal practices resonated with the experiences of women with whom social workers worked. Barbara Collins (1986) links the feminist mantra 'the personal is political' with the 'person in environment' principle – both mean that private woes are public issues. Feminist perspectives and theories offer paradigmatic ways of understanding patriarchal culture, but this conflicts with what feminists and social workers 'want for humanity and society' (Collins, 1986: 214), which includes men.

For Roberta Sands and Kathleen Nuccio (1992), all strands of feminist thinking share the political project to end women's oppression. For them, postmodern feminism, with its emphasis on deconstructing categories, acknowledging difference and rejecting essentialism, recognizes the diverse constitution of the client (sic) population and unique individual needs. They reject criticisms that postmodernism negates or undermines the political project or there has to be a unified category, perspective or standpoint on which to base political action. While recognizing that this might be problematic for social work, which has used categories such as race, gender and class to legitimize their action against oppression, they argue that awareness of difference within the category 'woman' means that workers can act in concert with an individual as a member of a special population and as a person in her specific environment.

Their individualized approach redefines the nature of subjectivity – basing it on the conscious and unconscious thoughts and emotions of individuals – and 'the person in environment' – that is, their sense of self and ways of understanding their relationship with the world. Therefore, subjectivity is not 'essential' or stable but contradictory and changing (Sands and Nuccio, 1992).

Important links can be made between the political nature of the subject – which may be the 'feminine' – and the way in which the world is constructed and experienced – which includes subjective interpretations of being female. Feminist social work, therefore, works with women to raise consciousness. For some, this involves not only political awareness but also feminist psychoanalytic theory (Mitchell, 1974), which informs continuing work on identity, sexuality and abuse (Hollway and Featherstone, 1997; see also Chapter 5).

The complex link between theory and practice, therefore, highlights tensions and contradictions (Orme, 2003). Collins (1986) was clear that feminism was a philosophical perspective or way of visualizing and thinking about situations to explain women's oppression. For Sands and Nuccio (1992), what differentiates postmodern feminism from postmodernism is the link between theory and practice (or praxis). However, neither they nor Collins (1986) went so far as to prescribe practice.

Feminist prescriptions for practice

A number of texts have explored feminist social work practice as a unified phenomenon, focusing predominantly on working with women either generically (Dominelli and McCleod, 1989; Hanmer and Statham, 1988) or via particular approaches, such as group work, that could be 'converted' to feminism (Cohen and Mullender, 2003). They identify with the political project of feminism from a standpoint or position (see Glossary). They acknowledge differences, but accept a commonality of experience, such that all women can agree on principles to eradicate gender inequality (Dominelli, 2002b). They challenge the operation of power between women workers and women service users by recognizing commonalities and differences (Hanmer and Statham, 1988). Commonality of experience – as victims of oppression – is both a source of identity and the basis on which relationships between women workers and service users can be built.

Questioning the feasibility of this egalitarian approach, Sue White (1998) suggests that it fails to recognize the operation of power in relationships within statutory social work, even those between women. Equally, Sue Wise (1990) suggests that exhortations to listen to women and focus on women's contributions and experience, while laudable, do not address the complexity and messiness of women's lives or acknowledge that women themselves are capable of unacceptable and antisocial behaviour. Working with these women, not men, poses an immense challenge to feminist social workers (Crinall, 1999).

These critiques challenge the assumption that it is possible and desirable to homogenize the category 'woman' in social work practice. Doing so denies the presence of power differentials created by being a provider of State services and implies that women are only ever offended against. This essentialises passive, non-violent femininity, limits the emancipatory project associated with women-centred practice and has implications for women who do not conform to gendered prescriptions – for example, abusing women involves theorizing in a feminist minefield (Crinall, 1999; Orme, 1994).

Not all who write about working with women argue for purely women-centred practice. Judith Milner (2001: 66) advocates solution-focused therapy based on the 'naturalness' of women's use of discourse, but acknowledges that narrative techniques might also enable men to learn to 'talk like women, negotiate, value relationships and embrace complexity'.

Understanding gender dimensions

A further development of women-centred practice involves focusing on women while working with men as part of the feminist project. For example, Kate Cavanagh and Viviene Cree (1996) try to destabilize men to ensure the protection of women. Others use concepts of masculinity emerging from feminist theory (Segal, 1990) for working with men to help them understand how their behaviour oppresses women (Orme et al., 2000) and children (Featherstone and Fawcett, 1995b). Mainstream male social theorists have 'adopted' feminist theory to explore the impact of gender oppression on men (Connell, 1994; Hearn and Morgan, 1990) and social work (Christie, 2001; Scourfield, 2002).

Significance for social work practice

In attempting to identify the significance of feminism for social work, a nihilistic view would be that it has made little lasting contribution because no single method has emerged as 'feminist social work practice'.

A more accurate perspective sees feminist theories as fundamental in highlighting the oppressive conditions of women and the ways in which social work can exacerbate or alleviate them. Feminist thinking has led to a reappraisal and reconfiguration of core social work principles and micro practices through understandings of power and gender, ethics of care and the use of empathy, identity, individualization and so on.

The breadth of feminist theory encompasses social, political, theoretical and practical considerations of the position of women, women's social and economic progress (or lack of it) and the subjugation of women through mechanisms of physical and sexual violence. Issue politics for feminism involve all aspects of social life – public and private.

Critical analysis of women in the paid labour force leads to the deconstruction of the notion of family built on motherhood, femininity and women's innate capacity to care. It has led to theories on the feminization of poverty (Lister, 1997; Pateman, 1987) and feminist campaigns against pornography (Dworkin, 1981), prostitution (McKinnon, 1992) and male violence (Hester et al., 1996).

One challenge is how to negotiate complex issues surrounding women's relationships with men. Some find 'oppositional politics', which depend on particular constructions of femininity that run counter to the overarching feminist project to understand the human condition and produce knowledge to enhance women's welfare, problematic (Oakley, 2005).

Power

Rowbotham (1983) eschews oppositional politics because it entails adopting male approaches to theory and action in favour of understanding the operation of power within and between categories.

Foucault's (1980b) analysis that power exercised and experienced at the micro levels of society makes it the site for resistance by marginalized and subjugated groups has been influential in feminist thinking (Bryson, 1999). Foucault saw power as both repressive and productive, operating through, rather than on, individuals and, therefore, being significant at both the local and global levels. Not only are personal issues politicized but also the personal and local become the site of political action – 'the personal becomes *the* political'. That is not to say feminists are not interested in the macro organization of power. Early feminists in the suffragette movement constantly challenged the power of the State and its denial of women's suffrage. Friedan's (1986) writing stimulated second wave feminists to organize themselves politically. However, power does not only mean domination. From a liberal feminist perspective, Naomi Wolf (1999) argued that 'power' feminism could resist male abuses of power and promote equal rights for women while not subjugating those of men.

Engagement with the State is necessary because of its power to legislate aspects of women's personal lives, such as outlawing domestic violence (Bryson, 1999), but, for social workers, working at the intersection of the State and women's lives, the influence of the State is more pervasive than this. The multitude of health and social care policies that inform the legislative duties of social workers are based on constructions of femininity – as represented in motherhood, caring, sexuality and so on – and restrict women's lives and their capacity to define their own welfare needs (Dale and Foster, 1986). In State social work, the law not only defines the ends but also the means by which social workers intervene in service users' lives as they exercise their statutory duties (White, 2006).

Ethic of care

Equally important for social work is feminists' deconstruction of the concept of care.

Carol Gilligan's (1983) 'different voice' feminism identified differences in women and men's moral reasoning: women operate according to an *ethic of care* and men according to an *ethic of justice*. What was significant was not just the differences but also the privileging and, therefore, dominance of masculinist, rational, logical ways of thinking that devalued women's ways of negotiating based on connectedness and relationship.

She concluded that the 'different voice' of women prevailed in personal and public relationships via an ethic of care, but the problem was that women's 'care work' was devalued in the personal and public spheres (Dalley, 1988; Ungerson, 1987).

Feminist theorists have questioned misconceptions about caring as unreservedly positive (Koehn, 1998; Orme, 2001), highlighting that a proper reading of an ethic of care could bring new understanding to professional practice (Parton, 2003). Some have explored male roles in caring (Fisher, 1994) and theorizing an ethic of care has been central in rethinking understandings of ethics and justice (Held, 1995; Orme, 2002b) and its links to identity (Young, 1990).

Identity

The 'politics of identity' was one consequence of feminism's relationship with postmodernism and notions of difference. It is not identity per se that leads to oppression, but the processes of oppression linked to how any one group is defined in relation to other groups. This has particular significance for social work as it works with people whose identities are prescribed in a number of different ways.

While people might identify strongly with a group, they may also have associations with many different groups, which suggests that identities shift in relation to context (Young, 1990). Identity has also complicated notions of gender. Judith Butler (1990) argues that, if there were no one, universal, homogeneous category of 'woman' and, therefore, no one perspective, standpoint or way of being represented by women, then there could be no one category of 'man' (see Chapter 5). These analyses are being applied to deconstructing the category of 'men'.

Individualization

The notion of the individual is core to social work but has also been contentious because working at the level of the individual was seen as a conservative and constraining approach. Early casework was said to pathologize individuals. Developments in community care have led to a focus on the individual in terms of personalized packages of care, but in bureaucratic ways that construct people as belonging to categories – 'old', 'disabled' or 'mentally ill', for example.

Debates about whether the focus should be on the individual, to alleviate problems and bring about change, or the social structures that constrain, constrict and construct individuals within them have been at the heart of social work.

Developments in feminism emphasizing diversity and difference are seen by some as privileging the individualistic approaches of postmodernism over the collective approaches of feminism (Dominelli, 2002b). Others argue that encouraging critical thinking facilitates more positive individualized work, enabling practitioners to respond to particular situations rather than the traditional social work 'methods' approach, where predetermined decisions often guide practice (Fook, 2002).

The use of narrative and discourse in person-centred approaches recognizes multiple identities and the complexities of peoples' lives. Hence, individuals are not seen as fulfilling certain types and paradigms (Plant, 1973), nor do they represent some sort of natural order. Rather, they are constructed by historical and social conditions (Weedon, 1999).

Whether the mantra is the feminist 'the personal is political' or the social work 'person in environment', both place the individual at the centre of theory and practice, such that social work mediates between the individual and the social. Feminism's emphasis on identity helps to reconcile these tensions by suggesting that the personal, individual and private experiences of women are a legitimate focus for, and site of, political action.

Empathy

Linked to individualization, the concept of empathy highlights paradoxical positions that can emerge for feminist social work. While recognizing the objective conditions of those with whom they work, social workers are expected to understand, accept and respect individual understandings and expressed wishes. This has implications for working with the most marginalized – that is, men who abuse women and children. Empathy does not mean agreeing with abusive behaviour, nor does it involve imputing wants and needs to individuals, nor constraining them by assumptions based on gender stereotypes, but, rather, being prepared to hear the conflicts and confusions.

Sandra Harding's (1987) suggestion that differences can be reconciled by the recognition that 'your claims are valid for you, but mine are valid for me' adds an important dimension to empathy and acceptance that can illuminate social work and gender.

Feminism, social work and gender

Social work shares with feminism the project of enhancing the welfare of citizens (Oakley, 2005). The problematic element for feminist social work has been how to foreground women and recognize how gender impacts on the material resources, life chances and experiences of women without either essentializing women into some form of passive femininity or compromising social work values when working with men and boys.

The contribution of notions of identity and difference (Williams, 1996) from postmodernism and postmodern feminism to social work has been transformative (Pease and Fook, 1999). The focus has been widened from women-centred practice to include the impact of gender relations on social work with both women and men (Christie, 2001; Featherstone, 2004; Scourfield, 2002) and has led to understanding of how gender impacts on all aspects of social work (Orme, 2001).

This chapter has sought to explain the complexities of feminist theory and its relationship with social work practice. In identifying multiple strands of feminist thought and their applications to social work practice, the aim has been not to criticize or judge negatively, but, rather, to explore how the shared aim of analysing and eradicating the oppression of women can lead to solutions.

Feminism offers explanations at macro and micro levels and the fact that there is often no prescription for how to 'do' social work is both frustrating and exciting. For students, practitioners, researchers and theorists alike, it means that they have to reflect on the situations in which they are involved from a variety of perspectives, and consider the impacts of any interpretations of that situation and their implications for action. This is good social work and one of the major contributions of feminist theorizing is that it has enriched and improved social work practice.

Study questions

1. Consider the different 'political' approaches of feminism. Which one resonates for you and why?
2. Think about a particular piece of work in which you have been involved and identify all the gender dimensions. In doing this, remember that constructions of femininity and masculinity can impact in complex and different ways on women and men service users, carers and workers.
3. What are the arguments for and against working with men who have committed acts of violence against women and children?

Glossary

Difference Influenced by the work of French feminists, notions of difference challenge political activities based on the idea of a single and unified category of 'woman'.

First wave feminism This term is applied retrospectively to the emergence of the feminist suffragette movement in the late nineteenth and early twentieth century in the UK and USA. However, women had been writing about 'women's issues' long before the emergence of these movements, so first wave feminism began much earlier than this (see Wollstonecraft, 1975, 1792).

Patriarchy Refers to social arrangements within the private and public realms that privilege and give power to men. It emphasizes the social and economic systems that impact on the relationships between women and men rather than differences as 'naturally' given.

Postfeminism Implies a discontinuity with the feminist project, suggesting either that feminism has achieved its aims or that past feminist approaches are no longer relevant, restrictive and descriptive of beliefs and behaviours.

Second wave feminism Acknowledging the political activities of women at the beginning of the twentieth century who were striving for equality in public life, second wave feminism is associated with 'the women's movement' from the 1960s onwards – that is, with women writers and activists who drew attention to and sought to explain how women were oppressed and subjugated in their personal lives.

Standpointism Initially pertinent to a Marxist perspective, particularly significant for feminism was the idea that the world is perceived from a particular standpoint. Though not uncontested, feminists privileged the standpoint of oppressed groups. The question is whether the 'standpoint' involves an automatic correlation between the social location and the standpoint. This becomes problematic when recognizing the different experiences and standpoints of women and men and the complexity and diversity of women's experiences, as influenced by their race, age, (dis)ability and economic status.

Select bibliography

A valuable collection of feminist writing, illustrating the central principles of feminist thought, is Humm (1992). With regard to feminist social work, I recommend Orme (2001) and White (2006).

Critical Social Work

Mel Gray and Stephen A. Webb

Introducing critical social work

Does social work thinking have any influence on real-world events? This issue of 'real-world' influence is posed with particular acuity in social intervention-driven fields. Social work is just such a field and 'practice relevance' has become an oft-cited slogan among key stakeholders.

While social work is an intervention-driven discipline, researching the relationship between social structure and individual agency requires a high degree of interdisciplinarity. This has undoubtedly been an obstacle in establishing the relevance of social work thinking about real-world events.

Such interdisciplinarity is required as the question of practice relevance is situated at the confluence of a number of dimensions of thinking, the approaches of which are similar, but their preoccupations are diverse. These include direct concerns with the desirability and feasibility of practice-relevant research itself, a focus on the relationship between theory and practice and the role of researchers in policy formation processes, as well as higher-order questions, such as the role of critical intellectuals in social work.

The important role of critical thinkers in modern societies ultimately rests on their critical position in relation to mechanisms of domination and analyses of hierarchies of power. The analysis of power figures centrally in the preoccupations of critical thinkers. In this regard, the French sociologist Pierre Bourdieu's distinction (see Chapter 3) between three types of practitioner lends itself neatly to social work. These three types are the critical intellectual, the professional expert and the servant to the Prince.

In this chapter, we are very much concerned with thinking about social work in ways that, on the one hand, draw attention to the significance of the critical intellectual and, on the other, juxtapose this position as a means of demonstrating the problems associated with those social workers who fall into either of the other two positions – professional experts or servants to the prevailing dominant system.

'Critical social work' has a narrow and a broad meaning in social work. In this chapter, we refer to these two meanings as Critical social work and critical social work. In the following discussion, Critical social work, when capitalized, refers only to the narrow definition and use of the term. All other uses are meant in the broader sense and, thus, are not capitalized. When used in a broader sense, some aspects of the perspective may have obvious relations with its counterpart as they have components to which some key thinkers have contributed.

Critical social work in the narrow sense designates several generations of key ideas, themes and commitments originating in a progressive political stance that emerged in the 1970s. According to this perspective, a 'critical' theory is distinguished from traditional social work approaches according to a specific set of values: a theory is *critical* to the extent that it seeks social transformation as forms of justice and emancipation.

Critical social work in this narrow sense, then, seeks to explain and transform various circumstances that social workers and service users find themselves in, while connecting this to a structural analysis of those aspects of society that are oppressive, unjust and exploitative. In this respect, Critical social work (with an upper-case 'C') emerged in connection with various intellectual movements, including feminism, race theory and Marxist criticism, that identified dimensions of economic and political domination in modern societies.

Critical social work in the broad sense (with a lower case 'c') is indicative of a much more generic approach that attenuates the necessary attributes and characteristics for effective interventions. While it is sensitive to core social work values, this broader sense is much more concerned with developing 'best practice' agendas that can maximize the potential for social workers and clients. Typically, the emphasis is on 'being critical' as a crucial disposition and in relation to existing practices, organizations and ideas. It draws attention to the value of using criticism as a capacity to contrast, reformulate or challenge existing practices. It contends that social workers *should necessarily be critical* and reflective in all their dealings with other human beings.

Payne's (1996) 'critical constrastive approach' is an almost perfect embodiment of a critical social work perspective with a little 'c', wherein he accentuates the need to engage in 'critical reflection using theory'. The main emphases are on finding alternatives, recognizing clients' strengths and resilience and identifying the inadequacies of resource provision. While it is still reconstructive, unlike the narrower sense of Critical social work, this perspective does not couple a structural analysis of, say, oppressive regimes in modern societies with a set of militant commitments, engagements and resistances to change.

In this sense, critical social work, while recognizing existing institutions and policies as obstacles to the emergence of better forms of engagement with service users, remains committed to the prevailing liberal democratic mode of political rule. Indeed, the unifying element of critical social work is its adherence to a liberal humanist sentiment. Thus, transformation is concerned with the incremental modification of individuals, resources and interventions within the current state of affairs rather than wholesale economic and political change. In this respect, critical social work, unlike structural social work (see Chapter 8), tends to focus on the cognitive work of the practitioner, emphasizing change at the individual or community level rather than demanding the necessity of widespread structural change.

Critical social work theory

Critical social work

We conceive of the broader critical social work as encompassing a range of eclectic perspectives that invoke the aura of Critical theory (see Introduction and Chapter 1) without marshalling the normative requirements of structural explanation. The relation to Critical theory is, however, largely impressionistic, with the uses of the term 'critical' being casual and loose.

A host of various critical perspectives that loosely align themselves to Critical social work are representative of this tendency, including reflective practice (Schön, 1983), critical best practice (Ferguson, 2003c), the service user movement (Beresford, 2000; Beresford and Croft, 2004), strengths-based perspectives (Saleebey, 2002) and empowerment and advocacy (Braye and Preston-Shoot, 1995). We wish to draw attention, also, to the way in which some Critical social work thinkers inadvertently cross over into critical social work once they adopt the postmodern turn.

What these various positions share in common, as critical social work, is an appeal to progressive liberal democratic ideals and an emphasis on certain humanistic social work values. The most obvious example of this in the social work literature is Robert Adams, Lena Dominelli and Malcolm Payne's (2002) *Critical Practice in Social Work* (see also Ferguson, 2008). In only partially accommodating the stricter and more authentic aspects of Critical social work, this softer set of persuasions, in fact, has the tendency of neutralizing the systematic political intent of the more progressive elements.

Donald Schön's (1983) *The Reflective Practitioner* has had a major influence on both Critical social work and critical social work (see, for example, Fook, 1996, 2002; White, Fook and Gardner, 2006). Jan Fook (2002: 42) notes 'the similarities between a reflective approach and postmodern and critical ways of thinking' as well as qualitative research (Fook, 2004). Following Carolyn Taylor and Susan White (2000), she sees deconstructive techniques as similar to reflective processes (Fook, 2002: 42) so that the client's 'story' told to the social worker is a 'text' that can be subjected to reflective analysis: 'Deconstructive questions can be used to assist in reflecting upon written (or verbal) accounts later in time (or ... at the same time), in a similar way' to that used by a qualitative researcher when analysing interview transcripts or 'texts' (Fook, 1996, 2002). In this way, reflective questions enable the social worker to research experience to uncover the theory implicit in action, understand or construct the situation, and discern gaps, biases, themes and so on, engaging in a process of 'deconstructing' experience and, in so doing, reconstructing the situation.

Empowerment is a theme developed by Suzy Braye and Michael Preston-Shoot (1995) in their *Empowering Practice in Social Care*. Graham McBeath and Stephen Webb (1991) note that empowerment used in this sense is thoroughly ambivalent and can be read either as endorsing a critical approach to social work or one that evokes neoliberal affinities based on individual responsibility and choice in a market economy of social care provision. They perceive much theorizing about empowerment in social work as typifying the latter and falling into an exclusively individualist account of change.

The mantra of empowerment has been deployed in a number of misleading ways, thus enabling easy appropriation by commentators of various political persuasions and, most often, simply as an acid test of service users' ability to make their own choices and decisions free from protectionist social interventions.

Taking a different approach, Harry Ferguson (2003c, 2008) developed what he calls a 'critical best practice' (CBP) approach, wherein he uses critical theory as an interpretative framework to develop a more positive perspective on critical social work. Like Dennis Saleebey's (2002) strengths perspective, CBP seeks to move beyond a deficits approach to focus on strengths, capacities, capabilities, resilience and so on, as constructed by a range of stakeholders in the practice situation.

Like Jan Fook (2002), Ferguson is attempting to establish examples of best practice inductively – that is, from the ground up or from the practice experience or situation.

For both Ferguson (2003c) and Fook (2002) knowledge is constantly developing as practice improves through reflection-in-action. Like Fook (2002, see also Napier and Fook, 2000), his aim is to provide exemplary cases as to 'how to engage service users, promote protection and well-being, establish empowering relationships and conduct long-term therapeutic work in an anti-oppressive manner' (Ferguson, 2003c: 1006).

Given the more systematic exegesis of Critical social work, the remaining parts of this chapter concentrate on addressing the distinctive contribution it has made to thinking about social work. This is followed by a summary critique drawing on the work of McBeath and Webb, (2005) and Stephen Webb (2006).

Critical social work

Key contributors to Critical social work are Jan Fook (2002), Karen Healy (2000, 2005), Steven Hick (Hick, Fook and Pozzuto, 2005), Jim Ife (1997), Peter Leonard (1997, 2001), Robert Mullaly (1993, 1997, 2002, 2007), Bob Pease (Pease and Fook, 1999; Allan, Pease and Briskman, 2003) and Amy Rossiter (1996).

The growth of Critical social work, especially in Canada and Australia in the last decade (Allan et al., 2003; Fook, 2002; Healy, 2000; Ife, 1997; Pease and Fook, 1999; Rossiter, 1996), has its roots in the lasting influence of radical social work (Bailey and Brake, 1975; Brake and Bailey, 1980; Corrigan and Leonard, 1978; Galper, 1975, 1980; Jones, 1983; Langan and Lee, 1989; Reisch and Andrews, 2002) and community work in the 1970s within the UK (Mayo, 1977).

In its socialist and Marxist guise, radical social work 30 years ago cast itself within the problem of the identity of the worker qua social worker. More precisely, the question was about the reconciliation of the contradictory identity of the community worker as part agent of the State and as part agent and advocate of the working class (the 'client' base). An intelligible dialectic of dominant and subordinate forces, State social worker 'against' the people, professional language versus the vernacular and so on emerged from this. What theory was used was essentialist in its appeal to defined identities and reductionist in its pressing the case of the working class.

Within social and cultural theory in the late 1970s, however, there emerged theories that rejected *universalizable* explanations based on a single or delimited set of foundations – self-consciousness (rationalism), class consciousness (Marxism) or raw observations (empiricist positivism), for example. Though coming late to social work, such perspectives led to a reevaluation of social work's universalist and Marxist approaches and the organization of generic social work agencies (McBeath and Webb, 1991). As we shall see, the claim of Critical social work that there are multiple starting points of equal status from which to assess the validity of social work interventions rather than a single one embraces what can be identified loosely as the 'postmodern' turn. This resistance to the idea of a unity or foundational 'ontology' (existences and their status), such as God, human nature and 'reason', out of which all else is derivable, expresses postmodernism's best-known figure: 'fragmentation'. If we have multiple, equally basic starting points, then we do not found explanations on a single factor or whole – 'the unity' – but on 'difference'. We shall show that 'difference' is basic to Critical social work theory. What it is, though, and how it is used in social work theory and practice may be subject to argument.

We have noted that Critical social work tends to use postmodernism and Critical theory as strategies of thought rather than as specific theories. This allows for a variety of readings and engagements. As Fook (2002: 17) notes, 'There are clearly many points of similarity between postmodern thinking and a critical approach'. While Critical social work carries with it an idea of an intellectual whole, it is clear that there are divergent approaches within it. Critical social work theorists share certain key concepts and theoretical ideas. As Healy (2000: 13) comments:

> despite their obvious variations, what these critical approaches to practice share is their foundation in the critical social science paradigm … there is a general endorsement of critical social science understandings about the nature of the social world and human existence.

Postmodernism and critical theory provide Critical social work with the theoretical and political resources to deal with contemporary issues, particularly in relation to social justice, emancipation, power relations, oppression, exploitation and domination. Pease and Fook's (1999: 2) foreword to *Transforming Social Work Practice* captures these emphases when they ask:

> How can we maintain what was positive and liberating in the critical tradition in social work, the emancipatory side of the Enlightenment, but still use postmodernism to deconstruct the problematic elements in the metanarratives of feminism, Marxism, and other critical perspectives to the point where reconstruction becomes possible?

Critical social work seeks to understand how dominant relations of power operate through and across systems of discourse and deconstruct and reconstruct these discourses. We have noted that Critical social work has high hopes of a better and more expansive future for modern societies. In summing up the characteristics of the postmodern and critical approach to social work, Fook (2002: 18) says that a 'postmodern and critical approach to social work is primarily concerned with practicing in ways which further a society without domination, exploitation and oppression'. In referring to the ideology critique of the Frankfurt School of critical theory, Richard Pozzuto (2000, unpaginated) explains that 'the task of Critical Social Work is to lift the veil of the present to see the possibilities of the future'. Similarly, in his influential book *Challenging Oppression: A critical social work approach*, Mullaly (2002) proposes a psychology of emancipation for social work so that oppressed groups might resist the dominant hegemony that encourages them to internalize and blame themselves for their oppression by accepting as normal and inevitable the present society and its oppressive social institutions.

A critique of Critical social work

It is ironic that there has been little by way of sustained critique within the Critical social work perspective itself. In their essay 'Post-critical social work analytics', McBeath and Webb (2005) undertook a close analysis of its central claims. They raised three doubts about the validity of Critical social work. They contended that these problems leave Critical social work in a difficult position, unable to achieve the degree of intellectual challenge to established social work theorizing that it aspires to, especially in relation to the analysis of power. The three doubts are as follows.

1   Critical social work mixes incompatible theoretical sources, particularly those of Foucault, postmodernism and Critical theory. The mixing of Marxism and Critical theory on the one hand with those of Foucault with postmodernism on the other, has produced a confused state of affairs. The muddling of theoretically incompatible sources has left Critical social work bereft in undertaking the important task of analysing *actual relations of power* in social work. Thus, it seems that Critical social work misuses Foucault's work while being happy for it to signal its commitment to postmodernism. Rather than acknowledging Foucault's tension with Marxism for what it is – that is, a very different treatment for the analysis of power – Critical social work seizes on certain Foucauldian slogans – such as 'power from below' and 'resistance as always already' – as well as the convenient replacement of ideology for dominant discourses, to create affiliations with postmodernism, particularly around the 'celebration of diversity' and the 'politics of difference'. McBeath and Webb (2005) show that the emphasis on difference signals the birth of a postmodernism from the womb of his earlier class reductionist account in Marxism. Now class is seen as one, if particularly influential, variable among many. This displacement of class as a universal signifier of oppression permits Critical social work a retheorization in terms of alliances between relatively diffuse oppressed groups.

2   In so far as Critical social work makes dominant discourses a theme, it aligns itself with Foucauldian terms, but, in aspiring to emancipating selves, it is working on a plane of freedom and redemption. As we shall see, this is a dubious position to adopt as it implies that there is something already out there – 'emancipation' or one's true self – that has been repressed by power and simply needs to be released. Fook (in Fawcett, Featherstone, Fook and Rossiter, 2000: 118) notes:

> expert professional social workers are able to create critical knowledge which potentially challenges and resists current forms of domination, and they are able to maintain commitment to a system of social values which allows them to work with, yet transcend the contradictions and uncertainties of daily practice.

From a critical theoretical viewpoint, Fook is offering a very bourgeois model – namely, the dominance of the concept (value systems) over the object (daily life). This kind of 'totality thinking' provides for a liberal utopian politics wholly out of sympathy with Foucault, but it is even more worrying and old-fashioned than that in some cases. Fook, for example, trades on a tired, imprecise, but 'critical', notion of 'false consciousness' – a term that is rooted in binary thinking if ever there were one.

3 Critical social work's 'Foucauldian' appropriation rests on an inadequate model of power that is organized by a rather fixed, narrow set of oppositions and so ignores the importance of complex power relations and more fluid operations and flows of power that are central to Foucault's analysis. Critical social work is happy to seize on historical and methodological grounds for evidence of fixed systems of power – such as identifying 'oppressive structures' along the lines of race, gender and class – but is reluctant to grasp the significance of the 'becoming' of historical events as a function of the proliferation of complex strategies and flows of power. Thus, the analysis of power cuts across two incompatible sources: Marx and Foucault. While, for Marx, power is a universality tale of class division and conflict, for Foucault, the structural dynamics became more fluid across time. This point is not recognized by Critical social workers, who apply Foucault's analysis of nineteenth-century rather fixed systems of disciplinary power to what is arguably far more fluid – namely, modern societies today. Critical social work seems to believe that Foucault persists in using his disciplinary model of modern power for late twentieth-century conditions and this provides a warrant for them to theorize power similarly.

Given the centrality of power for analysing regimes of domination, Critical social work does not let loose the full methodological force of Foucault's 'analytics of power' on the issues at hand. Foucault's theory of power is closely linked to concrete empirical studies that, in turn, contribute to the refinement of his theoretical tools. Critical social work fails to produce detailed analyses of micro power relations that are constituted by wider systems of domination and leaves largely unaccounted for the formation of social work divisions within agencies and the relationship between discursive and non-discursive power. A stronger emphasis on relations of power as 'governmentality' would help offset this bias.

Emerging towards the end of Foucault's life, the notion of 'governmentality' spawned a mass of secondary literature from many of Foucault's closest collaborators (see Burchell, Gordon and Miller, 1991; Mitchell, 1999). What Foucauldian studies of governmentality do is identify the terms of sociopolitical programmes that, via subtle power relations, have attempted to shape the 'conduct of conduct' – the management, and, thus, regulation, of populations and then analyse the 'capillary action' of these programmes on the various strata of society at which they are aimed. Critical social work has not looked deeply at the relations of power as the conduct of conduct and of power/knowledge within the domain of social work agencies. Critical social work assumes an ideological mode of operation by social workers on an oppressed population – service users. Such accounts tend towards the deterministic and do not take seriously enough the flowing variable character of the formations of practice. This weakness provides Critical social work with an all too easy link to the strategy of critical theory that gives a picture of a standardized practice constituting and repeating patterns of injustice.

Critical social work practice

We have shown that there is a distinct – though not always clearly perceptible – difference between those who advocate Critical social work and critical social work. As mentioned previously, Critical social work has an interesting symbiotic relationship with critical social work. The large 'C' has been referred to by some as the 'beginning' of critical social work (Fook, 2002). We have implied that a 'radical' or Critical approach to social work is weakened by a broader critical social work. Even though the term 'radical' is problematic, as the early writers themselves pointed out, the legacy of this 'early' writing is evident in various critical social work discourses, such as the literature on critical thinking skills, the questioning of dominant ideologies, locating one's own values and social positioning – reflexivity – in relation to particular issues, organizational and social change strategies, caution over language use and traditional structural analysis. Gone is the questioning of the profession's propensity to enact *radical* social change. This has been traded for structural analyses that underestimate the capacity of the individual – social worker and client – to enact change while working 'within the system' (see Chapter 2) or else for 'critical reflection' and language analytics that focus attention on the social worker's subjective construction and deconstruction of the client's situation as determinants in their analysis (see Chapter 15).

Significance for social work practice

We would like to end by making some positive recommendations for Critical social work that draw attention to its significance for practice.

In providing analyses for practice contexts, it would benefit from concentrating on two related levels:

- paying closer attention to the minutiae of governmentality as practices and flows of power, as 'the conduct of conduct'.
- moving beyond orthodox Marxism to theorize 'the State' and its apparatus as biopolitics, policing and regulatory power.

The postmodern turn does not facilitate such an analysis and impedes serious empirical investigations of power.

Critical social work's contribution to a progressive Left agenda would also be less hindered if it focused its analytical lens on ideology and ideological formations, in the spirit of Antonio Gramsci and Nicos Poultanzas, rather than the neologism of dominant discourses.

If we are correct in saying that Critical social work is both a symptom of and reaction to modernity, it should drop its postmodern pretensions by concentrating on the acute and deleterious effects of late modernity – particularly those of neoliberalism – on social work. As noted by John Solas (2002: 128), 'if postmodernism is such a thoroughly baseless, reductive and inert doctrine, then why persist with it? The poverty of postmodernism prompts a timely return to the rich legacy of Marxism'.

(Continued)

The lasting importance of Critical social work is that it has provided a theoretical foundation for articulating the complexities social workers often experience in practice, especially in seeking to achieve change. Indeed, unlike many other theories in social work that are either politically neutral or servants to dominant systems of power, Critical social work is affirmative about the possibilities of transformation. This is undoubtedly part of its strength and appeal.

The political critique undertaken by Critical social work centres on the theoretical implications of concepts that sustain a transformative tradition of engagement, commitment and action that posit the possibility of new social and political forms. This entails its opposition to mainstream forms of social work theory and practice that find their legitimacy as either examples of professional expertise or servants to the Prince. The aim of Critical social work is practical, but its grounds of justification are political and ethical. In this sense, Critical social work is superior to mainstream theory *as theory*, by which we mean that it is superior in terms of its knowledge. This is most evident in the way that Critical social work takes the important steps towards a reflexive turn of theory that conceives of itself as an agonistic event in the life of modern societies.

Notwithstanding the criticisms raised above, what Critical theory in social work is, above all, then, is derived from the level of engagement it achieves *through its thought* in permitting a 'self-awareness' as the first step in engaging in processes of social and political transformation. To return to the insights offered by Pierre Bourdieu (1998: 8), he made no secret of the significance offered by the role of the critical practitioner when he noted that:

> What I defend above all is the possibility and the necessity of the critical intellectual, who is firstly critical of the intellectual *doxa* secreted by the doxosophers. There is no genuine democracy without genuine opposing critical powers. The intellectual is one of those, and of the first magnitude.

Study questions

1. Read Orme on feminism (Chapter 6) and Hick and Murray on structural social work (Chapter 8) and identify three key features from each chapter, explaining why they lend themselves to Critical social work theory.
2. Is Critical social work theory compatible with evidence-based practice in social work?
3. Does 'postmodernism' make a positive contribution to Critical social work theory?

Glossary

Alienation Refers to the negative effects for individuals of living in certain types of modern society. The concept is often used to refer to a person's estrangement, loneliness and dissatisfaction that are felt especially in everyday life.

Critical theory Originated as an organizing concept in the work of German social and political scientists, particularly those working at the Frankfurt School, including Theodore Adorno, Walter Benjamin, Herbert Marcuse, Jürgen Habermas and Max Horkheimer.

Critical poststructural theory is a variant of structuralism in anthropology and literary theory that derives from the work of Ferdinand de Saussure and Claude Levi-Strauss. Poststructuralism encompasses the intellectual developments of Continental – French – philosophers. This is often referred to as the 'linguistic turn' in philosophy, whereby meaning, beliefs and values were seen to be determined by and reduced to linguistic or language systems as expressed in text, narrative and conversation (see Chapters 13 and 15).

Deconstruction Derives from the philosophy of Jacques Derrida and has been particularly influential in literary criticism and social theory. The operation of deconstruction is a method that shows how unifying and enduring concepts in Western philosophy – such as truth, reason, universality and progress – are, in fact, rhetorical constructions based on the function of language. It shows how dominant meanings and symbols that we assume are the truth are little more than textual manoeuvres and shifts that demonstrate the value-ladenness of the author's intention.

Doxa The fundamental, deep-founded, unthought beliefs, taken as self-evident universals, that inform an agent's actions and thoughts within a particular field. Doxa tends to favour the particular social arrangement of the field, thus privileging the dominant and taking their position of dominance as self-evident and universally favourable (see Wikipedia).

Governmentality This feature of Foucauldian analyses of power, which has been more recently developed in the work of Nikolas Rose, Dean Mitchell and Pat O'Malley, is different from other analyses of power in its emphasis on the micro power of concrete social relations, which is often referred to as 'the conduct of conduct' – that is, how individuals monitor, regulate and observe themselves in ways that conform to the normalizing requirements of dominant systems, such as schools, religions and the State.

Ideology An organized set of ideas or beliefs formed by normative regimes of power that purport to form a comprehensive vision of the truth. Marxist analysis of ideology shows it to be a set of ideas proposed by the dominant class of society to all members of society. In this way, it is constructed as a normative truth. Hence, the main function of ideology is to maintain the existing social order through normative processes.

Liberal humanism Derived from liberal theory, which affirms the individual dignity and worth of people based on their ability to determine right and wrong by appealing to universal human qualities, particularly the use of reason. It entails a commitment to the search for truth and morality through rational means to support human interests and emphasizes the importance of free will, self-determination, respect for persons and positive freedom.

Select bibliography

The social work journals that endorse a Critical social work stance are *Social Work & Society, Critical Social Work* and *Journal of Progressive Human Services*. Key texts are Fook (2002), Healy (2000), Leonard (1997) and Taylor and White (2000).

Structural Social Work

Steven F. Hick and Kate Murray

Introducing structural social work

Emerging in Canada during the mid-1970s, the structural approach challenged the individual-level focus of conventional social work and emphasized emancipation and social justice (Carniol, 1992). The approach's historical and critical analysis challenges the dominant social and economic structures of patriarchal capitalism, colonialism, racism, heterosexism, ableism and ageism and emphasizes how these structures are the 'root' cause of social problems in that they produce and reinforce oppression.

Drawing on a range of sometimes competing perspectives, including Marxism, feminism, anti-racism, radical humanism and postmodernism (Carniol, 2005a; Lecompte, 1990; Lundy, 2004; Mullaly, 2007; Payne, 2005), structural social work seeks the transformation of society towards values of freedom, humanitarianism, collectivism, equality, self-determination, and popular participation. It emphasizes social transformation, but does not neglect personal issues and individual difficulties. Individual and structural changes are addressed simultaneously, because each of these levels is related to and affects the other. Hence, structural social work has the twin goals of alleviating the negative effects of an exploitative and alienating social order on individuals, while simultaneously aiming to transform society.

Structural social work theory

Structural social work falls into a larger category of approaches that are considered 'progressive', 'radical' or 'transformative' rather than 'conventional'. Conventional approaches emphasize client adaptation and support provision within the dominant social order. Structural social work, however, questions the legitimacy of institutions and economic systems, suggesting that real advances in social welfare cannot be achieved without fundamental changes to the way in which global society organizes the distribution of resources and power.

The structural approach to social work should not be confused with the broader theoretical concept of 'structuralism'. While structural social work initially built on structuralist sociological theory, it has since developed an increased emphasis on human agency (see Chapters 2 and 15).

Structural social work is grounded in critical sociological theories. Originating in the late 1930s from the Frankfurt School, the ideas of early critical theorists questioned conventional modes of enquiry, which assumed the existing social order to be 'natural'. Max Horkheimer (1937) accused traditional theory of being merely descriptive – seeking to explain how society functions but falling short of exposing and challenging the way in which 'society' itself is constructed. This thinking, along with the contributions of others such as Jürgen Habermas, Antonio Gramsci and Ulrich Beck, emphasized how cultural, political and moral beliefs and structures were essential aspects of 'hegemony' – that is, unquestioned assumptions about 'the way things are', which function to maintain the existing social order. Critical theories hold that liberation requires a recognition of that which dominates people or 'imprisons the mind' as persons cannot be free from that about which they are ignorant (Sabia and Wallulis, 1983).

Based on this interrogation of the social environment, several elements emerge as key conceptual features of structural social work:

- a problematization of dominant social and economic structures through adoption of a 'conflict' or 'change' perspective;
- a focus on multiple, intersecting forms of oppression produced and reinforced by structures;
- a concentration on the dialectical nature of the interaction between individuals and macro-level structures.

Problematization of dominant social and economic structures

An 'order' perspective views social problems as a 'disruption' of society's natural equilibrium and suggests institutional fixes to re-establish stability. In contrast, conflict or 'change' perspectives view society as comprised of many different individuals and groups between which there are complex tensions and areas of agreement and disagreement. Thus, structural social work highlights issues of power, inequality and how social structures are constructed and reinforced by powerful elites to ensure their own continued dominance while exploiting less powerful groups.

Based on an historical and contemporary critique of dominant social orders, structural social work understands the purpose of the capitalist economic organization of paid and unpaid work to be the maintenance of patriarchy (male dominance), profits and private property. The result of this system is that rights, resources and rewards are allocated differentially on the basis of, inter alia, gender, class and race (Moreau with Leonard, 1989). As capitalism became increasingly neoliberal and globalized in the latter part of the twentieth century, every part of the world saw a drastic transfer of global wealth from poor to rich countries and from the less affluent to the wealthy. Participation in capitalist social relations is reinforced by institutions of socialization, including schools, the Church, the media, the family and social agencies. Also required are institutions of regulation and correction, including the police, armed forces, courts and social services.

Maurice Moreau with Lynne Leonard (1989) described how social institutions and policies function to maintain particular forms of group living and sexuality that reinforce the economic structure – for instance, the nuclear family and heterosexuality. A critical awareness of how these dominant institutions function reveals possibilities for their dismantling and suggests a vision of social transformation.

Mullaly (2007) views social work values are fundamentally incompatible with contemporary capitalism and calls for a transformation towards a socialism others such as Hick and Carniol do not prescribe a specific social order, but rather see it as arising from the transformation process.

Multiple forms of oppression

Structural social work highlights the way in which dominant structures decrease access to opportunities, resources and power for certain groups, resulting in individual and collective experiences of oppression. The approach's critical examination of the modern economic system has, at its base, a class analysis that views economic power as monopolized by a decreasing number of wealthy elites. Over time, structural social work has incorporated a more comprehensive, contemporary analysis of the social relations underpinning oppression, along such lines as gender, racialization (socially constructed racial categories), cultural identity, (dis)ability, age and sexuality.

Feminist analyses of patriarchal family structures and women's work have profoundly influenced structural social work. From feminists, the approach gained the pivotal insight that 'the personal is political' – that is, 'private', personal interactions and roles are both shaped by, and serve to reinforce, larger, gendered, dominant institutions and relations of power (see, for example, Baines, Evans and Neysmith, 1998).

Theory concerning oppression based on racialization or ethnicity exposes how language, religion, nationality, ancestry and skin colour continue to be the basis of exploitation and inequality (Satzewich, 1998). Often, racism goes unnoticed – embedded within taken-for-granted structures and assumptions of 'whiteness' (Frankenberg, 1993).

Other writers highlight how social structures are infused with heterosexism and homophobia based on assumed heterosexuality and gender 'norms' (Carabine, 1996; O'Brien, 1994; Richardson, 1996).

(Dis)ability movement activists emphasize how 'disability' is socially constructed through assumptions of a young, able-bodied, healthy male. While existing supports or arrangements for such individuals are seen as 'entitlements', people requiring a different kind of help are assumed to be 'needy' or 'dependent' (Wendell, 1996).

In attending to those who document these many forms of oppression, structural social work recognizes the multiple categories by which individuals are exploited. This has enriched the approach's understanding of how emancipation might occur and the inclusive transformation to which it aspires.

A dialectical approach

In understanding that 'the personal is political', structural social work emphasizes that social and political change begins within the social relations of people's everyday lives, such as in sexuality, family roles and the workplace. In this way, the approach overcomes the perceived duality between 'structures' and 'individuals'. Traditionally, this perceived duality has resulted in an emphasis on individual self-determination and the capacity for self-help, but it also enables personal blame for social problems.

A second, opposite response to this supposed personal–social duality has been the structuralist–determinist tradition, which views individuals as 'victims of structures that cannot be changed'. This latter outlook negates any possibility for social workers to engage in meaningful, emancipatory practice (Pease, in Moreau with Leonard, 1989).

Rejecting this assumed 'duality', however, structural social work takes a 'dialectical' approach, seeing 'individual agency' and 'social structures' as related, co-existing constructs engaged in a mutually reinforcing relationship where one organizes and perpetuates the other. Thus, oppressive structures are understood as not static or immovable but subjective – that is, constructed by human actions according to particular ideologies and relations of power. The major principles of dialectics can be understood in the following way:

- everything is related, such that nothing can be understood in isolation;
- change is constant – nothing is absolute or immutable; old forms are replaced by new forms while preserving some older viable elements;
- change is gradual, incremental and cumulative; small changes eventually aggregate to significant and radical transformations;
- change results from the unity and struggle of opposites; there is common ground even within binary opposites, such as good or bad, true or false, capitalist or socialist; that which is seemingly 'unified' contains opposing forces or tensions and it is those tensions or contradictions that become the basis for social change (adapted from Naiman, in Mullaly, 2007: 237–8).

Thus, structural social work understands the formation of dynamic and shifting social structures involving both personal and collective elements. While highlighting oppressive structures, the approach attends to the multilayered forces that comprise them, producing an awareness of oppression at interrelated structural, cultural and personal levels.

This dialectical interaction between individuals and macro-level structures is often described in terms of 'social relations'. Dorothy Smith (1987: 155) defines social relations as 'concerted sequences or courses of social action implicating more than one individual whose participants are not necessarily present or known to one another'. She describes how social relations are evident in everyday settings as people act competently but unconsciously to coordinate their actions in accordance with standards, expectations or rules.

The dialectical nature of structural social work also responds to the recurring question of whether one should change the system from within or work outside or against the system. While activism is commonly associated with social movements, the vast majority of social workers find themselves working in government-funded institutions or agencies. Against this backdrop, some argue that politics and social work should not mix, that 'professional' non-directiveness and value-neutrality require radicals to leave their politics at home. Others argue that, as a sanctioned 'profession', social work is not capable of engaging in any activity that fundamentally challenges the dominant social order of which it is part. Structural social work, however, challenges this false separation between a person's 'professional' and 'personal' life. The approach highlights action outside the institutional contexts of social work practice yet emphasizes that, even while acting as agents of government, social workers can provide oppressed groups with access to knowledge and State power, thereby using contradictory relations to contribute to social change.

Structural social work practice

Structural social work has developed and matured through time, influenced by evolving social and economic contexts, discourse analysis and reflexivity in practice (see Chapter 15).

Historical development

Until the 1960s, the dominant approach to social work practice was social 'casework' – a pseudo-medical methodology for diagnosing and treating individual behaviours that came to incorporate Freudian psychoanalytic principles.

In the 1960s and 1970s, economic and political upheaval and the heightened consciousness of oppressed groups increased the focus on collective aspects of social problems. Systems and humanistic theories began to challenge diagnostic categories and medical concepts of 'causality'. Conflict-based theories rooted in feminism and Marxism criticized dominant institutions.

Moreau with Leonard (1989) noted that critical sociology, including labelling and deviancy theory, exposed the social control functions of social work, thus encouraging the development of radical approaches (Bailey and Brake, 1975; Corrigan and Leonard, 1978; Galper, 1975, 1980). Radical authors criticized social casework as ineffective, elitist, forcing an adaptation to injustice, pathologizing social problems and valuing professional self-interest over client needs (Moreau with Leonard, 1989). Carleton University students, embracing these critiques, demanded the school's recognition of institutional injustice, fostering structural social work's simultaneous focus on individual change and longer-term structural transformation (Moreau with Leonard, 1989).

While Ruth Middleman and Gale Goldberg's (1974) 'structural social work' identified the social environment as the source of social problems, they attributed those problems to 'disorganization' rather than 'oppressive structures' (Mullaly, 1993). However, Peter Leonard (1997) demonstrated that 'consensus-focused' ecological theory was irreconcilable with materialist accounts of society. Thus, while both 'eco systems' and 'transformative' approaches were once considered to be 'structural' (Davis, 1991), societal transformation is now recognized as a definitive tenet of structural social work.

Despite the energetic birth of structural social work in the 1970s, conservative global trends in the 1980s led to the declining visibility and perceived impracticality of transformative approaches. However, in 1993, Mullaly situated structural social work as providing social workers with a nuanced analysis of contemporary sociopolitical and economic issues and a coherent framework for radical practice. Further, Fook's (1993) *Radical Casework* advanced transformative methods for practice.

Since then, there have been several significant contributions to this discourse within social work (such as Carniol, 1992, 2005a, 2005b, 2005c; Dominelli, 1997b; Hick, Fook, and Puzzuto, 2005; Ife, 1997, 2001; Leonard, 1997; Lundy, 2004; Mullaly, 1997, 2002, 2007; Pease and Fook, 1999; Reisch and Andrews, 2002). However, Michael Reisch and Janice Andrews (2002) note that such progressive perspectives are in the minority, serving to represent 'the road not taken' by the profession as a whole.

Advances and controversies

Under names such as 'critical social work', 'political social work', 'progressive social work', 'radical social work', 'structural social work', 'anti-discriminatory' and 'anti-oppressive' practice, there exists a common vision of societal transformation. However, there are different understandings of the precise mechanics through which 'oppression' and 'liberation' occur. Thus, several qualities stand out as 'distinguishing features' of structural social work.

First, the approach is noteworthy because of its analysis of interconnected societal structures, how these are constructed and how they may be dismantled (Carniol, 2007, personal email correspondence). Carniol notes that this analysis differs from many versions of 'anti-oppressive' and 'critical' social work approaches that try either to homogenize the different harmful structures into a 'vague mush', to ignore class analysis entirely, or characterize 'oppression' as a subjective, individual experience.

Some approaches identify a particular category, such as 'class' or 'gender', to be of primary importance (Bishop, 1994, for example), suggesting a 'hierarchy of oppressions'. However, structural social work avoids identifying a single fundamental source of oppression. Instead, it is equally critical of all oppression and concerned with all oppressed groups. It draws attention to how multiple structures intersect and experiences of oppression are viewed as complex and multilayered, often shared by entire groups, but also unique to each individual circumstance.

The structural approach provides a window through which to explore these 'points of intersection' between different forms of oppression, which Colleen Lundy (2004) describes as multiplied, 'tangled knots'. However, Mullaly (2002) calls for more theoretical development to explicate multiple identities, the fluidity of group membership, contextual variables, individual or psychological factors, status within an oppressed group and individual variations in experience. He notes that social workers must be aware of the heterogeneity of all groups and recognize oppression between and *within* oppressed groups.

A second distinguishing feature relates to how structural social work's analysis of intersecting oppressions and dialectical personal–structural interaction is inclusive of a myriad of perspectives, enabling the integration of various concepts and practices, such as radical and feminist approaches (Fook, 1993). This enables disruption of the conventional, artificial distinction between 'direct intervention', 'community development' and 'policy analysis', as well as the perceived choice between working 'within' or 'against' the system. Hence, structural social work has the potential to act as a unifying approach within radical social work (Carniol, 2007, personal email correspondence; Mullaly, 1993).

There is disagreement in some areas, however – for instance, the extent to which structural social work is informed by postmodern and poststructural thought. Among other criticisms, there exist concerns that postmodernism may obscure structural domination, limit the potential for solidarity and coherent social change or enable an 'anything goes' relativism (Agger, 1998; Harvey, in Mullaly, 2007; Leonard, 1995). For a fuller discussion of postmodern and poststructural theory, see Chapter 11.

Nonetheless, several authors describe valuable postmodern contributions, including postmodernism's attention to a multiplicity of perspectives, realities, positions and experiences that enhances a recognition of the legitimacy of each individual's 'voice' within an analysis of social issues. Postmodern critique has enabled the deconstruction of modernist concepts embedded within structural social work, such as those prescribing one 'linear track' to emancipation (Carniol, 2005a; Mullaly, 2007). Ben Carniol (2005a) notes how postmodernism and poststructuralism have enhanced the exploration of multi-interactive layers of internalized oppression and privilege across local-to-global structures. An attention to discourse and the social construction of knowledge is also a postmodern contribution (Mullaly, 2007). As in feminism, power is seen to be enacted not only through the State but also by everyday actions in ongoing, situated contexts. This understanding provides another lens for examining the individual–structural dialectic and the location and subjectivity of social workers and clients. Such awareness becomes an empowering foundation for transformed, non-oppressive relationships and solidarities seeking social justice (Carniol, 2005a).

Ben Agger (1998) argues that it is possible to pursue a critical postmodernism, incorporating the helpful aspects of this perspective while avoiding extreme relativism. Steven Best and Douglas Kellner (1997) and Steven Hick et al. (2005) see postmodernism as a 'turn' rather than a break or shift from modernity to postmodernity. Hick (2005) suggests that a more 'indeterminate' engagement with postmodernism may allow structural social work to retain its fundamental premise of social transformation. Carniol (in Hick et al., 2005) and Mullaly (2007) concur that postmodernism can contribute to a healthy climate of accepting differences and enabling greater solidarity in resisting the multiplicity of illegitimate privileges.

Practice and critique

Analyses of 'state theory' and 'dialectical' human–structural interaction seem a world apart from the everyday activities of child welfare, hospital discharge planning or youth counselling. Thus, social workers have voiced dissatisfaction with structural social work's lack of emphasis on practical skills, such as techniques for assessment and interviewing. This critique stems from the approach's development in reaction to the overemphasis on 'casework skills' that dominated the field for so long (Moreau with Leonard, 1989).

This concern is commonly addressed by emphasizing how existing practical skills can often be adapted and enhanced by the structural approach. Moreau (in Moreau with Leonard, 1989: 21) suggested that 'one could use a number of techniques ... as long as ... problems were not psychologized or depoliticized and use of a technique did not further mystify a client'. Lundy (2004) provides an assessment guide for family intervention and Colleen Lundy (2004) discusses the use of genograms, contracts and communication skills from a structural perspective.

While these illustrations are helpful, Moreau with Leonard (1989) reframes the assumed need for practice models. Too great a concern with 'skills', notes Moreau with Leonard, reinforces dominant beliefs that locate social problems – and solutions – within the realm of 'the individual' – that is, responsibility for problem solving thus becomes centred within individual social workers' abilities to perform a particular 'technique'.

Significance for social work practice

In discussing social work assessment, Fook (1993: 74–5) states that 'not *all* personal problems are *totally* structurally caused ... there is *always* a structural element in any experienced problem'. Thus, structural social workers consider *all* the dimensions of personal problems, but are particularly attuned to the less visible structural elements.

Moreau with Leonard (1989) identified four practices of structural social work and Moreau and Frosst (1993) added a fifth. Carniol (1992) and Hick (1998) each discussed six elements while Mullaly (1993) described eight. The following list summarizes seven key, interrelated elements of these conceptualizations of structural social work practice:

- defence of the client;
- collectivization or collective consciousness;
- materialization;
- unmasking oppressive structures and critical consciousness-raising;
- increasing the client's power in the worker–client relationship;
- empowerment through personal change;
- social activism and political change.

Defence of the client

Clients' difficulties often relate to restrictive and unfair institutional procedures, such as the way in which information is recorded or bureaucratic time constraints. Social workers are equally capable of reinforcing – or questioning – these practices. Structural social workers ally with clients, using their institutional power to defend or promote clients' interests, both within and outside social agencies. This could involve providing insider information, subverting rules or initiating organizational change to maximize clients' access to resources and rights. Such actions require the negotiation of ethical decisions and potential personal risks, including job loss.

Collectivization or collective consciousness

A lack of class consciousness among the working class enables the maintenance of a stratified society (Naimen, in Lundy, 2004). Structural social work encourages the formation of groups to highlight the collective causes of problems and affirm individuals' collective identity. This fosters the analysis and planning of actions to resist oppressive practices and facilitates links to larger progressive movements.

Materialization

'Materialism' emphasizes that economic resources and material goods are central in defining relations of power within capitalism. Structural social work grounds clients' problems in their access to resources and fosters an understanding of how thoughts, feelings and behaviours are linked to material conditions, such as work, community breakdown and economic pressures. Priority is given to clients' survival needs, including food, shelter and access to services. The approach makes explicit the limits of self-help, mutual aid or 'counselling' when these don't address societal change.

Unmasking oppressive structures and critical consciousness-raising

Paulo Freire (1970) believed that oppressed people needed to gain a 'critical consciousness' of oppressive social structures in order to challenge them. He suggested that this 'conscientization' occurs as people engage in praxis – that is, a critical dialogue merging activism and discussion wherein social analysis and practice inform each other in a dialectical cycle of action–reflection–action. Structural social workers use critical questioning, reframing and the disputing of myths to assist clients in exploring how oppressive power relations impact on their daily lives.

Increasing the clients' power in the worker–client relationship

Instead of viewing client–worker interactions as top-down or expert-prescriptive, the structural approach seeks egalitarian and democratic relationships by exploring power relations – especially the systemic power or authority that resides with the worker (Carniol, 2005a).

Reproduction of oppressive social relations is minimized by:

- engaging clients in a dialogical rapport (Freire, 1970); downplaying professionalism; acknowledging personal biases and values; self-disclosing; the open sharing of information; demystifying social work 'techniques'; involving clients in decisions;
- alternative service delivery models where decisions (such as hiring personnel) are made democratically both by staff and service users.

Such models cultivate support for structural practice and the legitimization of demands for social justice. These two practices maximize clients' agency within interventions.

Empowerment through personal change

A positive client self-image is supported by normalizing fears and reactions and validating strengths or successes. Clients are helped to identify the contradictions between thoughts, feelings and behaviours and to link these with the social context in relation to themselves and others. Clients' and others' contributions to problems are clarified within a structural context to foster a healthy understanding of 'self' and help clients change their feelings, thoughts or behaviours when these are harmful to themselves or others.

Social activism and political change

An involvement in social justice organizations, social movements, alternative services and the use of non-violent tactics, coalitions and solidarity work is emphasized because of its unique role (translation from Corbeil et al., in Moreau with Leonard, 1989: 30):

> autonomous groups are important precisely because they are outside the institutional network where they enjoy a greater degree of freedom to criticize and to act. Social workers should avoid co-opting these groups by trying to integrate them in the institutional network thus cutting off their essential margin of manoeuvre.

Elizabeth Whitmore (2007, personal email correspondence) calls for a renewal of structural social work, noting that a key determinant of its future will be the ability to actively engage practitioners in defining how the approach relates to their daily work. For instance, Purnima George and Sara Marlowe (2005) describe a structural approach taken in rural India to demonstrate the approach's operationalization and viability. By using direct and legal action, social care initiatives to empower service users, innovative resource generation projects and organizational networks, one grass roots organization alleviated immediate poverty and violence while contributing to the systemic abolishment of 'untouchability'. This account from India demonstrates the emancipatory potential of structural social work that must be recognized and cultivated 'on the ground'.

Carniol (2007, personal email correspondence) notes that a second key to ensuring that the importance of structural social work lasts lies in its receptivity to new areas of critical awareness and a proven ability to serve as a unifying approach within the progressive, critical and radical social work movement. However, Carniol notes that its future relevance depends on its adherents' capacity to act coherently within or against broader social forces. He highlights the importance of solidarity in bringing people together in organized democratic and accountable efforts to change society.

In our minds, this appears to be the key challenge. Progressive movements and schools of social work often emphasize small differences at the expense of solidarity. A change in this tradition towards a more unified approach will be instrumental in ensuring structural social work's lasting importance and the possibilities for effecting meaningful societal change.

Study questions

1. Betty is a 39-year-old Indigenous woman who grew up in a reserve community. After leaving an abusive husband, she stayed at her mother's building for senior citizens, but was evicted because her children were not allowed there. Now, her children have been apprehended by Child and Family Services because she was not providing appropriate shelter. Using structural social work practice principles, how might you work with Betty?
2. Is it desirable to seek a societal transformation away from oppressive social and economic relations? Why or why not? Could a social worker really influence such a change?
3. Working as a welfare caseworker, how could you use a 'dialectical understanding of person–structure interaction' to influence social change through your work? What challenges might you face as you tried to do this and how would you confront these?

Glossary

Collectivization A structural social work practice strategy wherein the social causes of problems are highlighted to foster both client identification with others and the group planning of actions for social change.

Dialectics A way of understanding processes that views everything as related. Change occurs incrementally and constantly through the interaction of many different forces and actions that can be complementary or opposed. Thus, social structures are always shifting, dynamic and formed by the interplay of many personal and collective elements.

Materialization A practice strategy that involves helping people to make connections between personal problems and emotions and their material living and working conditions.

Multiple oppressions A framework that understands oppression as occurring at personal, cultural and structural levels according to factors such as class, gender, racism, (dis)ability, sexuality and age. Various forms of oppression are thought to intersect – affecting each other but remaining distinct and equally important.

Structures of oppression Include social, cultural and institutional practices that decrease access to opportunities, resources and power for certain groups. 'Primary' structures of oppression include patriarchal capitalism, heterosexism, colonialism, racism, 'ableism' and ageism.

Select bibliography

Moreau's (1979) 'A structural approach to social work practice' reflects the birth of structural social work, and his *Empowerment through a Structural Approach to Social Work* (1989, with Leonard) illustrates the development of practice principles.

Starting in 1993, Mullaly's texts entitled *Structural Social Work* (1993) and *The New Structural Social Work* (2007) advanced the approach based on state theory, ideological value bases, the changing context of globalization and the incorporation of critical postmodernism. Mullaly's *Challenging Oppression* (2002) provides an in-depth exploration of the central concept of oppression.

Hick began writing about structural social work in 1997 and integrated this in discussions about anti-oppressive practice (2002) and critical social work (2005).

Carniol's (2005a) article, 'Structural social work (Canada)' in *Encyclopedia of Social Welfare History in North America* provides an excellent brief overview of the approach's historical and contemporary development and practice elements. Carniol's various editions of *Case Critical* (1987, 1990, 1995, 2000, 2005b) address the merger of structural social work theory with practice, as does his 1992 article 'Structural social work: Maurice Moreau's challenge to social work practice' and Colleen Lundy's *Social Work and Social Justice: A structural approach to practice* (2004).

Multi-culturalism

9

Purnima Sundar

Introducing multiculturalism

Rapid global change is a fact of life in the twenty-fist century. Technological advances, expanded economies and enhanced systems of communication have facilitated and supported immigration on a massive scale throughout the world. As a result, the industrialized nations continue to experience growing ethnic, racial, cultural and religious diversity (see Glossary). Such shifts have prompted writers and policymakers to study, discuss and debate the multiculturalism that has come to characterize cities and towns across the globe.

In both popular and academic texts, multiculturalism is distinguished from monoculturalism (where there is one homogeneous group in society) and assimilationism (where a majority group establishes political, behavioural and social norms that newcomers must emulate to ensure inclusion) (James, 2003). Multiculturalism is a philosophy that acknowledges and values diversity in society and describes the various tangible (that is, economic) and intangible (for example, social) benefits that result from different ethnic, cultural, racial and religious groups living together. Its goal is to support the full political, social and economic integration of all members of society. Both philosophically and practically, multiculturalism has unsettled traditional notions of collective national identity and exclusion and inclusion in society.

Multiculturalism is more than a simple way to describe culturally plural societies and how they function. Instead, multiculturalism is an *ideology* related to ethnic, cultural, racial and religious diversity that influences people's identities and behaviours. This ideology plays a critical role in shaping a country's nationhood and its reputation on the global stage. It is also reflected in a country's institutions and official policies. Finally, it guides the way that social workers understand and respond to diversity as helping professionals working in multicultural societies.

In this chapter, I explore the ideology of multiculturalism, its impact on institutional policies and its influence on the way social workers think about and shape their practice. I review the work of key thinkers, discuss how this ideology influences knowledge production and the development of practice guidelines in the field of social work and conclude by summarizing the major controversies related to multiculturalism.

The theory of multiculturalism

Formal reflections on multiculturalism began to emerge in the late 1800s as intellectuals considered the cultural pluralism resulting from the European colonization of North America and Africa. Writers such as the sociologist W. E. B. DuBois and the pragmatist philosopher William James adopted the view that such societies would create opportunities for people to embrace diversity and work towards a humanistic and egalitarian social world.

Today, ideas about multiculturalism vary considerably. Most of the debate centres on notions of identity, equality and difference. Multiculturalism presents a unique challenge to contemporary liberal democracies that strive to ensure equality for all members of society, such that they are viewed and treated in the same way, while at the same time making certain that diverse identities are valued and supported (Gutmann, 1994; Rattansi, 2004). The question then, is: within multicultural societies, is it possible for people from diverse groups to experience full economic, political, social and educational inclusion (that is, to be perceived as equals), while at the same time sustaining the traditions and practices unique to their cultural group (that is, to honour their differences) (Abu-Laban, 2002)?

The 'difference blindness' perspective

Some would argue that, in order for a liberal democracy to function as intended, people need to practice a 'difference blindness' that ensures individual rights and privileges are applied to everyone in the same way, without reference to one's cultural background, ethnicity, race and/or religion. This allows the State to maintain its neutrality in decisions about the allocation of resources, the application of the law and the general treatment of society's members.

This view is clear in the writing of Canadian author Neil Bissoondath (1994), who suggests that focusing on people's differences emphasizes how they are *dissimilar* to one another and weakens a broader commitment to national unity. He argues that, in Canada, rather than promoting a shared sense of 'Canadianness', the emphasis on multiculturalism pits one group against the other. According to this perspective, remaining committed to the 'homeland' identity prevents people's full inclusion in the country in which they live and reinforces the inequality that exists between diverse groups and mainstream society.

Although sound in theory, the 'difference blindness' point of view has practical limitations. Despite an articulated commitment to equality, policies and laws are differentially applied to people and resources are unevenly distributed. This results in the sustained marginalization of diverse groups and, ultimately, works in favour of the interests of the dominant group in society (middle- and upper-class white men) (Abu-Laban, 2002).

Clearly, differences based on culture, ethnicity, race and religion are real because they are real in their consequences (Dei, Karumanchery and Karumanchery-Luik, 2004). Society must, then, consider the various histories of oppression experienced by diverse groups, understand how they have has significantly disadvantaged them in the past and decide how to repair this damage so that full inclusion and participation are ensured for the future.

The 'recognition of differences' perspective

As an alternative to the above perspective, it has been suggested that true equality and the protection of individual rights can only exist when there is the 'recognition of differences' between people and these differences are valued.

Canadian political philosopher Charles Taylor has played a key role in developing this view. In his seminal publication 'The politics of recognition' (1994), he traces the historical and theoretical roots of 'identity' and 'recognition' and applies them to the modern, liberal challenge of multiculturalism. Taylor draws on George Mead's (1962, 1934) view of identity as a *process* that emerges through human interactions (rather than an objective 'thing') and the shared meanings that arise from such exchanges. Taylor describes human life as 'dialogical' and suggests that the way in which we are recognized by others is important because this influences the way we see ourselves. This has particular consequences for self-esteem and self-confidence (Taylor, 1994: 36):

> The understanding that identities are formed in open dialogue, unshaped by a predefined social script, has made the politics of equal recognition more central and stressful … Equal recognition is not just the appropriate mode for a healthy democratic society. Its refusal can inflict damage on those who are denied it … The projection of an inferior or demeaning image on another can actually distort and oppress, to the extent that the image is internalized.

Ethnicity, culture, race and religion are critical aspects of our identities that help us to navigate the complexities of the modern world. External recognition of these identities, however, results in the creation of a hierarchy in which some groups (read white, middle class and male) experience advantage while others (read people of colour and immigrants) experience marginalization. As a result, it is difficult to maintain self-esteem, self-confidence and self-respect when one's ethnic, cultural, racial or religious background is used as the grounds for exclusion, at both interpersonal and systemic levels in society (Honneth, 2001; Schuster and Solomos, 2002).

According to Taylor, a necessary foundation for democracy is equality, with no one identity being privileged over another. At the same time, however, people need to be recognized as *having* a unique identity in order to feel an authentic, strong sense of self. The question is, then, how can we resist homogenizing individuals in the name of ensuring equality, but acknowledge difference without creating such hierarchies of identity?

In order to move forward, Taylor (1994: 72) argues that further reflection and debate are necessary in order to find a reasonable compromise or midpoint between 'the inauthentic and homogenizing demand for recognition of equal worth, on the one hand, [and] the self-immurement within ethnocentric standards, on the other'.

Canadian political philosopher Will Kymlicka suggests a practical solution to this dilemma. In his work *Multicultural Citizenship* (1995), Kymlicka, like Taylor, highlights the importance of recognizing and valuing diverse identities. He argues that liberalism has, historically, been focused solely on the rights of the individual at the expense of group rights. Further, political processes continue to reflect the interests of middle-class white men, whose views are consistent with this liberal notion of an emphasis on the individual. Such processes do not support the needs of an increasingly diverse population as they exclude people of colour, women, people who are economically disadvantaged, people with disabilities and so on from full participation in society. Therefore, the goal of a liberal democracy in the age of heightened cultural pluralism should be to introduce a focus on group rights. These 'special representation rights' would eliminate barriers that prevent people from marginalized groups from participating in the political by designating spaces that would secure their role in shaping society. In this view, particular groups that have been historically disadvantaged need special privileges to restore equality.

The 'recognition of differences' perspective has been critiqued for its fixed view of identity and its lack of in-depth attention to the ways in which particular elements of our identities, especially for women and people of colour, intersect to produce marginalization and oppression (Abu-Laban, 2002; Bannerji, 2000). For example, by simply creating 'special interest rights' for people of colour, we do not fully acknowledge the way that gender and class can intersect with race so that poor women of colour continue to be marginalized. Therefore, the effects of a history of colonialism, empire-building and displacement on our identities, as well as the oppression that can result, require more attention.

The radical alternative: a critical multiculturalism

Critical scholar Peter McLaren argues that the 'difference blindness' and 'recognition of differences' perspectives are both inadequate to deal with the challenges posed by cultural pluralism. He offers an approach he calls 'critical multiculturalism'.

This view emphasizes the need to acknowledge the ways in which race, class, gender, nation and sexuality have been constructed within a particular sociohistorical and capitalist context (that is, through a white, middle-class, male, Western, heterosexist lens) and how this is the key challenge of multiculturalism.

By interrogating both the conditions of 'otherness' and 'whiteness' in depth, McLaren (1994) suggests that members of society can become aware of and address the ways in which hegemonic norms continue to marginalize and oppress people with diverse identities.

Linking the ideology to official responses: multiculturalism across the globe

While it is important to distinguish between the *ideology of multiculturalism* and *official approaches to multiculturalism*, the two are clearly linked. The way a country thinks about multiculturalism (difference blindness, recognition of differences and critical multiculturalism) informs responses (or non-responses) to diversity. Together, this ideology and the presence or absence of official approaches to cultural pluralism shape a country's national identity and influence the ways its citizens interact with one another and its institutions. While critical multiculturalism is not yet visible in State structures, a 'difference blindness' approach and 'recognition of differences' perspective are evident in various national responses to cultural pluralism.

In her book *The Dark Side of the Nation: Essays on multiculturalism, nationalism and gender* (2000), scholar Himani Bannerji distinguishes between 'multiculturalism from below' and more official approaches to diversity. In the former, multicultural activities are rooted in an anti-colonial or anti-racist project initiated by 'the people', while, in the latter, policies consistent with the goals of a multicultural ideology are created at the level of society's institutions.

'Multiculturalism from below' appears most prevalent in places such as the UK and USA, where a 'difference blindness' approach to multiculturalism predominates. Here, the emphasis is on individual opportunity and the need for 'civic integration' (read assimilation) in which immigrants are expected to adopt the language and the cultural norms of the majority (Soroka, Johnston and Banting, 2007). This is particularly true of the USA, where the term 'melting pot' describes a nation in which diverse groups have come together and shed their ethnic identities to create an entirely new 'American' society with particular attitudes, norms, beliefs and behaviours that differ from the traditional identities 'back home' (Kivisto, 2002). While multicultural-type initiatives have been introduced in both the UK and USA (particularly to deal with discrimination in housing and employment), these have not been formalized at the federal level.

'Official' responses to cultural pluralism (where a strong policy framework accompanies a well-articulated, government-endorsed vision for a diverse society) tend to be associated with countries that adopt a 'recognition of differences' approach. For example, Canada's growing ethnic, cultural, racial and religious diversity prompted the introduction of the Canadian Multicultural Policy in 1971 and the Multiculturalism Act in 1988. These national strategies – the first of their kind – were developed in part to promote cultural diversity as an intrinsic component of Canada's social, political and moral order (Calliste and Dei, 2000). The goal of such initiatives has been to encourage the diverse groups in Canadian society to participate fully in its social, economic and political life, especially in areas such as employment and education (Kobayashi, 2005; Wood and James, 2005).

Similarly, in 1996, Australia articulated a vision for multiculturalism for the new century through a Statement on Racial Tolerance. This vision formed the basis for policy recommendations that emphasized inclusion and focused on four core principles: civic duty, cultural respect, social equity and productive diversity (*Australian Multiculturalism for a New Century: Towards Inclusiveness, 1996*). Today, multiculturalism is presented as an approach with cultural, economic and political benefits for all members of society, with the 'core of Australian identity embedded in the notion of diversity' (Kivisto, 2002: 110). These policies and related initiatives reflect multiculturalism as a fundamental aspect of the national character of these countries and have prompted important policy changes (especially in relation to employment and education) at the federal level.

Multiculturalism and social work practice

In addition to affecting a country's national identity and shaping its official policies, the ideology of multiculturalism affects the way in which we interact with one another. This happens both informally, within our communities, and in the context of formal, professional, 'helping' relationships.

In the next section, I describe how ideas about multiculturalism have influenced the field of social work, both in terms of its theory and practice.

Trends in social work theory

In recent decades, various theoretical frameworks have emerged in social work in order to understand the ways that diverse groups experience the world and interact with one another. In North America, prior to the late 1960s, a commonality of needs was assumed and issues related to diversity were mostly overlooked (Al-Krenawi and Graham, 2003). Since that time, different perspectives have been influential, including the colour-blind approach and different models of cultural pathology and inferiority.

Presently, theories that view race, racism, inequality and oppression as central in the lives of people of colour are most influential in social work (Tsang and George, 1998). The anti-racist perspective, for example, focuses on how racial inequalities are manifested materially at the individual, organizational and structural levels of society (see, for example, Calliste and Dei, 2000; Dei, 1996). Similarly, critical race theory (which originated in the field of law) has been used by social work scholars (see, for example, McDowell, 2004; Razack and Jeffrey, 2002) to understand the existence of racism in interpersonal relationships, as well as within public structures and institutions (Delgado, 1995; Singer, 2005). These perspectives view race as central in the lives of people of colour, as whiteness is understood (both historically and in the present) as being the optimal, privileged standard in society (Ladson-Billings, 1998). Also popular are anti-oppressive (Dominelli, 2002a, for example) and critical approaches to understanding power and oppression (such as Mullaly, 2002), which broaden discussions of domination and subjugation to include other types of identity (including age, gender, ethnicity, nationality, race, ability, religion, sexual identity and class) that form the basis of inequality in society.

Shifts in social work practice

The ideology of multiculturalism has also created an increased awareness of the challenges that cultural plurality introduces to social work practice. Of particular interest, then, is the impact of racism and oppression on diverse groups and the ways in which people can be supported in responding to these challenges. Indeed, professional associations responsible for overseeing the education and accreditation of social workers throughout the world have made explicit commitments to addressing the issue of social work practice with diverse groups in multicultural contexts (such as the Central Council for Education and Training in Social Work in the United Kingdom, the National Association of Social Workers in the United States of America and the Canadian Association of Schools of Social Work in Canada).

A popular concept to emerge in the area of cross-cultural social work is 'cultural competence'. This term describes strategies used by social workers to increase self-awareness, knowledge and skills in working with members of diverse groups (Williams, 2006; Yan and Wong, 2005). Developing cultural competency is seen as *necessary* for social workers engaging with diverse clients in multicultural environments and, according to the National Association of Social Workers in the USA, neglecting to become so is considered a violation of one's ethical responsibility. American social work professor Doman Lum (1999: 29) suggests that four elements are key to providing a service that is culturally competent:

> acceptance of and respect for cultural differences, analysis of one's own cultural identity and biases, awareness of the dynamics of difference in ethnic clients, and recognition of the need for additional knowledge, research, and resources to work with clients.

In addition to the emphasis on knowledge and skill, vital to becoming culturally competent is one's capacity for self-awareness. As human beings, social workers have particular biases, values and beliefs that are informed by their culture. These necessarily seep into work with clients, including those with diverse backgrounds. Therefore (Yan and Wong, 2005: 183, emphasis in original):

> to overcome the ingrained effect of their culture and to respect their client's differences, culturally competent social workers should *analyse* and maintain a high level of *self-awareness* of their own cultural background … [which includes being aware of one's] own cultural values, biases, preconceived notions, and personal limitations.

Despite its influence on social work practice, the concept of 'cultural competence' has been critiqued extensively. For example, Ruth Dean (2001: 624) argues that it is an untenable goal, a myth 'located in the metaphor of American "know-how". It is consistent with the belief that knowledge brings control and effectiveness, and that this is an ideal to be achieved above all else'. Also Charmaine Williams (2006) argues that cultural competency is presented as an objective 'technique' rather than a way of approaching social work with clients that is rooted in a strong theoretical foundation. In addition, Miu Chung Yan and Yuk-Lin Wong (2005: 181) question the extent to which it is possible for social workers to actually 'suspend their own cultural influences' and maintain neutrality when working with clients as the use of self – which includes cultural aspects of identity – is seen as key in these professional interactions.

Perhaps most problematic, however, is that cultural competence is based on a particular understanding of what culture *is*. The term 'culture' is used in a commonsense way, without critical examination or debate (Park, 2005). It is seen as fixed, unchanging and consistent across all members of a group, which is what makes it knowable and controllable (Dean, 2001). This essentialist view of culture emphasizes differences between those who practice social work (and who are assumed to be 'cultureless') and clients from diverse backgrounds who 'have culture', which is at least partially responsible for their problems (Keenan, 2004). Those *with* culture are constructed as 'other' and judged as deficient against the mainstream, hegemonic norm of white culturelessness (Park, 2005). Implicit in these assumptions is that social workers should 'intervene' to resolve the problematic influence of culture on the lives of diverse clients (Park, 2005).

In light of such critiques, there are several suggestions for how the field of social work might shift its approach to work within multicultural contexts. First, rather than attempting to 'know the other' prior to assessment/intervention, social workers might seek to gain understanding *through* the therapeutic relationship (Dean, 2001). Prototypical understandings of the habits, behaviours and values of diverse groups will always be incomplete because one's culture is in a constant state of change and evolution. Therefore, our practice might be guided by a genuine curiosity and openness to learning about another's complex lived experiences and thoughtful reflection on how to build positive relationships within a dialogical space (Yan and Wong, 2005). Adopting a critical multicultural approach (as described earlier) may be helpful here.

US social work scholar David Nylund draws on Peter McLaren's 'critical multiculturalism' as a way of teaching social work students how to work across differences from an anti-racist perspective. Critical multiculturalism (Nylund, 2006: 30):

> 1) recognizes the sociohistorical constructions of race and its intersections with class, gender, nation, sexuality, and capitalism; 2) creates pedagogical conditions in which students interrogate conditions of 'otherness'; 3) challenges the idea of social work as an apolitical, transhistorical practice removed from the power struggles of history; and 4) makes visible the historical and social construction of whiteness.

This and similar approaches attempt to unsettle the 'centre – margin' and 'mainstream – other' relationships that tend to predominate in mainstream social work (Keenan, 2004) and move towards creating inclusive therapeutic settings in which mutual learning and critical reflection can take place.

Significance for social work practice

In the field of social work, the topics of multiculturalism, anti-racism, anti-oppression and so on remain important issues to consider. The extent to which these themes are discussed in mainstream social work, however, varies from country to country. For example, in the USA, as well as throughout many parts of Europe, interest in multicultural issues in social work have been relegated to special subdisciplines, such as 'cross-cultural' or 'anti-racist' and 'anti-discriminatory' social work practice, as the main emphasis throughout the field has shifted to 'service user perspectives'. This trend expands the focus beyond culture and ethnicity to include human rights more broadly. In Canadian social work, however, cultural pluralism, diversity and anti-racism have remained very much at the forefront of social work discourse. Indeed, academic research, writing and debate continue at a national level in order to stimulate discussion and work towards reasonable, appropriate responses to the issues raised.

Critiquing multiculturalism: identifying the disjoint between the 'ideal' and the 'real'

In general, few people in liberal democracies disagree with the fundamental goal underlying the ideology of multiculturalism – that is, to create an inclusive society in which people are both viewed as unique and treated as equals and with respect. We tend to believe that immigration has more positive outcomes than negative ones (Hiebert, 2003) and diversity can enrich a country significantly. Most criticisms of multiculturalism are rooted in the disjoint between what we imagine as the 'ideal multiculturalism' and the way this is experienced and practised in people's everyday lives.

For example (as described earlier), some would argue that multiculturalism highlights *differences* between people rather than emphasizing what *unites* them (see, for example, Bissoondath, 1994; James, 2003). The ideology of multiculturalism suggests that liberal democracies are places where people can sustain their ethnic/cultural/racial and religious traditions and values *while also* participating fully economically, socially and politically in mainstream society (Dewing and Leman, 2006). The reality, however, according to Canadian scholar Carl James (2003: 210), is that 'multiculturalism promotes a discourse of "difference", signalling that culture is primarily carried in and exhibited by people with "foreign bodies" who are "linguistically different" … and "do not look and sound Canadian"'. The term 'Canadian', then, is used to refer to people who are white with European backgrounds. These individuals serve as the norm from which people of colour are said to deviate. People in these 'different' ethnic, cultural, racial and religious groups are also *homogenized*, or lumped together, so that similarities between group members are exaggerated and individual differences are ignored. A related concern is what British scholar Tariq Modood (1997: 10) calls the practice of *cultural essentialism*, in which 'each culture (or ethnic, racial, and religious group) has a unique, fixed essence that can be understood independently of context or intercultural relations, and which makes a … group act the way it does'. 'Essentializing' tends to privilege – or, more often, problematize – certain groups based on characteristics all members are assumed to share. When these differences intersect with global events (such as 9/11), the resulting exclusion and marginalization of people from certain groups are disastrous (Abu-Laban, 2002).

Another common criticism of multiculturalism is that it is a superficial treatment of diversity that is mostly focused on festivals at which ethnic trinkets, foods and cultural music and dance are presented for mainstream consumption. This has been called the 'saris, samosas and steel band syndrome' (Dei, 1996; Khan, 2000) or a 'shallow' approach to multiculturalism (Bissoondath, 1994; Hiebert, 2003). In addition to trivializing the rich histories and customs of diverse groups, this practice undermines the very principles that the ideology of multiculturalism claims to support.

At the root of most of these critiques is the argument that, despite the admirable goals articulated by decisionmakers and politicians in liberal democracies, the ideology of multiculturalism is a set of beliefs that is used by those in positions of power to reap the economic rewards of immigration, while at the same time 'containing' and controlling cultural diversity (Bedard, 2000; Bhabha, 1994; Hage, 2000). According to Canadian scholars Frances Henry, Carol Tator, Winston Mattis and Tim Rees (2006: 49), the policies and practices of multiculturalism:

position certain ethno-racial groups at the margins, rather than in the mainstream of public culture and national identity. While 'tolerating', 'accommodating', 'appreciating', and 'celebrating' differences, it allows for the preservation of the cultural hegemony of the dominant cultural group.

It has been argued that, despite promises of inclusion and equality, official multiculturalism sustains an arrangement in which there is one dominant culture with access to political, economic and social power, and several multicultural groups with little (if any) access to these (Bannerji, 2000). This happens because people in positions of power promote a discourse that embraces multicultural values and goals, but then neglects to establish an appropriate framework to ensure accountability (Henry et al., 2006).

According to Canadian writer Clifford Jansen (2005: 31), 'words like "promote", "encourage", "recognize", "ensure", "develop", and "reflect" are used in legislation and public discourse ... but there seem to be no sanctions [to enforce this]'. For example, in Canada, despite policies and practices designed to promote employment equity, people from diverse groups (including visible minorities and Aboriginal people), although increasing numerically in the workforce, tend to be concentrated in low-level, lower-paying jobs (Kobayashi, 2005). Without a mechanism in place for monitoring and evaluating the success of such policies, there is little hope of achieving true change.

A final criticism of multiculturalism is that the language used is incongruous with the very real existence of racism and xenophobia in society. Within liberal democracies, a national commitment to a multicultural ideology projects the image of benevolence and charity towards 'others' on the global stage. In such a context, a 'celebratory' view of diversity becomes a commonsense, unquestioned way of approaching diversity (Bedard, 2000). The problem, then, is that, if one accepts the classic multicultural rhetoric that we live in societies that value equality based on race, religion, nationality and so on, it is difficult to identify or take seriously claims that violate this 'norm' (such as racism, or biased hiring practices). Any discourse that challenges this taken-for-granted way of doing things is seen as an exception to the rule or the fault of the injured party (Dei et al., 2004).

In an increasingly global context, discussions about the nature and consequences of cultural plurality have become common, both in academic circles and within the broader society. In this chapter, I have presented multiculturalism as an ideology that informs State policies, shapes national identities and influences the way that social workers talk about and practise in relation to cultural diversity. The future of multiculturalism is unclear. The way we think about multiculturalism, the extent to which it is reflected in public policy generally and how it shapes the field of social work will likely change depending on shifting global conditions.

Study questions

1. What are some of the key arguments for and against multiculturalism? Which of these do you agree and disagree with and for what reasons?
2. Use the Internet to research multiculturalism in a country of your choice. What is this country's history in terms of cultural pluralism? What are some current trends in relation to the way this country handles diversity?
3. How might your view of multiculturalism impact on *your* practice in the field of social work – at the individual, family and group levels?

Glossary

Citizenship A framework of status, rights and obligations within a particular nation.

Culture The ideas, values, norms and behaviours associated with a particular group with specific geographic origins that shape how we interpret and act in the world. Culture is never static – it is constantly evolving and changing.

Diversity The range of ethnic, cultural, racial and religious characteristics of different groups in society.

Ethnicity Sense of 'peoplehood' based on common descent, language, religion and tradition.

Globalization The increased economic, sociocultural, technological and political interaction and interdependence that occurs between countries throughout the world.

Multiculturalism A philosophy that acknowledges and values diversity in society and describes various tangible (economic) and intangible (social, for example) benefits that result from cultural pluralism. Its goal is to support the full political, social and economic integration of all members of society.

Nationalism Identification with a particular nation state defined by the geographic boundaries that separate countries from one another. National narratives establish a sense of cohesion between those sharing a particular physical space (such Canadians v. Americans).

Race The observable, physical features that are shared by several people and distinguish them from members of other groups. Meanings associated with and classifications based on race are socially constructed.

Select bibliography

Besides Kivisto (2002) and Kymlicka (1995), I would recommend Taylor and Gutmann (1994).

Neo-liberalism

10

Sue Penna and Martin O'Brien

Introducing neoliberalism

A reading of the literature on contemporary social work yields reference after reference to the detrimental impact of neoliberalism on the delivery of social work services, yet it is often unclear quite what neoliberalism actually is. It is understood variously as an ideology, a hegemonic project, a policy framework, a set of initiatives and a government strategy.

Neoliberalism is all of these things and, at the same time, none of them because it has become an umbrella term – a shorthand reference to a set of theoretical orientations and institutional changes that, together, have altered the terms of reference of contemporary social work. For this reason, it is impossible in this short chapter to do justice to the wide sweep of ideas and changes encompassed by this term, so here we first outline two key theoretical contributions to the body of literature designated 'neoliberal' and then turn to some of the major institutional changes enacted within the policy agenda influenced by these theoretical contributions.

Perhaps the most important thing to grasp about the different theories gathered together under the banner of neoliberalism is that they have in common a central emphasis on the market as the organizing principle of social life. The theorists most commonly understood as proposing neoliberal social arrangements are principally – although not exclusively – from the discipline of economics and, therefore, social life and social relationships are viewed through the prism of economic categories.

It is not surprising, then, that they have little to say about social work per se. Rather, their interest lies in the welfare state – in particular, in this coupling of the terms 'welfare' and 'state', which is seen by neoliberal writers as detrimental to the efficient reproduction of societies. Why should this be the case? Well, there are several reasons, the most important being:

- the loss of freedom entailed in welfare states;
- the bias towards those who deliver services against the needs and wishes of consumers of services;
- the stifling of economic activity and its wealth-generating potential.

How is it that something which sounds as benign as 'welfare state' can generate such dysfunctional and sinister consequences? To answer this question, we need to take an excursion into the philosophy of the Enlightenment – the period in European thought that saw the development of secular and scientific worldviews.

One of these philosophies was liberalism – developed in the seventeenth and eighteenth centuries as a set of ideas that challenged the feudal structures of European societies, mounting a powerful critique of the idea of a monarch ruling by *divine right*. The arbitrary exercise of power inflicted on citizens and subjects of a king or queen was legitimated by a *theological worldview*, which held that a monarch was more or less enacting God's will on Earth. Liberalism proposed instead a secular understanding of social and economic life that emphasized the importance of protecting the *freedom of individuals from the State*. The defining characteristic of liberalism is a fundamental distrust of power exercised by the State.

Updating classical liberalism in the wake of the major expansion in the public sector that followed the Second World War (1939–1945), neoliberalism reiterates classical liberalism's concern with protecting the *liberty of individuals* against the arbitrary exercising of power by governments. However, in neoliberalism, this concern is developed in the context of a major extension of State responsibility, authority and activity during and immediately after the war. The war years saw key resources, such as coal and steel, nationalized and further nationalization programmes, together with the rapid extension of public services in the post-war period, accounted for a much enlarged State apparatus, provoking an ongoing and systematic set of critiques of these arrangements.

In the neoliberal view, the State's responsibility for welfare should be confined to maintaining a residual welfare system of last resort. The preference is for private forms of welfare services that are held up as not only the most efficient way of providing for collective need but also as harbingers of freedom, choice and consumer satisfaction. There is no explicit neoliberal theory of *social work practice and user–provider relationships*, but rather of *State practice and State–market–citizen relationships*. Since the late 1970s, the gradual adoption of neoliberalism as the basis of a comprehensive policy programme in institutions of global governance, such as the European Union, World Trade Organization, International Monetary Fund and World Bank, means that neoliberalism has fundamentally altered the conditions under which social work takes place and the conditions of life of service users. It is in this sense that neoliberalism is an important factor in understanding contemporary social work. As social work is one of the key operational embodiments of the welfare state (McDonald, 2006), so it is a main target of the perceived need to dismantle the latter's institutional foundations.

Key ideas

Friedrich von Hayek has to be acknowledged as a leading force in the development of neoliberal theory. An economist trained in Austria during the 1920s, Hayek was exposed to the 'subjectivist turn' in social theory and philosophy, which had its home in Austria. Rejecting macroeconomics, with its emphasis on large statistical databases, Hayek specialized in microeconomics – the micro dynamics of markets and the role of subjectivity in economic phenomena. Yet, more than that, Hayek understood economic activities within a philosophical framework, locating them within a theory of knowledge that underpinned his argument of how societies could best provide for their members.

Hayek acknowledges that government can and should play an important role in ensuring the material well-being of the least well off in society. Indeed, the target of Hayek's critique, and that of neoliberalism more generally, is not the *aims* of government in seeking to alleviate suffering or support those in need, but its *methods* of doing so (see Hayek, 1959). In particular, the proposition that government should, or even could, devise a system of social support that ensures each citizen is awarded the collective resources that he or she deserves is completely counter to the very idea of a 'free society'.

The road that aims at *social justice,* says Hayek (1959: 261–2), leads inexorably to an authoritarian socialism because it is 'sheer illusion to think that when certain needs of the citizen have become the exclusive concern of a single bureaucratic machine, democratic control of that machine can then effectively guard the liberty of the citizen'. It is sheer illusion partly because, citing Wiles's (1957) *Property and Equality,* Hayek (1959: 107) claims that the democratic control of parliament 'is and always has been the merest fairy tale'.

It may be worth noting here that this claim is not necessarily the cynical view of a right-wing ideologue. For example, Britain's New Labour government (during the period 1997–2007) has gone to war against Iraq, has been caught up in a cash for honours scandal, has manipulated behind the scenes to ensure the introduction of identity cards, has facilitated the 'rendition' of alleged terror suspects and has refused to reform the House of Lords – all of which have ridden roughshod over the wishes and demands of large segments of the electorate. The tendency in sociology and social policy to dismiss neoliberalism out of hand is strong precisely because of its attack on the welfare state, but that attack is not simply an unprincipled rejection of the goals of mutual support. It is, rather, a restatement and reworking of classic liberal principles of individual freedom, independence, choice and self-determination *against* the social democratic principles of social justice, social planning and State intervention.

Looking around at the planned economy of the Soviet Union, the theories of Maynard Keynes – whose economic prescriptions would form the basis for the welfare state in the postwar era – and the collectivist, State-planned socialism of the British Fabians – which was gaining intellectual ground during the 1920s and 1930s – Hayek despaired of what he considered to be a fundamentally flawed approach that would not only be unable to deliver the economic progress it claimed, but would also require an extension of State power that could have dangerous consequences. As Nazism gathered force in Europe during the 1930s and the persecution and murder of Jewish, homosexual, learning disabled and Roma people started to become apparent, Hayek was further convinced of the need to restrain State power. In Hayek's theoretical framework, the market can do everything the State can do, more or less, but more efficiently and with none of the political dangers associated with Nazism and Stalinism. The exceptions are the provision of defence (army, navy and airforce), a basic physical infrastructure and a *residual* welfare system for those in greatest need.

In this way, Hayek proposes an important distinction between two types of society: a 'spontaneous order' (the liberal society) and a 'constructivist', State-directed society (social democratic and communist). The former is considered to be the most efficient means of organizing social life, with the market providing the conditions by means of which overall social welfare is realized.

The market, left to its own devices, is the basis of wealth creation. While Hayek recognizes that market processes will generate unpredictable and unequal material outcomes, he argues that the overall benefit outweighs individual disadvantages. The wealth of the richest will 'trickle down' to all social groups in society, while the different values and preferences found in modern, pluralist societies can be realized more efficiently in a market system, making innovation and the effective distribution of desired goods and services possible.

Such preferences and values cannot be accommodated in a centrally planned, bureaucratic system that, by definition, has been devised precisely in order to achieve some vales and preferences rather than others. Thus, a 'spontaneous', liberal, market society is said to uphold the politics of individual freedom and self-determination, innovation and efficiency and a 'constructivist', socialist, planned society is said to uphold the politics of collective submission and dependency, economic stagnation and wastefulness.

Hayek's spontaneous order of society

The starting point of Hayek's theory of markets is a theory of knowledge. Hayek is a micro-economist who argues against the notion of economics as a predictive, objective science. In discussing the reliance on positivist methods of the social sciences in general, he argues that the belief in science as a neutral, objective force for progress is one of the great mistakes of the (French) Enlightenment philosophies.

Hayek's (1952, 1979) views on subjectivism and human knowledge led him to reject the claims of macroeconomics to be able to predict economic behaviour through the development of aggregate categories, stressing instead the role of interactions and subjectivity in economic processes (Hayek, 1979). For Hayek, as a subjectivist theorist, the idea that academics, or, indeed, anyone else, could arrive at a knowledge base that would enable governments to steer societies and plan economic activity was impossible. This is because the vast amount of knowledge that exists in the world is too fragmented and dispersed to collect into a statistical model and, moreover, the knowledge that people use in their everyday lives is largely tacit and unspoken and, thus, not amenable to scientific discovery or representation. This tacit knowledge has developed over the course of human history, having an evolutionary function, and has enabled the successful survival and development of human societies – which progressed through millennia of change and development without the help of modern planners. It tends to be transmitted culturally via the family and other social institutions – notably commercial, religious and communal associations – and is dispersed most clearly through the market, where it serves a coordinating function, signalling where materials and skills are needed, for example, and matching prices to rates of pay. Thus, for Hayek, the institutions of the market and the family are highly important because of the role they play in maintaining functioning, orderly societies.

What is crucially important for this theoretical framework, then, is the proposition that all order in the social (and physical) world arises from the spontaneous formation of self-regulating structures. In the course of evolution, tacit knowledge becomes embodied in certain practices and institutions. In turn, the latter are the products of the natural selection of rules of action.

Hayek sees this development as a process of cultural adaptation through competition. That is, of the multiple sets of practices and rules that develop during the evolutionary process, those allowing the most functional adaptation to the external environment become dominant. All evolution is seen as a process of continuous adaptation to unforeseeable events, contingent circumstances that cannot be predicted.

Competition is seen to be a key element in this process because of Hayek's view that the sheer volume of information dispersed throughout society could never be centrally coordinated in an effective way. Competition simultaneously encourages the development of new products for which there is a demand, lowers costs due to the need for efficient production and sees off those products and services that society in general cannot use. Competition, levels of pay and prices within the market system enable a lucid response to the uncertainty of economic activities and social needs to be made, as well as enabling the most efficient utilization of resources in the economic process (Hayek, 1982).

Competition within the market, while allowing for the maximization of economic production and individual preferences and goals, also secures social solidarity through the interdependence of individuals. Each individual producer and consumer depends on a vast and unknowable network of other producers and consumers for the market to work. Hayek, and neoliberals generally, argue that social life flourishes most strongly and most effectively when the tacit knowledge of individual citizens, rather than the predictive knowledge of scientists, is allowed to thrive.

Public choice, collective loss

Hayek's sustained reformulation of classical liberalism is concerned to provide a moral and economic case for 'free market' capitalism, considered to be under threat from the development of social democratic structures in the post-war era. He was joined in this critique by Milton and Rose Friedman (1980: 309), who claimed that 'the greatest threat to human freedom is the concentration of power, whether in the hands of government or anyone else'. This 'greatest threat' arises because there is an 'invisible hand' at work in politics that results in individuals who, charged with promoting the *general interest*, actually end up promoting a *special interest* to which they are allied (Friedman and Friedman, 1980: 292; see also Greene, 1987: 81).

This idea of an 'invisible hand' in politics is the subject of work by the public choice school (see Buchanan and Tullock, 1962; Niskanen, 1987; Tullock, 1989). Public choice theory is a field of economics and, while there are various theoretical and empirical foci, as well as ideological variations, within this body of work, notwithstanding these differences, public choice approaches are generally known as the 'economics of politics'. This is because those working within this school apply economic analyses to, in particular, the behaviour of politicians, voters and those who work in State agencies.

Public choice theory considers peoples' actions and decisions as governed by rational and self-interested motivations and the formal political arena as a marketplace. Applying this view to political processes and institutions, the focus of much analysis is the 'demand side' of the political market and the 'supply side' of bureaucracies.

The political arena is, therefore, understood as a market, with voters being the consumers of policies and political parties 'firms' selling their policies to voters. In this arena, the 'vote motive' is considered to replace the profit motive. In contrast with normative theories of the democratic process, the public choice school argues that voters have neither the expertise nor the information to select from the range of options presented to them. What voters are offered is a selection of policies put together as a package designed to appeal to a number of different interest groups (Harris and Seldon, 1979) – a process that is inevitable as, in order to be elected, parties have no choice other than to try and appeal to a variety of interests. In consequence, there is an inbuilt bias in the democratic polity towards increasing expenditure (and therefore political control over the economy) by governments. This increasing expenditure then fuels inflation, a situation that can only be avoided by keeping the public sector small and affordable. This also has the advantage of keeping taxation low and, hence, encouraging entrepreneurship.

The supply side analysis challenges the presupposition that is seen as inherent in the works of Fabian socialists – that public institutions will be staffed by neutral, disinterested public servants whose primary aim is to serve the 'general good'. Working from a model of human activity as rational and maximizing utility, the arguments suggest that employees of State bureaucracies have a vested interest in expanding services, which leads to pressure for increasing State intervention and expenditure. This is considered undesirable because of its inflationary potential, but also because individual preferences cannot be ensured – the consumer has no control and no redress with regard to the services provided. They are, therefore, producer-orientated, at the expense of consumers.

Public choice arguments, applied to welfare issues, were taken up in the United Kingdom by Ralph Harris and Arthur Seldon (1979) at the Institute for Economic Affairs (IEA). They studied electoral choices over some 20 years and argued that market transactions are always superior to State action. In all its manifestations, public choice theory challenges the notion that government can correct 'market failure' (unemployment, inflation and social need) through the political system, instead focusing on what are seen as the many instances of 'government failure'. The steady stream of publications from this school in the post-war period posed a serious challenge to the Keynesian economic theory that legitimated expanded State intervention in economic and social life through the nationalization of key industries, the manipulation of production and consumption through economic policy and the development of comprehensive welfare services, paid for through taxation and delivered via the public sector.

Neoliberalism and social work practice

Elements of these various neoliberal theories began to be taken up by policymakers and politicians in the 1970s. The general thrust of the views we have described – that the public sector was too big, too bureaucratic, too inefficient and failed to serve those who accessed it in a satisfactory way – seemed to gain legitimacy in the light of a series of problems affecting Western capitalism. In particular, the shift of manufacturing and the heavy extractive (mining) industries to the developing world left high levels of unemployment. The oil crisis of 1973 contributed to rapidly rising inflation, which had reached 26 per sent in the UK by 1976.

This combination of high unemployment and high inflation severely undermined the Keynesian economic theory that had underpinned the development of welfare states. Keynes had proposed that a country could have *either* rising unemployment *or* rising inflation, but not the two together. The phrase 'fiscal crisis of the State' began to be used by those on the left of the political spectrum, while, on the right, neoliberal ideas were taken up as a solution to the seemingly intractable problems facing government.

The eventual outcome was the production of a shifting interpretive framework, a neoliberal discourse that came to frame policy programmes in the 'advanced' nations (Cameron and Palan, 2004; Clarke, 2004b; McDonald, 2006) and was adopted in global governance institutions that affect domestic policymaking. This marked a change in policy regimes that was to affect most countries and was based on reducing the public sector in order to reduce inflation and taxation. Over time, various aspects of this ambition were developed and we turn now to the ways in which these developments have impacted social work services.

A necessary feature of any entrepreneurial, capitalist market economy is competition and, thus, the private, as opposed to the public, ownership of property must be a priority policy goal. One of the ways in which the public sector was reduced and ownership was transferred was through part- or full-privatization.

First was the privatization of the nationalized industries – an ongoing process now enshrined in policy in the World Trade Organization (WTO) and translated into domestic legislation via membership of regional bodies, such as the European Union (EU) or the North America Free Trade Agreement (NAFTA) group. Meant to boost Western capitalism, privatization has also been advocated as a solution to the anticipated 'crisis' of an ageing population placing financially unsustainable demands on pensions and health and social care providers.

The effects of privatization have been felt throughout the welfare state societies (Lorenz, 2006; McDonald, 2006), although the implementation is uneven across countries and displays operational variations. Apart from the wholesale transfer of assets to the private sector in the case of nationalized industries, and the use of private finance initiatives in infrastructure development, the 'dissolution of the public sphere' (Clarke, 2004b) and the introduction of the logic of market transactions into public services are effected through the separation of purchaser and provider functions, where service delivery is contracted out to third-sector or commercial organizations.

Another way of introducing a market logic is through the aptly named 'marketization' process, where fees are charged for services previously provided free of charge, such as home care, and internal markets introduced in public agencies. Increasingly, welfare agencies operate within networks comprising strategic and commissioning statutory organizations, third-sector and commercial service providers. These developments mark a significant shift in policy frameworks that impact social work (see Webb, 2006).

An equally significant development has been the introduction of 'new public management' techniques into the organization and administration of public services. It is here that we see the operationalization of neoliberal ideas in social work agency practice. Sweeping changes in the conditions of service delivery, control and accountability have taken place, including the introduction of performance measurement – a mechanism that, together with bureaucratic standardization, paradoxically enables the central control of service delivery by government. The adoption of a corporate management language and the prioritization of budget management and control through an intensive 'gatekeeping' of access to services (Jones, 2001) limit the role of social workers as they move away from face-to-face work with service users and towards the purchasing of care packages for those most in need. The fine balance which social work has always negotiated between, for example, care and control, rights and obligations (Lorenz, 2006) has shifted away from the aspirations of care and has turned towards policing (Jones, 2001).

Chris Jones's (2001: 552) research with social workers in the UK employed in the State sector examined the impact of these various changes on the work they did. He writes of:

> an interconnecting series of processes which created a new working environment within state social work: a new type of highly regulated and much more mundane and routinized relationship with clients which could not be described as social work, at least not in the terms that they understood it.

This routinization and regulation, according to John Clarke (1996: 54–5), are, in part, a consequence of the fact that social work has been stripped of many of its humanistic qualities, has been pushed into the 'interstices between organisations' and has been made to dance to the tune of private interest.

This rational, calculative quality in service provision alters the experience of frontline work. Social workers and service users become increasingly engaged in economic exchanges rather than reciprocal relationships and what drives their encounters is the value of service packages rather than a collaborative endeavour. It also expands the accounting, monitoring and audit requirements of service delivery and discourages 'free' State provision, except in the most desperate cases, and even here we are seeing significant gaps in service provision. Jones (2001) describes relentlessly growing caseloads, a rise in the proportion of 'heavy end' work – with 'at risk' children, for example – and an increasing sense of desperation about the apparently intractable conditions in which social work's 'consumers' are to be found.

As services are rationed and regulated according to market criteria, consumers of those services are to be found in increasingly desperate circumstances – for a key feature of the neoliberal policy agenda is increasing inequality and immiseration (Harvey, 2006). The aim of creating wealth through neoliberal policies has seen the increased production of poverty throughout the world, with a corresponding increase in inequality and all the attendant social problems that accompany it. In these circumstances, Walter Lorenz (2006) proposes that neoliberal pressure on welfare delivery systems results in former public care structures taking on increasing control functions, with the responsibility for caring getting pushed into the private domain.

These strategies for managing public services as though they were commodities lead to contradictory and unintended outcomes, depending on many factors – the culture of a particular organization, its management structure, tensions between service objectives and the socio-economic profile of the locality being served, for example (Boland and Fowler, 2002; Hartley and Pike, 2005; Martin and Davies, 2001). In basic terms, the drivers for the development of services and the criteria for success are so different for profit and not-for-profit organizations that perverse outcomes are generated by trying to transform the latter along the lines of the former. Indeed, these strategies generate as many problems as they are intended to solve and many argue that the process of change has, in fact, done a great deal more harm than good. The strategies of privatization and marketization, for example, have generated some sharp conflicts in the European Union. The passionate argument generated by the EU's Framework Directive on Services of General Interest, which proposes further commodification of health and social care services, highlights the inherent contradiction between, on the one hand, a neoliberal economic policy objective of developing an entrepreneurial, dynamic, competitive economy and, on the other, the objective of social cohesion and inclusion, of which public welfare is a key expression (Penna and O'Brien, 2006).

Significance for social work practice

The diverse ramifications of neoliberalism for social work practice derive from the structural processes immanent in its global deployment. Neoliberalism is now enshrined in global institutions that affect the domestic policy of all countries. It marks a significant shift away from an ethos of universal social insurance regarding personal and family obligations. The demise of the public sector is now so advanced in so many countries that it is almost impossible to conceive of a return to traditional styles of collective provision for collective risks as a viable alternative. The neoliberal pursuit of individualism and consumerism has formed a rigid discursive grip around the public sector's institutional forms. In these circumstances, the weight of uncertainty is redistributed downwards and increases the cumulative insecurities of the least powerful and most vulnerable in society (Marris, 1996), who tend to be the users of social work services. Of course, social work practice takes place not only in public agencies but also in many settings, but all of them serve a clientele whose material circumstances are set to worsen and whose status is not that which commands the attention of the contemporary captains of neoliberal capitalism.

In conclusion, we have provided an introduction to some of the main ideas in neoliberal philosophy. What happens when the private economic realm is expanded into the arena of public services is that winners and losers invariably emerge, the institutions of welfare find themselves under siege and frontline workers are subjected to incredibly stressful pressures. As eligibility for welfare services in the public sector becomes more restricted, these workers find themselves responsible for citizens with the most intractactable problems, but without sufficient resources to meet their needs. While it would be unwise to make broad generalizations across the breadth and variety of services engaged in social work delivery, research in the UK points to the difficulties involved in transferring notions such as 'competition' from the private, commercial sector to the public and not-for-profit sector (see Penna and O'Brien, 2006).

For Clarke (2004a: 92–3), welfare states are anathema to neoliberalism as they 'provide the symbolic and material expressions (however contradictory and limited) of forms of solidarity, collectivism and citizenship'. In other words, they stand against the individual calculation of cost–benefit ratios that characterize economic markets, while the privatization and marketization of welfare services is aimed at substituting the client–professional relationship with a buyer–seller relationship. Clarke (2004b: 35) appends, 'That which cannot be financially represented (economically valorized) is ruled inappropriate or irrelevant'. This is the logical outcome when all aspects of social life are expressed through an economistic model that is understood as the generic form.

Study questions

1. List and define four key concepts in neoliberalism.
2. How has neoliberalism changed the policymaking context?
3. What is the relationship between 'new public management' and neoliberalism?

Glossary

Divine right The idea that a monarch is enacting God's will on Earth.

Fiscal crisis of the State An actual or supposed inability of the State to raise enough tax revenue to pay for its expenditures.

Residual welfare state Residual welfare state provision is considered to be a safety net, available only to those defined as being most in need – usually when the market or family is unable to make the necessary provision.

Social justice The idea that a society ought to give individuals and social groups good treatment as well as a just and fair share of the benefits of society.

Theological worldview A widely accepted assumption that God is the creator of the natural and social worlds.

Select bibliography

Besides Penna and O'Brien (2006), we would recommend Ferguson (2007); and O'Brien and Penna (1998) and Webb (2006).

Post-modernism

11

Barbara Fawcett

Introducing postmodernism

Postmodernism, postmodernity and 'the postmodern' are all terms that have been used in a variety of ways. A common thread that runs throughout is the distinction made and the associated distancing from concepts relating to modernism, modernity and 'the modern'.

This chapter explores the terminology and the many ways in which the associated conceptual orientations have been developed. Given the size of the topic, three main areas are explored. These relate to the operation of knowledge and power, understandings of the 'self' and the different interpretations given to, inter alia, unity, fragmentation and contradiction. As a means of making links between modernism and postmodernism, a form of critical postmodernism is developed throughout this chapter and the implications for social work are explored.

The theory of postmodernism

Terminology

Fiona Williams in 1992 memorably referred to *postmodernity* as a way of referring to the postmodern condition and to *postmodernism* as a means of understanding the condition. This establishes a helpful distinction between postmodernity (and a postmodern era) and post-modernism, which can be seen to encompass a wide range of theoretical perspectives that both influence and inform the era or condition. In a similar way, 'modernity' can be regarded as a useful means of referring to the modern condition, with modernism being used to denote a range of theoretical orientations that characterize the modern period.

In relation to the timeframe we can currently be seen to occupy, there is wide-ranging variation and dispute, with arguments and associated terminology veering from modernity to late modernity to postmodernity with the imposition of the 'small certainties' of modernism (Bauman, 1992; Callincos, 1989; Fawcett and Featherstone, 1998; Giddens, 1990; Lyotard, 1994).

The relationship between postmodernism and poststructuralism is also contested, with some writers making a clear distinction between the concepts and others arguing that there are so many similarities that a conceptual blurring has taken place. Madan Sarup (1993), for example, maintains that it is difficult to maintain a distinction between poststructural theories and postmodern practices. However, others, such as Andreas Huyssen (1990), insist on a clear distinction being made between the concepts. It can also be argued that to concentrate on definitional issues and associations is to miss the point of the postmodernist project. However, in order to apply concepts as slippery as postmodernism to social work practice, there is a need to forge links and associations, however impermanent these may turn out to be.

Conceptual frameworks

In order to apply theoretical concepts to practice contexts, it is necessary, to some extent, to both simplify and generalize. In this, the importance of layering the analysis has to be recognized. Accordingly, there are the outer layers, which, in some instances, may be all that is required. However, there are also further layers that can be uncovered when further interrogation is called for. In this chapter, emphasis is placed on the outer layers, although certain areas are explored in greater depth. As highlighted above, these focus on the operation of knowledge and power, understandings of 'self' and the interpretation of concepts such as unity, fragmentation and contradiction.

Modernism

It is useful, although not a prerequisite, to start an exploration of postmodernism by looking at what *modernism* is broadly seen to represent.

Modernism is generally regarded as being characterized by the key ideas and values of the Enlightenment. These rested on strong notions of order and the belief in unity and included an acceptance of the importance and the inevitability of progress, the belief that rational scientific objective facts will continue to be revealed and that incontrovertible and essential truths relating to not only science but also social and psychological phenomena will continue to be discovered.

Drawing from the work of Zygmunt Bauman (1992) and Sarup (1993), modernism can be seen as being dominated by the operation of grand narratives or 'big stories' that are viewed as having a universal application and a universal set of principles. Examples of these grand narratives or 'big stories' include liberalism, Marxism, psychoanalysis, economic rationalism, biosocial determinism and structurally orientated analyses. These 'big stories', at various points, have claimed infallibility and have provided all-embracing explanations that have tended to ignore the possibility of large gaps or omissions or criteria that simply do not fit. These metanarratives have provided pervasive ways of seeing the world at particular points in time. Although Westernized concepts have dominated, there has also been a tendency to assume a global applicability or relevance. Said (2003), for example, presents the discourse of orientalism as a systematic way of demonstrating how European culture has been able to manage and produce the 'orient' politically, sociologically, militarily, ideologically, scientifically and imaginatively during the post-Enlightenment period.

Modernism, as writers such as Michel Foucault (1972, 1979, 1980b; see also Chapter 4) have highlighted, can be associated with a tendency to associate knowledge and power with expert knowledge. The intertwining of knowledge and power can then be used to draw a dividing line between the knowledge of the expert and that of the service user, client or consumer. As a result, experiential knowledge is downgraded and this can be seen in the ways in which, for example, various government documents, such as *The National Service Framework for Mental Health* (UK Department of Health, 1999) published in England and Wales, equates 'gold standard' research with the carrying out of randomized controlled trials and relegates research that focuses on the experiences of service users to fifth position. In relation to social work, the doctor, social worker or professional assumes the mantle of the expert and the accompanying power of position and influence is used to determine what constitutes acceptable and unacceptable knowledge. Psychiatric or clinical knowledge of schizophrenia, for example, is prioritized over other forms of knowledge relating to belief systems or experiential criteria. Since the onset of the Enlightenment in the eighteenth century, medicalized knowledge obtained by going to university has been ascribed a much higher status than that of the folk healer, even though, for a while at least, the levels of success were probably similar.

With regard to 'self', modernist understandings tend to refer to individuals as having a unified or essentialist core self. This 'self' remains the same in all situations and types of 'self' can be identified and categorized. This also allows personal experience to be referred to in a straightforward, factual and uncomplicated way. The feminist phrase 'the personal is political' (see Chapter 6) has clear modernist overtones, in that it is accepted that personal experiences have a unique validity that can straightforwardly lead to the adoption of political positions.

In a similar manner, language is regarded as comprising fixed meanings, referring to objects and events that are tangible and factual (Sarup, 1993). However, Ferdinand de Saussure (1974, 1916), who is seen as the founder of modern structural linguistics, moved away from this interpretation when he developed an analysis that presented language as structuring meaning rather than referring to something real and tangible. Saussure regarded meaning as socially generated and viewed language as an abstract system comprising signs, made up of a signifier (sound or written image) and signified (meaning). Prior to being combined in language, he maintained that signifiers and signified had no natural connection. However, once a signifier and a signified had been combined, a fixed meaning or a 'positive fact' (de Saussure, 1974, 1916: 120) was produced.

With regard to concepts such as 'unity', 'fragmentation' and 'contradiction', modernism focuses on *unity* and there is a marked tendency to make facts fit the perspective being presented, rather than emphasis being placed on exploring fragmentation, diversity and contradiction. Gendered binaries are perhaps one of the most significant examples. Here, the unity category 'man' is set against the unitary category 'woman' and there is a focus on homogeneity rather than heterogeneity within the gender categories. However, the establishment of these binaries has presented an opportunity to challenge devalued binary positionings and proponents of 'second wave feminism', to give an example, concentrated on re-examining, repositioning and revaluing the unitary category 'woman' in relation to the unitary category 'man'. This proved to be a very significant project and served to place women's rights firmly on the political agenda. However, like any rights-based movement, these constitute social movements embedded within the modernist conceptual frame of reference.

Postmodernism

Judith Butler (1995: 35; see also Chapter 5) asked: 'The question of postmodernism is surely a question, for is there, after all, something called postmodernism?' This is a pertinent quote for there are those who reject postmodernism for its relativism, fluidity and the difficulties involved in weighting criteria to separate 'the acceptable' from 'the unacceptable'. Stevi Jackson (1992: 31), for example, fiercely opposed poststructuralist critiques of radical feminism, stating that 'Women are being deconstructed out of existence'. Similarly, Christine Di Stefano (1990) raised concerns as to whether or not feminism without an essentialist subject and some kind of standpoint could survive. She drew attention to becoming 'an other amongst others' (1990: 77) in a pluralist world. However, there are feminists who have embraced forms of postmodern feminism and their work will be considered later in a discussion of 'critical postmodernism'. These matters aside, a key question to address at this point echoes the one posed by Butler above: what is postmodernism?

A range of authors (for example, Best and Kellner, 1992; Dickens and Fontana, 1994; Howe, 1994; Parton, 1994a; Featherstone and Fawcett, 1995b; Fawcett, 2000, 2007) have looked at the ways in which postmodernism has placed emphasis on areas such as deconstruction, plurality, relativity and anti-foundationalist methodology generally. Although, as highlighted, attempts at definition can be regarded as a modernist enterprise, postmodernism can be broadly characterized by an emphasis on deconstruction, or the questioning and taking apart of taken-for-granted assumptions and accepted theoretical frameworks. This lends itself to dominant understandings – clinical psychiatric criteria, for example – being deconstructed and interrogated. Accordingly, questions are asked about how, at a particular point in time, psychiatry became the dominant discourse, with 'discourse', drawing from Foucault, understood to mean the way in which, at specific historical junctures, power, language and institutional practices come together to produce taken-for-granted or accepted social practices.

Postmodern critique emphasizes that all knowledge claims – no matter how powerfully they are embedded in social, political and individual ways of viewing the world – have to be opened up for critical questioning. It also means that, to continue with the example given, opening up dominant discourse to critical scrutiny is not simply a question of mental health survivor perspectives replacing clinical psychiatric understandings. Postmodern perspectives place emphasis on the necessity for the operation of a wide range of understandings. However, a key point to restate is that, as a result of everything being viewed in plural terms, postmodern orientations render it impossible to give one perspective greater weight than another as all have claims to validity and all are relative. A consequence is that it becomes difficult to take a political, moral or ethical position and separate out what might be regarded as the unjust from the just. Similarly, in relation to modernist notions of 'expert knowledge', postmodern orientations draw attention to the way in which such forms of knowledge operate and dismantle the corresponding power relationships. As all knowledge is regarded as relative, it is no longer possible for one individual or group to claim particular expertise or justify their dominance.

It is, however, also important to note that postmodern orientations cannot claim a monopoly on deconstructive forms of analysis. Critical theory, for example, focuses on deconstructing accepted or taken-for-granted tenets, such as the claims made by economic rationalists or proponents of neoliberal managerialist frameworks. The difference is that Critical theory aims to uncover the truth of a situation or what is really going on (Harvey, 1992), while, as far as postmodern orientations are concerned, there is an absence of a central core, only an endless series of layers.

With regard to understandings of the 'self', postmodern perspectives replace a modernist 'core' unitary self that remains the same in all situations, with a fluid and fragmented 'self', which is continually constructed and reconstructed by social practices and the interplay of dominant discourses. This tends to result in a view of 'self' that is continually being constructed and where individual agency or will is limited. This conceptualization has been subject to considerable modernist critique. From a feminist perspective, for example, Seyla Benhabib (1995) notably said that postmodern concepts of subjectivity were not compatible with feminist politics. She differentiated between strong and weak postmodern analyses, equating strong positions with 'the death of the autonomous, self-reflective subject, capable of acting on principle' (Benhabib, 1995: 29). She regarded weak analyses as those that deconstruct to reconstruct and are amenable to being utilized as a form of feminist critique.

Language, similarly – drawing from Jacques Derrida's pivotal (1978) work on deconstructionism – is never fixed, not even when signifier and signified are combined. Rather, by means of what he called the concept of *différance*, meaning can only be produced by the never-ending juxtaposition of signified and signifier in discursive contexts. Accordingly, meaning and meanings continually change and are always in process, with the person producing the sound or written image playing no part in the creation of meaning. To give an example, the combination of 'hallucination' and 'psychiatric' temporarily produces one set of meanings, while the juxtaposition of 'hallucination' and 'spirituality' temporarily produces another. In short, there are no essentialist or immutable connections between language and meaning and both are in a constant state of flux.

Critical postmodernism

Zygmunt Bauman (1992: viii) asserted that:

> It seems sometimes that postmodern mind is a critique caught at the moment of its ultimate triumph: a critique that finds it ever more difficult to go on being critical just because it has destroyed everything it used to be critical about; with it, off went the very urgency of being critical.

The notion of critical postmodernism draws from postmodern feminisms, as well as those writers who have sought to apply postmodern perspectives to policy and practice. A selection of writers whose work has contributed to making links between modern and postmodern orientations include, in chronological order, Graham McBeath and Stephen Webb (1991), Nancy Fraser and Linda Nicholson (1993), David Howe (1994), Nigel Parton (1994a), Brid Featherstone and Barbara Fawcett (1995b), Fiona Williams (1996), Barbara Fawcett (2000), Jan Fook (2002) and Patrick Bracken and Philip Thomas (2005).

What critical postmodern perspectives do is to draw from both modern and postmodern orientations to produce forms of critical analysis that critique, interrogate, deconstruct and reject foundational underpinnings for particular conceptual frames, yet facilitate the identification of inequalities and the mounting of effective challenges in particular contexts.

Modernism and postmodernism are not opposite sides of the same coin. Postmodernism cannot be explained by simply looking at modernism and formulating antithetical positions. Critical postmodernism is about drawing from *both* orientations to produce a form of analysis that makes links and explores tensions (Fawcett, 2000). Accordingly, with regard to modernism, the universal 'big stories' based on rationalist foundations are rejected and claims related to the operation of expert knowledge are dismissed. With regard to postmodernism, the emphasis on relativism, pluralism and anti-foundationalism is challenged, as it becomes impossible to ground ideas or make distinctions between what is acceptable and what is not. As has been highlighted, within postmodernism all ideas and actions are plural and relative and, as a result, none can carry more weight than another, leaving power imbalances and oppressive forces, such as sexism, racism and 'disablism', to be dismissed as irrelevant.

When looking at the ways in which *critical postmodernism* differs from *postmodernism* in relation to the operation of knowledge and power, emphasis can be placed on posing a series of questions at macro and micro levels – that is, at the level of society and the level of the individual. Drawing from Fook (2002), these questions include the following.

- What constitutes 'acceptable knowledge'?
- Why are some forms of knowledge valued over other forms at particular points in time?
- How do we know what we know?
- What has informed what we know?
- How has the perspective of the knower influenced what is known and how it is known?

Interrogation of these aspects serves to deconstruct and dismantle accepted tenets and knowledge/power configurations. In terms of weighting criteria and addressing structural inequalities and social divisions, critical postmodern perspectives ensure that this is still possible, but only in specific contexts or particular situations (Fawcett, 2000; Fraser and Nicholson, 1993; Williams, 1996). This is important and is where critical postmodern perspectives differ most markedly from postmodern orientations. Accordingly, a social worker using a critical postmodern perspective – and addressing the questions outlined above – would acknowledge the operation of competing power and knowledge frameworks. He or she would do this by drawing attention to information that, it would appear, was being privileged and responded to and information that was being downgraded and ignored in a particular context or situation. The multiplicity of meanings an event can have for a particular person at a particular time and the way in which understandings can vary is another area to attend to as social workers and service users may not be making similar connections or sharing meanings. Similarly, in any interaction, both the social worker and the service user draw from a variety of underpinning conceptual frames – for example, from medicalized or social models of disability, child protection understandings, welfare orientations, rights-based underpinnings, 'commonsense' viewpoints and so on – and this also has to be acknowledged.

With regard to 'expert knowledge', Howe (1994) used a postmodern perspective that, in its application, can be regarded as similar to critical postmodern orientations. He rejected the modernist view of professionals as experts or agents who were uniquely equipped to determine meanings and prescribe solutions. He (1994: 150) stated:

> If there are no privileged perspectives, no centres of truth, no absolute authorities in matters of taste and judgement, then all truths become working truths and relative truths. The full participation of all those involved in decisions about what is going on and what should be done is the only way to define non-oppressive, culturally pertinent truths and working practical judgements.

This quote can be seen to contain a critical postmodern emphasis in that it highlights the importance of negotiation. Critical postmodernism emphasizes the significance of negotiatory mechanisms and inclusion, with all those who have an interest in a particular area being involved in discussion. This does not mean that all views are given equal weight, but ensures that all views are attended to and outcomes are negotiated in specific contexts or situations.

In relation to language and constructions of 'self', critical postmodern perspectives move away from modernist orientations where individual experience tends to be regarded as unique and the 'self' remains the same in all situations or contexts. It also revises the postmodern view of 'self' as being fluid, fragmented and continually constructed with individual agency being limited. Critical postmodern perspectives reframe this so that the 'self' is regarded as having many different facets, but, to use the analogy of a kaleidoscope, although the facets or the pieces change every time the kaleidoscope is turned, there is a temporary fixing of facets or pieces between turns. This means that there is a temporary fixing of 'self' in specific situations and, although the self is positioned by social practices and discourses, in any one situation or context, there *is* agency and the 'self' *can* also position (Fawcett and Karban, 2005). To give an example from the arena of mental health, in one situation an individual may be constructed as a 'schizophrenic', in another he or she may position him or herself as a 'voice hearer' and, in yet another, as a 'mental health survivor'. Links can also be made between situations or contexts and intercontextual or intersituational comparisons can be formulated.

With regard to concepts associated with terms such as 'unity', 'fragmentation' and 'contradiction', modernism is about making things fit, emphasizing unity and how all parts of a whole neatly fit together. This results in those symptoms that match a particular diagnosis, for example, being emphasized or those factors that fit a particular argument being privileged, with those aspects that do not correspond being ignored or given secondary status.

Postmodernism, in turn, by means of ongoing processes of deconstruction, explore those aspects that do not fit, drawing attention to gaps, contradictions and omissions. Anne Wilson and Peter Beresford (2002), for example, critique the categorization and classification of mental distress. They maintain that their experience of mental and emotional distress does not fit neatly into psychiatric DSM1V categories of criteria for psychiatric syndromes and that what is most important to them is often left out and ignored.

Postmodern perspectives turn a critical gaze on the gaps and omissions of modernist constructions, but critical postmodern perspectives draw attention to the utility of contradictions. Rather than gaps or omissions being seen to be a problem, as is the case with modernism, the highlighting of these areas – with attention being drawn to the resulting contradictions and paradoxes – is seen to be productive. Bracken and Thomas (2005), for example, both psychiatrists, draw from what could be regarded as critical postmodern conceptualizations in their development of 'postpsychiatry'. They critique adherence to the belief that science and technology can resolve human and social problems and question the unthinking prioritization of disease or medicalized approaches. They regard 'postpsychiatry' as providing the opportunity for doctors to redefine their roles and responsibilities and they challenge the notion that psychiatric theory is neutral and objective. They maintain as does Beresford (2006) that psychiatry has to engage with the perspectives of service users and consumers and emphasize importance of these views shaping the culture and values of those working in the arena of mental health. They particularly highlight the need to pay full attention to social and cultural contexts, place ethics before technology and minimize the medical control of coercive interventions. They also fully acknowledge the need to avoid Eurocentric notions of dysfunction and healing and, while recognizing the pain and suffering involved in severe mental ill health, regard an uncritical reliance on Westernized frameworks as unhelpful. Their exposition of 'postpsychiatry' prioritizes the promotion of positive citizenship, which they define as freedom from discrimination, exclusion and oppression. Positive citizenship also confers freedom on individuals to define their own identity in a number of different ways (Bracken and Thomas, 2005).

Within modernist perspectives, as has been highlighted, there is an emphasis on looking at the world in either/or, or binary modes – for example, rational/irrational, culture/nature, mind/emotion, sanity/insanity and able-bodied/disabled. These either/or binaries are regarded as having either/or implications. A binary that is often used in relation to disability, which has been critiqued in detail by Jenny Morris (1996) and Michael Oliver and Bob Sapey (2006), is that of 'carer and cared for'. Within modernist orientations, the terms 'carer' and 'cared for' tend to be used to divide people into two distinct groupings, with the meanings associated with each being ascribed universal applications. A positioning in the 'carer' category carries with it the assumption that the carer is able-bodied and possesses the physical and conceptual capacity to 'care'. The location of an individual in the 'cared for' part of the binary brings with it a different set of associations. These are those of dependence and incapacity.

As emphasized, postmodern perspectives reject such 'either/or' positions and look at different conceptualizations of 'self'. Accordingly, women and men, whatever their perceived 'problems', 'impairment' or 'incapacity', can be seen to occupy a wide range of caring positions and be involved in a diverse number of caring interrelationships.

Critical postmodern perspectives, in turn, take this further by placing emphasis on 'both and' and by relating this to context. As a result, an individual can be seen to have many different identities, relationships and caring interrelationships, with different relationships and identities being produced and prioritized in different situations.

Postmodern social work practice

Debates and controversies surrounding postmodernism – and the critical distinction between modernism and postmodernism – emerged in social work in the early 1990s. McBeath and Webb's seminal paper, published in 1991, set the tone for much of the discussion that followed in the work of writers such as David Howe, Jim Ife and Nigel Parton (see Hugman, 2001).

The implications of this rich debate for social work have been considered throughout this chapter. However, in terms of application, rather than an emphasis being placed on producing a particular model or approach, attention is drawn to how critical postmodern perspectives provide conceptual frameworks that can be used to both critique and guide and inform policy and practice considerations. These include never taking anything for granted and questioning all knowledge claims, no matter how powerfully presented or embedded they are, including those of the social worker.

There also has to be an acceptance that, in different situations, meanings and presentations of the 'self' differ. A social worker cannot expect a service user to be rational, consistent and present in the same way in all situations. Similarly, the social worker will come across differently in different situations, so meanings have to be continually negotiated as it cannot be assumed that understandings or meanings are shared. Emphasis has also to be placed on social workers working with service users on their own assessment of their situation as no one assessment can be regarded as being privileged and all have a particular contribution to make.

Critical postmodern perspectives also reject a 'one size fits all' concept or practice model. Universal theories, with universal applications – particularly those that operate in a top-down or expert-orientated way – are inappropriate. Accordingly, social work theories, policies and practices that claim to have a global relevance and applicability are regarded as unworkable. Rather, emphasis has to be placed on negotiation and what is viable in a particular context, although intercontextual links can be made.

Significance for social work practice

With regard to social work practice, postmodern orientations have been criticized for promoting fragmented rather than unified and coherent analyses. They have shifted the focus away from the big canvas of modernism and concerns with global poverty and inequality and have instead concentrated on relative and competing claims about small and, some would argue, insignificant and disconnected facets. However, the continuing importance of postmodernism – particularly critical postmodernism – can be seen to lie in the emphasis placed on context and process.

In modernist analyses, there is an element of the 'taken-for-granted' with regard to unquestioned underlying tenets or 'truths', expert opinion or the power and authority of established institutions. Postmodern perspectives question and deconstruct all prevailing power/knowledge frameworks, so that none can claim a privileged position or contend that there is a 'right' way forward or an enduring and incontrovertible fact. As a

(Continued)

result, nothing can be regarded as fixed and 'everything' has to be regarded as fluid and transitory, with a temporary stasis only being achievable in specific contexts. This can be seen to constitute a challenging and what can be described as a liberatory aspect of postmodernism. Indeed, it is in this irreverent and unremitting examination and exploration of 'everything' that postmodernism's more enduring and significant contribution to social work practice can be seen to lie.

In conclusion, postmodern perspectives have been explored using modernist and critical postmodernist orientations as a form of critique and a way of applying theory to practice. Critical postmodern perspectives have been presented as having the capacity to provide the conceptual tools to interrogate, deconstruct, construct and negotiate ways that are responsive to context, knowledge and power dynamics, and to the varying ways in which the 'self' is presented in different situations. Critical postmodern orientations draw attention to all aspects of a situation and focus on inclusion and negotiation, the weighting of criteria in context and the making of intercontextual links. These attributes, it is contended, can be seen to have an ongoing relevance for social work and its commitment to constructive critique, theoretically nuanced practice and the need for social workers to continually differentiate between acceptable and unacceptable social practices in a variety of complex contextual situations.

Study questions

1. What are the opportunities and constraints posed by modernist, postmodernist and critical postmodernist perspectives for social work?
2. What are the main negotiatory strategies that you would employ in particular contexts?
3. Address the questions drawn from Fook (2002) on page 124. Identify the ways in which these could inform social work practice.

Glossary

Critical postmodernism Perspectives that can be seen to make links between modern and postmodern orientations and emphasize the importance of context.

Modernism A range of theoretical orientations that characterize the modern period and focus on progress, 'truth' and metanarratives.

Postmodernism A range of theoretical orientations that emphasize relativity, plurality and deconstructive forms of analysis.

Select bibliography

Recommended reading is Fawcett (2000), Fook (2002), Foucault (1990) and Nicholson (1990).

Part III
Perspectives

Social Network Analysis

12

Deirdre M. Kirke

Introducing social network analysis

This perspective has developed over the past 80 years in various disciplines across the world.

Linton Freeman's excellent (2004) history of social network analysis gives details of the development and change in network research over time, from the use of simple network ideas to the complex science that network analysis has become (Hummon and Carley, 1993). He attributes some of the earliest uses of social network ideas to John Almack (1922), who studied homophily among schoolchildren, Wellman (1926) who recorded which children played with each other, Helen Bott (1928) who refined the methods of recording interaction data for children and Jacob Moreno (1932, 1934) who developed the sociometric approach to data collection and used the concept 'network' in the sense that it is currently used in social network research.

Freeman suggests that, over this time, numerous theorists and methodologists have developed different aspects of what has become integrated, at this point, into an organized paradigm for research. He outlines the four features of social network analysis as being:

- motivated by a structural intuition based on ties linking social actors;
- grounded in systematic empirical data;
- drawing heavily on graphic imagery;
- relying on the use of mathematical and/or computational models.

The first of these features relates to the theoretical and conceptual aspects of modern social network analysis, while the other three relate to methodological aspects.

Social network analysts adopt a distinctive approach to examining the social world: the theoretical approach is relational, the data are relational and the statistical tests focus on relational properties of networks, such as density (Wasserman and Faust, 1994).

Researchers from multiple disciplines are engaged in social network research, but the sociological approach to social network analysis is probably closest to the interests of social workers and it is the one I use.

Social structure is at the core of sociological enquiry, but it is examined quite differently in mainstream sociology and social network analysis. Like other sociologists, social network analysts assume that individual action can be explained by the social structures in which individuals are embedded and the processes at work in those structures. Generally, sociologists' methodological approach to this question is to examine individuals and their attributes, treat those individuals as if they were independent units, group the individuals by their attributes and relate those groupings to the individuals' behaviour, attitudes, political preferences and so on. This approach is, according to Barry Wellman and S.D. Berkowitz (1988), more psychological than sociological because it produces explanations that are based on aggregating individual motives for action, and not on the patterned connections between individuals that affect individual action or provide access to scarce resources.

Problems that social network analysts see with the individualistic approach are that it treats individuals as independent units when researchers know that they are likely to have relational ties and as if they were randomly connected when research shows that they are clustered in networks. Explanations are given based on similarity in attributes. This leads sociologists to accept behaviour as normative, or deviant, based on similarity in attributes rather than on the relational ties they share.

Key ideas

In contrast, social network analysts directly examine the social structure involved, collect data on the relational ties between the individuals in that structure, examine how those relationships are patterned and examine the individuals' behaviour in the context of the social structure in which it is embedded. They will usually also examine individual attribute data, but analyses of the structural connections between the individuals in the networks take precedence, while similarities between the attributes of individuals are examined within those networks.

Thus, relational ties are at the core of the social network perspective (Freeman, 2004). Repeated interactions between individuals result in the formation of relationships. Such relationships can be based on transactions (any exchanges), communication, boundary penetration (such as interlocking directorates), instrumental (using ties to get a job), sentiment (friendship), authority power or kinship and descent (Knoke and Kuklinski, 1982). As these relationships become linked with others, they form networks.

The concept 'social network' is used in social network analysis to describe a finite set of actors and the relationships between them (Wasserman and Faust, 1994). Social networks can vary enormously in size and type, from dyads to triads, from partial to complete networks, and their structure – that is, the pattern of the ties in the network – may change over time as new ties are formed or broken. While the relational ties will usually be between individuals, network analysts also study the connections between groups, organizations, communities or other units of different types that are connected.

Social network analysts examine social networks in order to explain how the social networks in which they are embedded affect individuals' actions, beliefs or attitudes, but they also examine how individuals' actions form, change and affect the social networks in which they are embedded. They are also interested in how resources flow through networks (Coleman, Katz and Menzel, 1957; Valente, 1995, 1996) and how networks can be used to search for resources (Granovetter, 1974). The social networks that have been of particular interest to social workers have been social *support* networks. Developments in social network thinking have ranged across three dimensions: theoretical, conceptual and methodological.

Theoretical approach

The theoretical belief permeating network research is the idea that the structure, or pattern, formed by the relational ties between individuals in social networks is central to our understanding of the social world. The principal aspects of this theoretical approach have been outlined by Barry Wellman (1988) as follows:

- structured social relationships are a more powerful source of sociological explanation than the personal attributes of system members;
- norms emerge from location in structured systems of social relationships;
- social structures determine the operation of dyadic relationships;
- the world is composed of networks, not groups;
- structural methods supplement and supplant individualistic methods.

Randall Collins (1988) confirms the value of network theory to sociological explanation, pointing out that it can explain network effects on individual action and belief, social exchange, inter-group integration, social mobility and economics. Those of most relevance to social workers may be network effects on individual action and belief, in which network theorists have developed concepts of cohesion and structural equivalence to explain behaviour (see Glossary at end of this chapter). Thus, for example, network research has demonstrated that cohesive networks tend to have homogeneous beliefs and behaviour (Kirke, 2006; McPherson, Smith-Lovin and Cook, 2001; Wasserman and Faust, 1994), individuals in cohesive networks tend to have better social support (Collins, 1988; Wellman and Wortley, 1990) and those with better social support will have better physical and mental health (Brugha, 1995; Oakley, 1994; Putnam, 2000).

Conceptual clarification

Although social network analysts have not been very active in developing network theory, they have been in clarifying concepts, which has been of direct relevance to network theory.

The advantage is that social network researchers use the same concepts and share the same meanings for those concepts.

John Arundel Barnes (1972) drew together various network concepts, such as reachability, defined them clearly and discussed the difference between the metaphorical and applied use of network concepts. In a marvellous little book, David Knoke and James Kuklinski (1982) defined numerous social network concepts, including network structure, egocentric networks, partial networks, whole networks and many more.

Further clarifications were given in a major social network methods textbook by Stanley Wasserman and Katherine Faust (1994). In this book, novice network researchers can find all the relevant concepts, their meanings and how they are applied in social network research.

One of my favourite teaching tools for clarifying concepts is Linton Freeman's (2000a) short paper, 'See you in the funny papers'.

Social network concepts that may be of relevance to social workers' research and practice are listed at the end of this chapter with their current definitions (see Glossary).

Methodology

The major emphasis in social network analysis has always been the methodological dimension. There were huge challenges. Researchers from disciplines as diverse as sociology, psychology, mathematics, statistics and computer science have worked together to overcome these challenges. The result is a very well-developed methodology, appropriate statistical techniques, mathematical models and computer programs, including the graphical imagery of networks, which are constantly undergoing development to answer changing questions. These researchers – from numerous disciplines, but sharing a common perspective – are members of the vibrant International Network for Social Network Analysis (INSNA), started in 1977 by Barry Wellman (see www.insna.org).

Newcomers to social network analysis will be pleased to know that it is used with all the conventional data collection methods, including survey research and ethnographic and documentary methods. The vital difference is in collecting information on relationships rather than solely on individuals and their attributes. Examples are Claude Fischer's (1982) scheme for collecting social support data, which asked questions such as who would take care of their home if they went out of town, with whom had they recently engaged in social activities and with whom had they discussed personal worries. The answers were combined to form a person's social support network. Fischer's scheme has been widely used in research on social support and personal networks (Campbell and Lee, 1991; van der Poel, 1993).

Some important aspects of social network methodology that mark it off from conventional methods are its emphasis on the structure and units on which it is dwelling and on the boundary it is placing on its structure. Thus, for example, in Deirdre Kirke's (1996) study, the *structure* is the complete network of teenagers in one community, the *units* are the teenagers and the *boundary* is both geographical (must live within the community chosen) and age-related (14–18-year-olds only).

Other major advantages of social network methodology are that it enables researchers to work at different levels of analysis singly, including personal networks, dyads, triads, partial and whole networks, and, more recently, to do longitudinal and multilevel analyses (Snijders, Steglich, Schweinberger and Huisman, 2005).

The social network analysis of data is different from conventional data analysis. The basic unit of analysis in social network research is the dyadic tie between units and each of these is coded separately with any associated data. Thus, each friendship tie is coded separately and associated data, such as when the friendship started and the strength and closeness of the friendship, are coded alongside it. Attribute data can be added for each individual in the friendship. Social network analysis programs, such as PAJEK (Batagelj and Mrvar, 2003) and UCINET (Borgatti, Everett and Freeman, 2006), are then used to identify the networks, measure their size, structure and network properties, such as density, distance, reachability, centrality and structural equivalence, and apply appropriate statistical techniques. Social network analysis programs also provide graphic imagery of the networks (see also Freeman, 2000b).

A number of social network methods textbooks elaborate on the various analyses used, as well as the appropriate statistical measures, depending on the needs of the researcher (Scott, 1991; Wasserman and Faust, 1994). Lists of further reading and appropriate software are available from the INSNA website (www.insna.org).

Application to social work practice

Social workers have been showing some interest in social network analysis for about the last 30 years. When the first edition of *Connections* was published in 1977, just four people from the discipline of social work were listed as members of INSNA: Diane Pancoast and Harry Wasserman from the Unites States and Mike Pennock and Harvey Stevens from Canada. Pancoast had published a paper, 'Natural Helping Networks', with Alice H. Collins in 1976, while Wasserman's research was recorded as 'doing studies of the Havurah phenomenon in Los Angeles Synagogues' (*Connections*, 1977: 11, 15).

Pennock's research interests included the analysis of social service delivery systems, while Stevens's were the development of record-keeping systems for private social service agencies (*Connections*, 1977).

A social network-related social work paper by John Garrison and Sandra Werfel dates from the same time. They discussed the use of the 'network session' in clinical social work, describing it as one in which social workers counsel a client in the presence of his or her natural social network in order to help the individual client and strengthen his or her network (Garrison and Werfel, 1977). Thus, they assumed, as current social network analysts do, that resources exist in an individual's network that may be drawn on for the individual's benefit. An extensive social support and, more recently, social capital literature has grown out of this simple idea.

Despite such evidence of some positive applications of a social network approach in social work, Elizabeth Timms (1983) and Graham Allan (1983) wrote papers a few years later expressing caution about professional social workers becoming involved in creating, or supporting, the development of informal caring networks for their clients. Such informal caring networks are what are currently known in the social network literature as social support networks.

Just a few years after these shaky beginnings, Philip Seed (1987, 1990) supported the use of social network analysis in social work research and practice and clarified how such tools should be applied in social work. Many social workers have embraced the social network perspective since then.

Use and critique by social workers

The principal application of the social network perspective in social work has been in the area of social support. I will use examples from this literature to demonstrate the use of social network analysis in social work. These examples are illustrative rather than exhaustive. While social support refers, more generally, to the support available to individuals from their informal social network, it can, of course, also include the support provided by a formal network of professionals, such as social workers, doctors, nurses, psychologists, psychotherapists or occupational therapists. Professional social workers have been using a social network perspective to examine social support networks that are informal caring networks only or a mix of formal and informal caring networks.

Informal caring networks

Research on informal support networks has ranged across topics such as mental illness, homelessness and immigrants in the USA and working mothers in China.

Joseph Walsh (1994) examined clients with severe mental illnesses who were being provided with rehabilitation services in their natural environments. He found that, although there were no differences between males and females in the size of their personal networks or in their perceptions of the adequacy of the social support they received, they differed in the support they received from different people in their networks, which Walsh described as different clusters.

Based on these findings, he suggested that social workers should review male and female clients' social networks by clusters before making interventions to improve their networks.

Another example relating to psychiatric clients is Eric Hardiman's (2004) examination of the social support received by adults with psychiatric disabilities from consumer-run mental health agencies. In particular, the agencies provided the participants with peer-focused networks of caring that were otherwise unavailable to them.

Hardiman suggests that service providers, including social workers, should take note of this way of encouraging the natural support of psychiatric clients in a community setting.

Related reading would be Traolach Brugha (1995), who demonstrated the value of social support networks in psychiatric illness.

In a study examining gender differences in support structures, frequency of support and satisfaction with support from parents, peers and other adults, Lisa Colarossi (2001) found that male and female adolescents differed in the proportion of supportive friends and adults they had and their satisfaction with that support.

The implications of these findings for social work are that social workers may be able to help adolescents to identify which network members are most helpful for particular kinds of problems, thus enabling them to use the different kinds of support available to them more effectively.

In a study of social support in homelessness, Karin Eyrich, David Pollio and Carol North (2003) directed similar advice to service providers. Those who experienced shorter- (12 months or less) and longer-term (more than 12 months) homelessness had different support networks. They suggested that service providers should, therefore, aim at different sources of support for the shorter- and longer-term homeless.

Other interesting examples from the social support literature include two papers on Chinese mothers in China and Korean immigrants in the USA.

Having examined the social support networks of Chinese working mothers in Beijing, Angelina Yuen-Tsang (1999) demonstrated that these mothers' support networks were communal in nature and differed from the support networks normally found in the West. She pointed out that social work interventions in Chinese societies should, therefore, adopt a whole network – rather than a personal network – intervention strategy.

Confirming the importance for social workers of being aware of cultural variations, Eunju Lee's (2005) paper on Korean immigrants in the USA highlights the need for social workers to be aware of the cultural differences between their Korean immigrant clients and other communities of clients.

In Korean immigrant communities, marital conflict – stemming in large part from cultural differences in the role of women in society – is a serious problem. She highlights the need for social work to reduce marital disharmony through culturally sensitive interventions, including education.

Formal and informal caring networks

Social workers have also been involved in expanding and improving clients' networks by linking the formal care provided by professionals with that provided by family, friends and neighbours.

By far the best example I have found of the formal and informal systems combining to provide social support for families in need is 'Wraparound'. The system, which developed to link the various forms of social support, formal and informal, needed by a family with children with special needs, is described very touchingly by a mother of such children (Hesch, 1998). The extensive, and appropriate, support provided by 'Wraparound' was directly geared to meeting the needs of families benefiting from the programme. The formal system provided the required professional care to the child and family that funding and time allowed, while the informal community support system filled in the gaps, providing the continued support over time that the formal system could not give.

The social support system described by Karen Hesch (1998) was originally developed in 1991 in Ontario, Canada, as a support cluster model for individuals with complex needs (Ochocka and Lord, 1998). Joanna Ochocka and John Lord evaluated the support cluster approach in 24 clusters and demonstrated the effectiveness of linking formal and informal support for individuals with complex needs. The support clusters effectively acted as a 'bridge' between the formal and informal support systems and between developmental disabilities and mental health.

Their findings demonstrate the value and potential of a multidimensional approach to support that involves citizens, families and service providers working together on issues rather than clinical interventions only.

Another example of social workers' efforts to create networks between the formal and informal is described by Caroline Cantley and Gilbert Smith (1983). They record how social workers attached to a psychogeriatric day hospital played a leading role in establishing a 'Relatives Support Group'. Monika Henderson and Michael Argyle (1985) also found that friends were the most important source of support for divorced and separated women, while Vikki Bell (2007) reported that families who experienced interprofessional collaboration in providing parenting programmes in a community setting found it helpful.

Implications for social work practice

As shown above, social network concepts have been used by social workers in their research and practice. However, they have not used social network analytic techniques when measuring social support networks. Researchers have usually discussed the size of the networks, but have not used social network techniques to examine the social structure of particular support networks in graphical detail, nor have they compared the impact of different structures on measures of density or cohesion.

Concepts, such as 'bridge', have been used (Ochocka and Lord, 1998), but, if researchers had drawn more closely on the social network literature, other insights into their role could have been provided – for example, Mark Granovetter's (1973) theory that strong ties create cohesion and weak ties reduce fragmentation in a community.

Another important insight is that 'bridges' can give individuals access to resources that are not available to them in their own network. This is important to social workers because it opens up the possibility of linking quite diverse networks to support their clients.

There is considerable evidence in network research that strong ties provide the most social support (Wellman and Wortley, 1990), various types of support are provided by different people in a person's network and women are the main providers of support to other women and to men (Fischer, 1982; Oakley, 1994; Wellman and Wortley; 1990).

These findings suggest that researchers in the area of social support should take account of the strength of the ties of potential, or actual, supporters as well as the role of gender. Although social work researchers have examined the role of gender in social support (Colarossi, 2001; Walsh, 1994), the relative strength of ties does not appear to have been examined directly. While strong ties are likely to be the most supportive, social work interventions may target weak ties, which can provide access to different types of support (Granovetter, 1973).

Research has usually focused on the personal networks of individuals with particular needs, but social workers might do well to examine networks that reach beyond the personal, to interlocking personal networks and whole networks. Research on 'support clusters' (Ochocka and Lord, 1998) may appear to do this, but its focus is on bringing together the significant people in personal social networks. Whole network research, however, would allow social workers to examine the natural clustering of family, friends, neighbours, co-workers and professionals that occurs in a community. This would enable them to build on community resources rather than solely on individual resources. Whole network research would also allow social workers to place their clients in the context of the networks in which they function. Yuen-Tsang (1999) pointed to the importance of doing this in Chinese communities because of the different cultural emphasis on communal networks in which individuals pooled and shared their resources.

The social support literature is geared primarily to demonstrating the *positive* aspects of social supports, but there can also be a negative side. For example, teenagers have been shown to support friends in their networks to use drugs (Kirke, 1995) and network members will share drug injection equipment with others, resulting in higher rates of HIV infection among those most involved in this risky behaviour (Curtis et al., 1995). Social work interventions may, therefore, sometimes need to focus on breaking network ties that carry such negative influences rather than building ties carrying positive influences. This suggests that social workers may, in such cases, need to intervene in the network of ties rather than just with individual drug users.

Closely allied to the social support literature is the social capital literature, to which social network analysts have made considerable contributions in recent years (Kadushin, 2004; Lin, 2001; Lin, Cook and Burt, 2001). Essentially, *social capital* is the social resources available in an individual's personal network or in a community setting. It is useful, therefore, to use social network techniques to examine research questions relating to social capital. As social capital has been shown to be particularly advantageous to people's health and well-being (Putnam, 2000), this may be a suitable topic for future social network-related social work research.

Future researchers in social work need to build on the achievements of their predecessors who have used a social network approach in research and practice. Useful directions would include being aware of the conceptual developments in social network analysis, moving beyond the metaphorical to the applied use of network concepts and using current social network techniques to measure these concepts.

About 20 years ago, Seed (1987) set out procedures for applying social network analysis in social services research and practice using social network ties to represent links between people, places, activities or events. More recently, Susan Murty and David Gillespie (1995) set out clear procedures for incorporating social network analysis into the social work curriculum. In an excellent short paper, they define network concepts and discuss their relevance to the social work curriculum.

Not being a social worker, I cannot say to what extent social network analysis has been incorporated into social work curricula, research and practice, but, as a social network analyst, I can say that, if social network analysis is widespread in social work, it is not apparent at the annual conferences of INSNA or in the *Social Networks* journal. The time seems right for social workers to build on the earlier social network efforts of those in their own profession. Social network analysis is relevant if ties of any kind are being studied between individuals or diverse groups. Social workers can do such research within their own profession or in collaboration with social network analysts in INSNA. In this way, they can be involved in the further development of social network analysis to suit the needs of their profession and the social network community more generally.

Study questions

1. Discuss the relative value of focusing on clients' personal networks or whole networks in social work practice.
2. Discuss the relative importance of strong and weak ties to the kind of social support available to social workers' clients.
3. Should social workers be expected to form networks for their clients that combine formal and informal networks?

Glossary

Bridge A bridge is a line – relationship – the removal of which would disconnect – break – the network into parts.

Centrality Relates to the extent to which an actor in a network is involved in relationships. Ties can be directed in to the actor or out from the actor. Alternatively, they may be undirected.

Cohesion Individuals become alike as a result of socializing bonds of interaction – for example, through ties of friendship. Cohesive subgroups are subsets of actors who have relatively strong, direct, intense, frequent or positive ties.

Complete network See under 'Whole network', below.

Composition of network Refers to measurements of factors relating to actors in a network, such as gender.

Density The ratio of the actual number of lines in the graph – network – to the number that would be present if all the points were connected to all the others.

Direct tie This is a tie linking two individuals – usually indicated by a line linking two nodes, which represent the individuals.

Distance The length of the shortest path between individuals in a network. Direct and indirect ties are counted to measure distance.

Dyad or dyadic tie This refers to a relationship between a pair of individuals.

Ego-centred network, egocentric network or personal network Comprises a focal actor, termed ego, a set of actors who have ties to ego and measurements relating to the ties between these actors.

Egocentric network See under Ego-centred network, above.

Indirect tie This is a tie that links two individuals who do not have a direct tie with each other, but who *do* have direct ties with one other individual (indicated by three nodes or individuals linked by two lines).

Link This is a tie or relationship between two individuals, or nodes.

Multilevel analysis This refers to the combination of data at different levels of analysis.

Network structure See under Structure of network, below.

Partial networks These are networks of various sizes between the triad and the complete network, such as a peer group.

Path Refers to direct and indirect ties that are used to trace the links between individuals in a network. The term also relates to distance, meaning the length of the shortest path between individuals in a network (see Reachability, below).

Pattern or patterning of ties See under Structure of network, below.

Personal network See under Ego-centred network, above.

Prestige The extent to which an actor is the recipient of relationships. Only relationships directed in to the actor count. See also under Relationship, below.

Reachability A measure of the extent to which the individual can establish indirect contact with other members of a network. Individuals are reachable if there is a path between them. See also under Path and Distance, above.

Relationship A tie or link between individuals. The specific set of ties to be investigated depends on theoretical considerations.

Size of social network This refers to the number of nodes, or individuals, who have ties in a social network.

Social network Comprises a finite set of actors and the relationships between those actors.

Strong ties Usually defined as those ties we have with family, relatives and friends, but the definition in any one case depends on theoretical considerations.

Structural equivalence Individuals who are structurally equivalent have identical ties to and from all other actors in a network.

Structure of network This is the pattern of the relational ties in the network and includes present and absent ties.

Triad These are ties between three nodes, or individuals.

Undirected ties The direction of the tie is not taken into account. It is sufficient that there is a tie between the two nodes.

Weak ties The definition in any one case depends on theoretical considerations. Weak ties are usually defined as those we have with people less close to us than family, relatives and friends. Examples include workmates and acquaintances.

Whole network or complete network A network in which all the relationships existing between all the actors within a particular population are identified.

Select bibliography

As well as references cited in this chapter, a good general text on social network analysis is Wasserman and Faust (1994).

Ethnomethodology

13

Gerald de Montigny

Introducing ethnomethodology

Ethnomethology (EM) originated primarily in the creative work of Harold Garfinkel, who combined Talcott Parsons' (1937) voluntaristic theory of social action with the phenomenological sociologies of Alfred Schütz (1962a, b, c) and Aron Gurwitsch (1964, 1966). Harold Garfinkel developed his distinctive reworking of Parsons' (1937) 'problem of social order' by attending to the 'life world' (Husserl, 1970). Attention to the 'life world' allowed for an analysis that could draw out the relations between the taken-for-granted presence of an everyday world and our practical, situated and lived forms of social action.

The publication of *Seeing Sociologically: The routine grounds of social action* (2006), which Garfinkel had written as a thesis proposal in 1948, further reveals his debt to phenomenological sociology. Anne Rawls (2006: 6), who convinced Garfinkel to publish this text, explains: 'Seeing sociologically, in Garfinkel's view, requires a focus on the routine details that comprise the coherence of activities, not a focus on the beliefs and motives of actors: seeing in new ways – seeing society anew – and in details'.

Harold Garfinkel was born in 1917 and grew up in Newark, New Jersey. He began his studies in accounting at the University College of Newark, then migrated south to the University of North Carolina where he completed his MA in 1942 before he was drafted into the army.

Following his discharge, he studied for his PhD at Harvard, where he was supervised by Talcott Parsons until he completed it in 1952. Through Parsons, Garfinkel took up the structure–agency debate in sociology – that is, whether attention should be given to so-called structural determinations or to individual and group actions.

Garfinkel, along with others in the post-war environment, shifted attention from structures and rules towards people's practical activities for ordering their everyday lives. He believed that Parsons had dealt with 'action' only incompletely (Heritage, 1984; Hilbert, 1992) and, as a result, Garfinkel turned away from a functional analysis of norms and values as underpinning social structures to examine instead 'experience structures' (Garfinkel, 1988: 104; Heritage, 1984: 9; Hilbert, 1992: 10).

Garfinkel's new sociology relied on Parsons' (1937) attention to the Hobbesian problem of order (Buxton, 1985). Thomas Hobbes (1958, 1651: 186) in *Leviathan* saw people as natural pursuers of individual wants (competition, diffidence and glory) and believed that, in an unregulated state of nature, the life of man is 'solitary, poore, nasty, brutish and short'.

Hobbes reasoned that there must be a sovereign power to rein in people's passions in order to ensure cooperation and social stability. Parsons countered that Hobbes incorrectly subordinated reason to the passions and proposed, instead, a distinctly modern and American 'theory of action', wherein order was achieved as a population voluntarily adhered to social norms and morals. Parsons presented his social theory, which synthesized rational (utilitarian) means and ends with 'action systems', as the culmination of social philosophy and sociology that began with Hobbes and Locke in the seventeenth century and proceeded to Marshall, Pareto, Durkheim and Weber in the nineteenth century.

For Parsons, writing in the 1930s while at Harvard, in a democratic America, it was clear that the 'common power' to maintain social order and peace could not be a sovereign king or queen. Equally distasteful were the forms of Nazism, fascism or communism he saw evolving in Europe. When Parsons wrote *The Structure of Social Action*, his country was not only suffering the social disruptions caused by the Great Depression but also could see the breakdown of social order across Europe. For Parsons, the solution to the problem of order rested in people's 'voluntary' adherence to norms and values that promoted social cohesion and cooperation (Buxton, 1985; Hama, 1999).

Garfinkel directed his attention not to action as an abstraction, but as effected in the mundane work of people in the day-to-day course of their lives. For Garfinkel, writing in a very different post-war America, order was ubiquitous as the stable, lived, worked and congenial forms of life evidenced in everyday public and private routines. Order was realized as people lined up for buses, drove to work, passed through the checkouts at supermarket or conducted classes in a university. Thus, while Garfinkel began with Parsons' concern with the problem of order, he believed that the 'problem of order' was no problem at all.

Garfinkel (1991: 11) argued that order was a palpable fact of what he would later call 'immortal, ordinary society'. The congregational production of social order – of whatever form – is achieved continuously day after day. For people living in the world, there is 'no time out', no interruption and no escape from life as a member of society. Thus, Garfinkel's (2002: 254) description of society as 'immortal' signals that what society is comes to be because it is continually 'staffed' or performed by members whose work creates various orders that will be there 'after the local staff leaves to be replaced by those who succeed it'.

Garfinkel's attention to 'immortal, ordinary society' resonates with Alfred Schütz's (1973: 218–20) sociological phenomenology, which recognized that the 'world of daily life' is an 'intersubjective world' in which 'we grow older together'. Schütz's phenomenology differed from Edmund Husserl's (1962) as Husserl proposed a philosophic 'disconnect' or 'bracket' of the 'natural attitude', while Schütz argued that, because experience is comprised of 'multiple realities', 'specific shock' experiences could disturb our paramount reality. Multiple realities include such things as falling asleep and a world of dreams, drama and stage plays, a painting that fills our visual field and participation in the fiction of the joke. Schütz's attention to 'shock experiences' provided Garfinkel with the insight to develop 'breaching exercises' to disrupt taken-for-granted routines.

In breaching exercises, Garfinkel (1967: 42) instructed students to enter the familiar scenes of their daily lives and undertake actions that would 'breach' the 'stable structures' of those settings. For instance, students were 'to engage an acquaintance or friend in an ordinary conversation ... and to insist that the person clarify the sense of his commonplace remarks'; to spend time 'in their homes viewing its activities while assuming that they were boarders in the household' (1967: 45), 'to engage someone in conversation and to imagine and act on the assumption that what the other person was saying was directed to hidden motives' (1967: 51); or to 'bargain for standard priced merchandise' (1967: 68–9). Garfinkel reported that the effect of these assignments was that students complained about anxiety, awkwardness and discomfort, as well as the angry, dismissive and confused reactions of others.

Key ideas

The distinctiveness of EM

To the novice, EM – and, in particular, Garfinkel's writings – often seem to be noticeably strange or odd. Further, unlike other contemporary theoretical giants, such as Michel Foucault, Jürgen Habermas, Gilles Deleuze, and Pierre Bourdieu, Garfinkel does not present an 'encyclopaedic range of ... investigations', nor does he 'attempt ... large-scale theoretical synthesis' (Heritage, 1984: 3). Richard Hilbert (1995: 158) notes that, unlike other sociologies:

> To its everlasting credit, ethnomethodology has been remarkably free of ... syntheses and groundings in tradition. Indeed, early characterizations of ethnomethodology specifically contrasted it with everything that had gone before, all of it, glossed into the general category not-ethnomethodology i.e., 'traditional sociology'.

In contrast to others' grand theorizing about general or global matters, Garfinkel, in *Studies in Ethnomethodology* (1967), turns his attention to practical and mundane matters, such as decisionmaking by jurors, 'passing' and achieved sex status in a transsexual male and good reasons for the production of 'bad' clinical records. Garfinkel (1967: 32) explains:

> Procedures and results of water witching, divination, mathematics, sociology, whether done by lay persons or professionals, are addressed according to the policy that every feature of sense, of fact,

of method, for every particular case of inquiry without exception, is the managed accomplishment of organized settings of practical actions, and that particular determinations in members' practices of consistency, planfulness, relevance, or reproducibility of their practices and results, from witchcraft to topology, are acquired and assured only through particular, located organizations of artful practices.

Whether it is the work of mathematicians, witchdoctors or social workers, EM leads us to examine the actual coordination of interactions as a practical matter. For social workers, EM makes remarkable the taken-for-granted performance of the orders of their work as files, reports, assessments, waiting rooms, interviews and so on.

At first blush, social workers might misunderstand Garfinkel's (2002: 115) claim that EM and formal analysis (FA) – the type of work that social workers do when assessing, diagnosing and treating clients – are 'simultaneously incommensurably different and unavoidably related' as a potential criticism of professional practice. Yet, a close reading reveals that Garfinkel, although committed to EM, refuses to claim analytic superiority for his discipline. Rather, he recognizes that, always and everywhere, people engage in ordinary moments of practical theorizing, generalizing and explanation (essentially the procedures for doing FA) and the essential reflexivity of such activities becomes taken for granted as background. Attention in EM to the 'essential reflexivity' (Lynch, 1993) of practice brings into focus the relations between social forms and situated work. Uncovering Garfinkel's view of the FA–EM relation requires a subtle reading that is sensitive to the contribution of EM to revealing the 'instructed' features of action.

Rawls (2006) explains that Garfinkel recognizes learning to do EM demands more than just reading. To learn to do EM, Garfinkel developed 'tutorial problems', or exercises, that disrupt the taken-for-granted routines of everyday life. In similar fashion, Garfinkel, by seeming to erect a divide between EM and FA, forces those who are interested to figure out how to do 'getting to the other side'. That they can get there is not in dispute, but what is of interest is *how* they get there.

Garfinkel argues that all people are potential ethnomethodologists as they are already continually engaged in the performance of sensible and accountable actions and orders. It turns out that EM has praxeological utility as a tool for explicating how practitioners, such as social workers, cooperatively enact various forms of social organization. EM can provide a detailed analysis of how such work comes to be 'in and as lived doings' (Garfinkel, in Rawls, 2006: 43).

Garfinkel (2002: 116) explains: 'The achievements of formal analytic theorizing and investigations are always accompanied by ethnomethodological alternatives, and they are accompanied everywhere. Wherever in an actual investigation one is found the other is also found'. Social workers can recognize that, as they work in mental health, child protection, family counselling, alcohol and drug rehabilitation or a local welfare office, they work up or insert the myriad inchoate and ineffable details of clients' lives into at hand, albeit formal, institutional categories. Social workers can recognize the artfulness, and the practical work of accomplishment, out of which emerges sensibility, order and organization as 'social work', our 'agency' and 'helping'.

In *Ethnomethodology's Program* (2002), Garfinkel provides a clear definition of EM's relation to 'formal analysis' (FA). He affirms that EM is concerned with 'remedial expertise' and that it does have something 'to promise or deliver', though he insists that 'its remedial transactions are distinctive to EM expertise'. He adds (2002: 114),'EM's remedial expertise is indifferent to the use of policies of generic representational theorizing and methods of constructive analysis'. For Garfinkel, EM is concerned with the ways that generic representational theorizing (or, as in our case, social work theory) as a practice gets done by members as *their practice*, as their work of dealing with practical matters at hand, as their day's work.

Garfinkel's (2002: 171) caution 'not to decide in advance what the phenomenon consists of on the basis of prior formal analytic studies' should be canonical for social workers. From EM, social workers are led to question and explicate taken-for-granted methods for producing the order and sense of day-to-day work with clients. EM directs social workers to attend to the actual forms and shapes of their work and clients' lives before leaping into theory. By using EM, social workers can examine the ways that their work produces a taken-for-granted organization in a local site. EM forces social workers to go beyond the traditional recognition that 'agency function' shapes social work practice (Robinson, 1949; Smalley, 1967; Taft, 1944) and recognize that it is *their practices* which accomplish the organization and its functions. EM allows social workers to recognize the 'essential reflexivity' (Lynch, 1993) of practice so that agency function is revealed to be a congregationally produced effect of members' actual work.

Rawls, in her introduction to *Ethnomethodology's Program* (Garfinkel, 2002: 19), claims that the purpose of EM is:

> to bring sociology from the realm of conceptual theorizing into the hands of practitioners, in order that we may understand and improve upon both the quality of individual human experience and the possibility of providing high-quality lives for all human beings. Social change requires, first and foremost, an understanding of social processes.

The claim that EM is motivated by a desire for 'high-quality lives for all human beings' is consonant with social work. Through EM, social workers are instructed to attend to actual practices, coordinated social relations and, ultimately, individual and collective responsibility for enacted forms of social order. EM provides tools to reveal that that which emerges as a client's problems, concerns and stories arises in and through, albeit not exclusively, the interactional, in situ and face-to-face work of producing a coherent and ordered account with a social worker. The emergence of 'candidate correct' (Pollner, 1974: 40) categorizations is recognized as satisfying practical and at hand purposes, rather than universal, decontextualized truths.

The nature of EM

John Heritage (1984: 4) explains:

> The term ethnomethodology ... refers to the study of a particular subject matter: the body of common-sense knowledge and the range of procedures and considerations by means of which the ordinary members of society make sense of, find their way about in, and act on the circumstances in which they find themselves.

At root, EM is quite simply about studying how people – that is, you and I – go about producing an often taken-for-granted, relied on and accountable order as our cogent and sensible everyday world. It is about how people in a supermarket, for example, queue up at a register, how people find a place on a bus, how a social worker ushers a client into her office and proceeds to do an interview and how, through ceaseless and endless repetition of such practical activities, coherence and sense arise. Behind 'ethnomethodology' is the simple idea that that which is familiar, taken-for-granted, common sense, routine and expected in our everyday worlds arises from a series of 'procedures' or methods by which all of us, in concert, congregationally achieve those features as our working and workable social orders.

Garfinkel's interest in everyday activities coincided with Harvey Sacks's interest in the ways that close analysis of recorded talk between people demonstrated their shared reliance on and deployment of standard devices for accomplishing local orders. Sacks's work, although clearly rooted in EM concerns, evolved into a distinct type of study known as conversation analysis (CA). Michael Lynch (1993) notes that the original ethnomethodological project became transformed into two closely related but different branches: EM studies of work, carried on by Garfinkel and those around him, and CA, as developed by Sacks.

Studies of work stimulated broad-based research into both formal and informal forms of action (see, for example, Baccus, 1986; Garfinkel, Lynch and Livingston, 1981; Girton, 1986). Garfinkel initiated this tradition with his analysis of good organizational reasons for 'bad' clinical records, Don Zimmerman (1976) followed with studies of the intake process and record-keeping in a welfare office and Egon Bittner studied the effects of policing on people on 'skid row' (1967a), people with mental illness (1967b) and young people (1976).

Conversation analysis

Sacks developed CA through early engagement and collaboration with Garfinkel (Garfinkel and Sacks, 1970). Although CA has evolved into a distinctive field of study, it remains affiliated with EM. Sacks died in a car accident in November 1975, however his lectures, dating from 1964, survived. These were published posthumously (1995) and reveal Sacks's abiding interest in the ways people use talk to get work done.

Sacks's interest in talk culminated in the 1974 paper that he wrote with Schegloff and Jefferson entitled 'A simplest systematics for the organization of turn-taking in conversation'. Lynch (2000b: 527) calls the paper a 'landmark', both in its rendition of detailed transcripts of 'naturally occurring conversations' and its argument 'that its findings were intrinsic to the data and not imposed by the analyst'. The paper took up the seemingly simple question of how turns are distributed between participants to a social occasion – an economy of turns – and proposed the examination of what the authors called the 'turn construction component' – use of sentences, clauses and phrases – and 'turn allocation components' (Lynch, 2000b: 702–3) – whereby one speaker selects the next speaker or self-selection for the next speaker occurs.

Through the presentation of transcribed segments of naturally occurring conversation, the paper demonstrated how people practically and interactively produced not just the order of a conversation but also the social order, accountability and warrant of an occasion. The paper launched research that led analysts to look beyond talk and meaning, to examine talk-in-interaction as productive of social orders. This period of study was a radical redirection away from the classic attention to the respectable study of 'language' – de Saussure's (1983) *lange* – and towards what had been regarded as the disreputable, chaotic, random, non-systematic use of 'talk' or 'conversation' – *parole* – and its productive functions in everyday life.

Just as EM and CA have become increasingly differentiated, CA has itself become internally differentiated, with some interested in analysing everyday or ordinary conversations and others focusing on 'institutional talk'.

Despite the emergence of such a division, the attention to 'institutional talk' has led to important clarifications of CA's foundations. Of note is Emmanuel Schegloff's (1992) demand that categories establishing the member's identity – or, more properly, identities – be demonstrably derived from and relevant to the participants in the talk. He insists that analysts should forswear simply asserting that the conversation has taken this form because, say, Joe is male, white, middle-aged, conservative and Catholic unless they can show, 'from the details of the talk or other conduct in the materials' (Schegloff, 1992: 110), that such identities are relevant and relied on as orientated to by the parties to the talk. Schegloff (1992) also extends this directive, stating that he is against the promiscuous use of identity categories and the rather common reliance on 'context' as explanation. He argues (1992: 111), in a fashion resonant with EM, that analytic work must 'show how the context or the setting … in that aspect, is procedurally consequential to the talk'.

Despite differences in approach and attention between EM and CA, at the root of both methods are fundamental commitments to explicating the interactive practices that produce forms of social order, coherence and accountability as practical and at hand matters. Thus, both EM and CA unite in affirming that there is 'orderliness at all points' (Sharrock, 2000: 536). Whether the production of order is pursued through detailed analysis of practical activities for sense-making or detailed attention to talk-in-interaction, then, the objective is to create knowledge that is deeply attentive to members' practices. In both EM and CA, analysts eschew imposing analytic order through the application of scientific categories and forms. Whether the interactional object for analysis is a 'family supper' or a social work interview, both EM and CA are committed to explicating just how such forms come to be produced by and for members.

Application to social work practice

Social work, EM and CA

The relevance of EM to social work arrives along two primary trajectories. First, social workers in the routines of their work – home visits, street outreach and counselling sessions – struggle to understand the ordinary and everyday worlds of their clients. Second, social workers have had a historical fascination with 'practice'.

Clearly, the focus of EM on everyday practical activities resonates with the core concerns of social workers. Social workers are deeply interested in just how people make their lives into families, friendships, work relations, neighbourhoods and so on. They are not indifferent to the mundane, ordinary and everyday ways and mores of clients' actions and interactions and, in this, their attention overlaps – albeit, often unrecognized as such – that of EM. The necessary curiosity of social workers with the taken-for-granted, commonsense, ordinary and everyday matches that of those who do EM.

By recalling Garfinkel's breaching exercises and the experience of discomfort it created for his students, we can better understand the experience of many social work students when they find themselves moving from familiar worlds to entering into the alien worlds of clients' lives. Unlike Garfinkel's students, who became strangers in familiar worlds, social work students find that they are strangers in unfamiliar worlds. They are obliged to enter those worlds not only as strangers but also as agents of extra-local (Smith, 1990) policies, legislation and codes. While social workers may appear to be 'present' in their work with clients, they are also continually orientated towards hidden or invisible background contingencies, expectations and agendas (Hak, 1995) in the forms of organizational mandates, policies and procedures which characterize their work environment.

EM, CA and social work

Therapy, counselling, psychiatry, medical practice, diagnosis and social work were of considerable interest to the first generation of EM and CA sociologists: Roy Turner (1972) studied 'therapy talk'; Don Zimmerman (1976) examined routines in a welfare office; Howard Schwartz (1976) explored the reliance on practical reasoning in psychotherapy; D.R.Watson (1981) took up the problem of use of 'proper' names in counselling; Gail Jefferson and John Lee (1981) analysed convergences and differences between ordinary 'troubles talk' between friends and 'troubles talk' in 'service encounters'; and Miller and Silverman (1995) examined troubles talk in counselling discourse.

The interest in such matters continues into the present as Ian Hutchby (2005) has examined active listening and eliciting 'feelings-talk in child counselling'; Douglas Maynard and John Heritage (2005) have examined doctor–patient interaction; Ilkka Arminen (2004) has looked at stories told at Alcoholics Anonymous (AA) meetings; and, Charles Antaki (2006) has explored the use of idiomatic expressions or clichés in work with mental health clients.

In recent years, a number of counsellors and social workers have reciprocated by taking up the tools of EM and CA. Increasingly, research is being developed that applies tools taken from CA to the examination of practice domains. For example, Anssi Peräkylä (1998) has analysed doctor–patient interactions and the accountable nature of the delivery of a diagnosis. Michael Forrester and David Reason (2006: 40) have examined psychoanalytic sessions to explore whether or not CA could be a useful tool to explicate 'the conduct of the psychoanalytic therapeutic interaction'. Michelle O'Reilly (2005) has examined therapy with children to provide a fascinating look at differences between adults and children in their use of onomatopoeia, while Karin Osvaldsson (2004) has focused on the use of laughter in a Swedish youth detention home.

CA has also been used to examine specific practice tools, including empathy (Wynn and Wynn, 2005), talk about feelings (Forsberg and Vagli, 2006), use of self-disclosure (Antaki, Barnes and Leudar, 2005), workers' management of their own moral evaluations (Kurri and Wahlström, 2005), helping clients to be self-directed (Vehviläinen, 2003), active listening, use of authority, managing emotions and so on. In all these studies, the attention to the detailed analysis of talk moves analysis past idealization and generalized theory on to the empirical examination of actual practices.

In recent years, social workers at the University of Tampere in the Department of Social Policy and Social Work, in Finland and at Huddersfield in the UK, have combined social work concerns with CA. Particularly noteworthy is their text *Constructing Clienthood in Social Work and Human Services* (2003). Throughout the text, detailed transcripts are examined to develop analyses of fundamental puzzles and problems in the delivery of child welfare. For example, in the book, Christopher Hall, Arja Jokinen and Eero Suoninen (2003) examine the tension between a social worker's attribution of inadequacy to a mother whose children are in care, and the mother's attempts to project personal moral integrity. Similarly, Stef Slembrouck and Christopher Hall (2003) examine parents' deployment of devices that 'make out' that they genuinely care for their children, but are unable to cope.

After more than 40 years since the inception of EM and CA, some social workers have begun to apply tools from these disciplines to analyse their practice (de Montigny, 2007). Any social worker can audio or video record his or her work and, by reading some excellent but simple primers on CA (Hutchby and Wooffitt, 1998; Psathas, 1995; Schegloff, 2007; ten Have, 1999), they can learn the basics of how to transcribe and analyse interviews. Indeed, for some years, I have had students complete conversation analysis assignments in my practices classes. Although there are predictable complaints about the amount of time it takes to do a proper transcription, students who work at the exercise and approach talk-in-interaction with a sense of curiosity find that they can begin not only to learn a great deal about the art of talk but also to grasp the essential reflexivity at the heart of practice. Students are able to make novel discoveries about the constituents of interaction and, hence, how turns in talk work, how a speaker signals readiness for another to take the next turn, how listeners use response tokens, such as uhms, yah, okay, mmhums, to shape a speaker's talk, how gaps, pauses and tone are used and so on.

If a student says to me, 'I recorded a chat with my friend', the questions I might pose are, 'What did you do interactively that made this occasion a "chat" rather than an interview, a debate, a lecture, a discussion, an appearance in court, and so forth?' and 'What can you see that helps you to understand how you and X went about doing "friendship"?' Such questions force an explication not only of familiar concepts but also of taken-for-granted practices.

For EM and CA, talk-in-interaction is not simply about words or about language. Rather, what is at issue is how people interactively accomplish sense and order. By making ordinary ways of working topical, the unnoticed becomes noticed and, in this way, social workers can only benefit.

Study questions

1. Locate a recently written account of a piece of work with a client, such as an assessment, a report or some paperwork. As you reflect on your interaction with the client and the written piece of work, can you identify slippage between what occurred and what came to be written? What did you include and what did you leave out? Who did you imagine or know would be reading your account and how did that shape your writing?

2. What background work, performed by others, was necessary for you to be able to enter your class and the classroom in social work? *Hint*: who is in the classroom with you? How did they get to be there? Whose work, and what work processes, preceded your entry to this class? What are the social relationships that are in place to allow this class to proceed?

3. Audio record talk at a supper table, or during a ride in a car with a friend, or when having a discussion with a partner. Transcribe about five minutes of it. What can you see in the details of the talk-in-interaction? How did you and the other person interact to produce a particular type of relationship? Can you identify instances where you let ambiguity pass or where you filled in an ad hoc or good enough understanding?

Glossary

Account, accounting Garfinkel's first degree in business accounting informed his interest in social 'accounting' practices and in the essential reflexivity of 'accounts'. Local practices are accountable as people accomplish the sensibility, good sense, haecceities or just 'thisness' of an occasion.

Ad hoc, ad hocing Means to rely on 'the infinite depth of detail' of interactive and organizational background features out of which a contingent, unfolding and good enough sense for practical purposes is accomplished.

Documentary method From Karl Mannheim (1952), but since transformed into a recognition that actors deploy a stock of at hand and taken-for-granted frameworks to take up particulars such that they become documents, or indicators, of the framework. A gestalt is derived from a pattern of occurrences and simultaneously discrete events become documents of the whole.

Indexical, indexicality Despite the problem of indexical expressions (pronouns such as he, she and it; deictic expressions – pointing words – here, this and there; Lynch, 1993), participants can and do make sense from each other's talk. Exploring how members resolve indexicality reveals 'ethno-methods' for sensemaking.

Reflexive, essential reflexivity The recognition that what is at hand, sensible and understood is as produced through practical activities. The essential reflexivity of practice unfolds the forms of order taken for granted in the world, such that ontology is as accomplished.

Sequence, turns In CA, sequence and turns are used to accomplish the order of social settings. Sense and coherence are achieved interactively.

Talk-in-interaction Talk is as accomplished in vivo, interactively, as a social engagement between participants. Talk-in-interaction attends to how these participants, here and now, produce the cogency, accountability and work of the occasion together.

Select bibliography

Besides Garfinkel (1967, 2002), Heritage (1984), Sacks (1995) and Silverman (1998), a good source is Schegloff (2007).

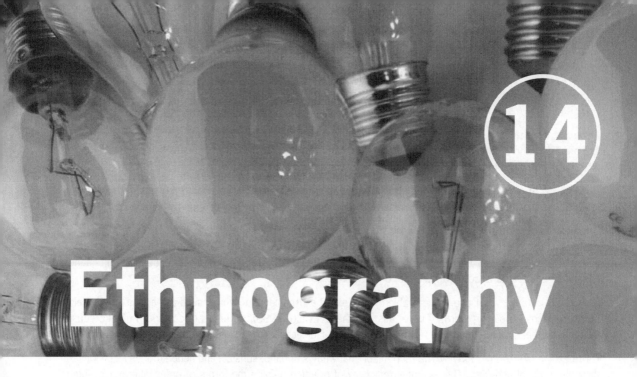

14

Ethnography

Jerry Floersch, Jeffrey L. Longhofer and Megan Nordquest Schwallie

Introducing ethnography

This chapter discusses how ethnography and social work practice share principles and methods. We broadly define ethnography first, describing its two primary features – holistic and inductive. Second, we compare ethnography with social work methods as it is argued that they have parallel traditions, both placing emphasis on the importance of context or environment. Third, illustrations of the use of ethnography to study social and mental health services are provided. Indeed, investigators from many disciplines have found ethnographic methods useful when studying topics of primary concern to social work. Fourth, we use an example of ethnographic research to demonstrate that practice research and sociohistorical research on social work can benefit from comparing social work's written narratives (such as case records and progress reports) with the in vivo work of oral narratives. Fifth, the inductive component of ethnography provides the opportunity to identify in social work the relationship between theory and practice, or what we call the phenomenological practice gap. Finally, we briefly discuss what it means when the social worker is ethnographer and practitioner, both the advantages and disadvantages.

Key ideas

Ethnography is an holistic and inductive method for studying people, places and processes (Creswell, 1994; Lincoln and Guba, 1985) which has a long history in the social sciences. It is most commonly associated with anthropology, but also has deep roots within sociology (Bernard, 2002).

About its *inductive* meaning, researchers 'do' ethnography in an attempt to capture, through description, experience and analysis, the bottom-up, lived experience of individuals (Agar, 1996; Burawoy, 1991; Hammerely and Atkinson, 1995). Inductive also means getting near the experience, as opposed to staying distant by seeing individuals through deductively derived (theoretical) categories.

The *holistic* component of ethnography is its focus on placing the inductively derived experience in the context of social and cultural phenomena.

Although participation and observation over time are the cornerstones of ethnographic research, ethnographers often draw from a deep toolbox of research strategies. These can include interviews, ranging from formal to informal, structured to unstructured; charts mapping community systems, such as kinship and/or hierarchy; survey-based research; the collection of life histories; the review of community texts and records; and the development of relationships with 'key informants' within a community. Similarly, ethnographers use multiple strategies for recording their data, including audio recording, filming, photography and, especially, copious field notes. Ethnographers combine the data gathered via these techniques with their direct observations to create an inductively derived, holistic representation of their objects of enquiry.

Indeed, a convenient way to think of this range of ethnographic strategies is to recognize that participant observation (a term often used interchangeably with the ethnographic method) means that the ethnographer might participate alongside an individual's everyday routines, while, at other times, only observe the routines. Many factors, practical and theoretical, determine why the ethnographer chooses some combination of participation and observation over another. However, whichever combination is applied, ethnography and participation observation mean (Bernard, 2002: 324):

> going out and staying out, learning a new language (or new dialect of a language you already know), and experiencing the lives of the people you are studying as much as you can. Participant observation is about stalking culture in the wild – establishing rapport and learning to act so that people go about their business as usual when you show up.

They are both (Bernard, 2002: 322):

> a humanistic method and a scientific one. It produces the kind of experiential knowledge that lets you talk convincingly, from the gut, about what it feels like to plan a garden in the high Andes or dance all night in a street rave in Seattle.

Application to social work practice

In several ways, the aims and methods of ethnography and social work are parallel. As a method, ethnography investigates how people live in their natural environment and the conditions and circumstances – both internal and external – that shape experience. This requires that the ethnographer goes to where the people live, purposively participating in and observing daily life in vivo or in open system.

Ethnographers strive to suspend moral judgments about the negative or positive aspects of experience. Instead, the aim is to examine local belief and practice as normative within a specific cultural context. Philippe Bourgois (2002), for example, shows how drug dealers functioned according to economic principles not unlike those governing formal economies.

When physical and mental health experience are the objects of enquiry, ethnographers seek to explain why one group or culture views behaviour as a disorder or disease (that is, a problem to be solved) while another experiences the same behaviour as conventional (Kleinman, 1988) or even normal (that is, as something to be understood, not solved). This approach resembles social work practice, which unfolds in open social systems, in the community, and with social workers' aims, which are to identify individual, group, family or community problems, solutions, needs and strengths. Social workers design interventions that help the client by starting with a careful analysis of where the client 'is', which means giving due regard to the client's views of the 'problem', the 'need' and the 'solution'. Indeed, the skills that produce good ethnography also produce good social workers: the ability to ask, observe, listen and even to participate in community life (Bohannan and Van der Elst, 1998). The practice of both ethnography and social work has been characterized as an art and the people practising as artisans. (For social work, see Unrau, Gabor, and Grinnell, 2007; for ethnography, see Bernard, 2002, and Wolcott, 2001.)

Even the criticisms of ethnography as a method or discourse and the practice model for social workers are similar. Social workers' active approach to problemsolving has sometimes been characterized as an attempt to police and regulate the poor, vulnerable and deviant (Margolin, 1997; Odem, 1995). In a similar way, ethnographers, particularly anthropologist ethnographers, have been criticized for 'otherizing' the 'natives' they describe or 'inventing' the culture of a group. Just as the objectivity–subjectivity debate has plagued the social work encounter, ethnographers have struggled with the issue of a personal voice in their accounts of fieldwork (Clifford and Marcus, 1986).

Ethnography and the human services

The use of ethnography to explore human services has provided fertile ground for interdisciplinary research among occupational therapists, anthropologists, nurses, sociologists, social workers and others in educational, medical and social service settings. The range of subjects for these investigations is broad, including child welfare (Aarre, 1998; de Montigny, 1995), homelessness (Connolly, 2000; Desjarlais, 1997; Wagner, 1993), drugs in the urban context (Bourgois, 2002), rural community life (Christensen, Hockey and James, 1998), individuals with disabilities (Davies, 1998), substance abuse (Alverson, Alverson and Drake, 2001), treatment for drug dependency (Carr, 2006; Skoll, 1992) and the effects of the policy of deinstitutionalization for those with chronic mental illness (Rhodes, 1991; Townsend, 1998; Weinberg, 2005).

Some researchers have concentrated their efforts on investigations of service provider perspectives and/or organizational cultures present in the human services (Baldwin, 1998; McCourt, 1998; Trevillion and Green, 1998; Warren, 1998). For example, anthropologist Tanya Luhrmann (2000) used ethnography to investigate the training of psychiatrists in the United States, analysing the dominance of biological explanations and cures for mental illness in mainstream psychiatry. Others have investigated the lived experience of clients and other vulnerable and disadvantaged populations. An example of this is Sue Estroff's classic (1981) ethnography of the lives of psychiatric clients enrolled in a program of assertive Community Treatment, which provides startling insight into 'living with' mental illness in the larger community. In a more recent study, Hoyt Alverson, Elizabeth Carpenter and Robert Drake (2006) have, similarly, used participant observation to explore jobseeking for people with severe mental illness. Similarily, through participant observation and in-depth semi-structured interviews, Tom Hall (2003) gives the reader the feeling that he or she is travelling through the daily lives of homeless adolescents in Britain.

Researchers have also used ethnography to develop meaningful, standardized measures in mental health services research. Norma Ware and colleagues (1999) used ethnography to investigate and define the common practice construct, the 'continuity of care'. Their work also highlighted the relationship ethnography can have with other methods, both qualitative and quantitative.

Ethnography (of both practices and institutions) is particularly useful in the study of human services because service provision is a process, occurring in open systems where circumstances, variables and experiences cannot be manipulated or controlled. Evaluations of service provision policies are particularly enlightening: how do policies actually play out in everyday practice settings? Ethnography can give voice to patient and provider perspectives by bringing us the local and experience-near conditions affecting service provision.

An ethnographic case study

Ethnographic methods might be used to evaluate social work by investigating differences between practitioner theory (that is, the conventional) and its application in practice (that is, the actual).

While written narratives, such as case notes, often reflect conventional institutional philosophies, oral narratives tend to be less restrained, revealing the creativity and flexibility regularly employed when providing services. Unfortunately, because many of the more intuitive aspects of helping in social work go undocumented, case records are often open to the criticism that they objectify the clients (Townsend, 1998). Case records have been viewed by many scholars as a mirror of what social workers 'do' to clients (Floersch, 2002).

Ethnographic methods can be used to overcome such difficulties by holistically investigating practice in context:

- its technical–rational or disciplinary knowledge – a prescribed theory dictating and defining normal, appropriate and successful management practices;
- its particular understandings of the client–consumer condition – situated knowledge or knowledge-in-action, which 'refers to the strategic, contextual, or practical' (Floersch, 2004a: 80).

Ethnography can thus illustrate how social workers perform different kinds of work, drawing on different types of knowledge.

Jerry Floersch (2002) observed and followed case managers providing social support services to individuals working with severely mentally ill clients. Within the institution, a 'strengths' model of case management was mandated and the majority of the managers observed had completed specialized training designed to 'assist people, who we will call consumers, to identify, secure, and sustain the range of resources, both internal and external, needed to live in a normally interdependent way in the community' (Floersch, 2000:173).

In the spirit of 'going native' (ethnographers immerse themselves in the community they are studying), Floersch attended trainings, learning the strengths lexicon for 'assisting people [the consumers] to get what they want' (Floersch, 2000: 173).

Having identified the key constructs of the dominant disciplinary, technical–rational knowledge used at the centre, Floersch collected both oral and written narratives of strengths case management events. In the context of both formal meetings with the team and staff psychiatrist and more informal hallway conversations and office chatter, the case managers used several routine phrases to describe their work with clients: 'doing for', 'doing with', 'gets it', 'high and low functioning', 'do him' and 'natural consequence'. Interestingly, none of these phrases correlated with the principles and language of the mandated strengths model. Instead, these situated diagnostic languages (examples of knowledge-in-action) evidenced a kind of intuitive, but nevertheless shared, measure of client progress. For example, in a team meeting, four case managers (abbreviated to CM1, CM2 and so on below) described their interaction with a client as follows (Floersch, 2002: 449):

CM1:   Did the cleaning crew get over there?
CM2:   No.
CM1:   They're supposed to go today.
CM3:   Who has got his daily med drop?
CM4:   I *do him* today at 1 p.m.
CM3:   OK, he's covered.
CM1:   What are we going to do about the damage to the bathroom ceiling?
CM2:   He's pretty good at repair work. Get him to do the research about the cost of the repairs.
CM1:   What happens if he doesn't do it?
CM2:   We can do it.
CM1:   No, we shouldn't.
CM1:   What about using the apartment maintenance workers?
CM2:   What if tomorrow I do a goal plan and fix the holes *with him?* I don't mind helping him. I like the idea that he would fix it himself. If he knows he has to pay for it, then maybe he will do it.

A conversation between two case managers about cleaning the apartment was observed a few days later (Floersch, 2002: 119):

> He amazes me how he doesn't catch that apartment on fire. I would like to see the cleaning crew go through it. I think we should give him the *natural consequences* about that because we co-subsidize the apartment.

In these oral narratives, the client was seen as a person with an illness and accompanying needs; the possibility of an irrational subject was acknowledged.

However, in the written narratives, the client was represented as a community member who possessed the 'strength' to be independent and even 'normal'. For instance, the medical chart listed the client's monthly goals as (Floersch, 2002: 113):

- 'I want to handle my money';
- 'I want to feel better emotionally';
- 'keep my apartment clean'.

The written narrative tended to confirm the policy of deinstitutionalization, reinforce the return of mentally ill patients to the community and the rational, strengths-based approach of assisting clients to get what they wanted.

In collecting these two forms of narrative of practice, ethnography allowed Floersch to see this example of strengths-based community mental health in context. In practice, things were not so clear-cut and the invented clinical language – or knowledge-in-action – of the oral narrative was needed to provide case managers with a medium through which they could discuss the difficulties of service provision that were not acknowledged by the strengths model of case management and the policy of deinstitutionalization. In short, studying case managers' fixed written narratives without also placing the oral narrative alongside them would have reified the practice model (that is, made it into something more real than it was.)

A more holistic and nuanced account of social work practice must therefore include practitioners' oral narratives and observations of in vivo practice events. Ethnography provides a vehicle for obtaining such accounts. Ethnographic investigations of this kind shed light on the openings that occur when 'theory fails to account for some part or all of the [practice] experience and where practice is open to influence outside of theory' (Longhofer and Floersch, 2004: 485). Jeffrey Longhofer and Jerry Floersch (2004) call these creative openings 'phenomenological practice gaps' and propose that studying such gaps provides insight into both the practical and intuitive knowledge base of practitioners and the limitations of leading theoretical perspectives and social policy.

Phenomenological practice gaps

Ethnography is especially suited to the study of open systems. What is meant by open systems? A good example of such a system is the human services sector.

Let us take the example of a young and single mother who enters a welfare office. Immediately she is confronted with a range of practices aimed at producing effects for her and her child. They may be aimed at income support, housing, education or employment or at supporting, promoting or regulating maternal and child health. This young mother, however, exists in an open system with many determinants, including race, class, kinship, gender, sexual orientation, neighborhoods, housing and educational opportunities. She has, as well, her own experience of these social forces and her own unique internalizations of these social worlds. Moreover, because the system is open, its qualities and characteristics cannot be stipulated in advance (a priori) – it can only be known as it unfolds through time (that is, with human agents and institutions in constant and dynamic interaction). Also, because the system is open, even from moment to moment or day to day, she and her child are constantly engaging these many and overlapping social forces, with one often cancelling out the effects of another, even during the course of a single day. Further, because she and her child are volitional, they may be engaging the system in such a way as to alter the very nature of the system and its determinants. Ethnography is a method that is suited to the production of knowledge in open systems such as the one in the example above. It is a method aimed at understanding dynamic interactions as they unfold through time. It is radically different from the experimental method, which operates in a closed system, where the variables can sometimes be controlled and manipulated.

Each practice the young mother encounters with her child has a stated aim or objective – most often mandated by regulatory and governmental agencies. As well, most practices are driven by theories or models (such as, strengths or empowerment). The distance one travels (the practitioner and the recipient of a practice) between the stated aim of a practice (a theory or model of practice) and the actual practice we have called a phenomenological practice gap.

We call it 'phenomenological' for several reasons. First, it is in the gap that everyday practices are lived. Second, every practice derives its meaning from related practices and resistances to them in unfolding webs through time. Third, we strive to understand the whole, not the part, and it is through understanding the relationships between the model and actual practices that this is accomplished.

Because practice unfolds in open systems, all models will, of necessity, produce gaps of varying dimensions with different consequences. Indeed, if there were no gaps, we would find ourselves in either artificially closed systems or situations where a practice is imposed without due consideration for the historical and cultural contingencies of human experience. Moreover, it is in these gaps where new knowledge can be generated and paradigm shifts are possible. It is also possible, however, that political and ideological commitments can close gaps where they should be maximally open.

We argue that ethnography is a method ideally suited to the study of the various conditions that produce, maintain and transform practice gaps. Indeed, using ethnographic methods, it is possible to discern the factors mediating the dynamic between model and practice, between the theory and realities of street-level practitioners and the recipients of their actions. Also, it is in the gap where street-level practitioner and the recipients of services push back against the model to open up a space for resistance, novel practice, transformative action and the emergence of new theory.

In conclusion, Russell Bernard (2002) summarized the central criticism of ethnography, noting that participant observation does not mean the ethnographer has a privileged standpoint that offers up a final or absolute understanding of the people studied. It is, therefore, important to comment here on the special meaning ethnographic research has for practising social workers, their agencies and the recipients of their services.

It is not uncommon to find social workers employed in agencies or settings where they also conduct research, thereby enjoying a unique kind of entrée and 'participation'. While in this duality of roles social workers may offer useful skills to institutional research, they may also produce potential conflicts. Bernard would call such social worker ethnographers 'observing participants' because they are employed as social workers (for an example, see Connolly, 2000). Unlike other observing participants, however (such as anthropologists trained as prison guards), social worker ethnographers may find themselves having to strictly monitor their observing so as not to violate the confidentiality of peers and clients (Bernard, 2002).

Floersch (2004a) noted that, in mental health research, clinician ethnographers have an insider position that enables access to actual practice because they are either licensed or have agency permission to be present during practice events. Indeed, the advantage of occupying practice and researcher roles is that it helps with the practical issues of ethnographic work, such as gaining trust, access and having insider knowledge of where to look and for what.

Does the combined role of social worker and ethnographer mean, however, that social worker ethnographers occupy a privileged 'insider' position with which practice can be authentically 'seen' or understood? They do not have the authentic view of social work, as opposed to the inauthentic view of non-practitioner researchers or social scientists. Practitioner researchers will always have biases and they should be reflexive about their findings, never assuming that practitioners will necessarily be better positioned to understand practice than non-practitioners.

Study questions

1. Imagine and then discuss examples of social work practice where the inductive method of gathering information is common. What aspects of the ethnographic method make it particularly well suited to the study of human services? Describe social work settings where you think ethnography would help in understanding human behaviour in context.
2. Think about your own practice experiences. Are there particular circumstances where textbook theory and prescriptions for practice are ill-equipped? If one were to conduct an ethnography of your field setting, what kinds of invented, situated knowledge might be revealed?
3. How might the skills you have attained as a social worker help as an ethnographer? Similarly, are there ways in which ethnographic technique might inform clinical or social work practice?

Glossary

Holistic In social work, this usually means viewing the person-in-environment, that is, seeing the internal (mind) and external (environment, culture and society) worlds simultaneously.

Inductive For social work, this means starting 'where the client is'. Ethnography is inductive by collecting real-time data by seeing, observing and asking about individual experiences (in historic and cultural time). Both traditions assume that a deductively derived theory cannot fully explain or describe a specific reality. Both traditions assume that deductively derived theories capture bottom-up experience, so, instead, ethnographers and social workers want their theories to be built from the ground up – they want the theory to be near the experience. Social work assumes that this method will help keep practitioners ethical because it is committed to empowering clients rather than using deductive theory to exert power over clients.

Knowledge-in-action Refers to the strategic, contextual or intuitive theories of social workers; knowledge that is derived from particular practice events or activities.

Objectivity and subjectivity The uncertain separation between one's personal observation and perception of external 'fact' and one's internal state, including thoughts, feelings, interpretations and cultural beliefs.

Open system Referencing the multiple determinants that may or may not affect processes as they occur in the natural environment and everyday life. Such systems can be contrasted with the closed systems of the laboratory.

Participant observation A research strategy involving active observation of and involvement in the lives of the people one is studying, the purpose being to gain direct experience of everyday life and culture as it occurs in a natural context. A cornerstone of participant observation is meeting people where they function regularly, meaning researchers go to the people or place they are studying.

Technical–rational knowledge A prescribed theory dictating and defining normal, appropriate and successful social work practice, which is usually produced in a 'scientific' milieu.

Select bibliography

Hammersley and Atkinson's (1995) and Agar's (1996) offer introductory books. Foote Whyte's *Street Corner Society* (1943) offers a glimpse into the ways ethnography has been used by urban sociologists and anthropologists as well as an engaging example of how ethnographic research can be presented.
Particularly useful when thinking about cultural competency in social work, Bohanan and Van der Elst's (1998) introduction demonstrates that ethnography requires asking and listening skills that assist in placing individuals in a cultural context.
Of interest to social workers are several recent investigations of social services (Edgar and Russell, 1998) and the intersection of psychiatry, social work and anthropology (Connolly, 2000; Estroff, 1981; Floersch, 2002; Hall, 2003; Lurhmann, 2000; Rhodes, 1991).

Discourse Analysis and Reflexivity ⑮

Sue White

Introducing discourse analysis and reflexivity

The social workings of social work depend on language and language in its everyday use is the concern of discourse analysts. Language is used by service users to tell their story and by social workers and other professionals to retell that story.

Language is not *everything*, though, and, at the extremes of emotion or circumstance, it often fails adequately to capture experience. Ludwig Wittgenstein (1961: 115) may have slightly overstated the case with his assertion that 'the limits of my language mean the limits of my world', but words undoubtedly *matter*, as do the order and manner of their delivery and the ways in which they are heard and interpreted. Yet, often this rich cultural resource is rendered immune from systematic analysis simply because it is so 'ordinary'.

In this chapter, I give a flavour of the debates in the eclectic field of discourse analysis (DA) and argue that the concepts and methods associated with the analysis of 'talk and text' can usefully be taught to social workers so that they may become reflexive analysts of their own affairs.

What the terms discourse analysis and reflexivity mean

DA involves the analysis of selected extracts of 'talk' or 'text' – that is, extracts of recorded or written words. These can be analysed in a number of ways. We can attend to the content and organization of communication or talk or we can seek to identify in this talk dominant and taken-for-granted ideas about particular phenomena, such as childhood, gender, race, the family or mental health, and how these reflect particular historical, political and/or moral positions. I shall describe in detail the debates between these approaches in due course.

Like 'discourse', the meaning of the term 'reflexivity' in the social sciences is contested (Lynch, 2000a: 26):

> Reflexivity is a well-established theoretical and methodological concept in the human sciences, and yet it is used in a confusing variety of ways. The meaning of `reflexivity' and the virtues ascribed to the concept are relative to particular theoretical and methodological commitments.

It is sometimes taken to have the same meaning as 'reflection' and, indeed, it has the same Latin root, *reflectere* – to bend back. As Michael Lynch notes above, there are many different definitions of reflexivity in the social sciences and, for him, we are all always and already reflexive. In this respect reflexivity refers to our intrinsic capacity to attend to what we are saying and doing in everyday situations – as evidenced, for example, in a preference for self-correction when we stumble over a word in conversation (Schegloff, Jefferson and Sacks, 1977).

Within social work, reflexivity is often conflated with reflective practice (see White, Fook and Gardner, 2006), which, at its simplest, means thinking about what we are doing and why. The concept of reflexivity I shall use here (after Taylor and White, 2000) adds substantially to reflective practice as it is conventionally conceived in social work (for a critique of conventional approaches, see Ixer, 1999; Taylor, 2006). The 'bending back' that the root of the word 'reflexivity' implies requires a sociocultural analysis of the kinds of ideas in which practice is embedded. So, what counts as 'knowledge' becomes a topic worthy of scrutiny in its own right.

Here, as we shall see below, DA can help by slowing down the action so we can reflect systematically and empirically on the language we use and which words and phrases assume power. In this way, we can start to understand the kinds of ideas that seem to carry currency and how practitioners deploy them in making sense of cases.

Key ideas

Being concerned with everyday language in use, DA often has a 'performative' orientation – a view that people 'do things' with their language; that talk *is* social action (Austin, 1962). A core idea is that speaking, listening, reading and writing are crucial aspects of the way in which we communicate and, through these micro practices, we construct our personal and social worlds. Yet, as I mentioned earlier, there is a sense in which the field of discourse studies is a site for disciplinary struggles (Slembrouck, 2006: unpaginated):

> [The] 'lender disciplines' [of discourse analysis] are to be found within various corners of the human and social sciences, with complex historical affiliations and a lot of cross-fertilization taking place. However, this complexity and mutual influencing should not be mistaken for 'compatibility' between the various traditions. Nor is compatibility necessarily a desirable aim, as much is to be gained from the exploration of problematical and critical edges and from making the most of theoretical tensions.

While DA is an empirical field that often involves the detailed analysis of extracts of 'talk', most texts on the subject devote copious pages to what can appear to be rather arid theoretical debates. It is worth considering why this may be. A single extract of talk can be analysed in a number of different ways. A core tension saturates the field, as Erickson (2004: viii, emphasis added) notes:

> The conduct of talk in local social interaction as it occurs in real time is unique, crafted by the actors for the specific situation of its use in the moment of its uttering, *and* the conduct of talk in local social interaction is profoundly influenced by processes that occur beyond the temporal and spatial horizon of the immediate occasion of interaction.

There is little doubt that both these statements are true. Frederick Erickson (2004) likens face-to-face encounters to the experience of climbing a tree that is simultaneously climbing you! They involve a complex reading of signals and cues and the operation of turn-taking rules that are often noticeable to us only when the rules are broken (Sacks, Schegloff and Jefferson, 1974), as well as the artful selection of powerful words and phrases to get us what we want!

In this situated, local context, talk can go in many different ways. In other words, it is not predetermined in any straightforward manner. Yet, neither do actors invent the world anew in each encounter (see Fairclough, 2005).

So, there are ongoing internal debates about the relative importance of analysing talk-in-interaction as against identifying dominant ideas in wider cultural circulation.

Analysing Discourse and discourse

I have noted that DA can be focused on the evolving talk-in-interaction (discourse) or on identifying historically situated, dominant ideas (Discourse). The use of upper and lower case for the terms in the heading above is intended to differentiate between 'discourse' as talk in action and 'Discourse' as a way of thinking or a body of knowledge (Gee, 1990; Walker, in Woolgar, 1988; see also Wetherell, 1998).

The macro reading of Discourse is related to Marx's concept of ideology. For example, Teri Walker (in Woolgar, 1988: 55) contends that Discourses (forms of thought and knowledge – for example, theories or political ideas) are reproduced within discourse (talk) at 'the point of its articulation'. Therefore, when analysing any conversation (discourse), it should be possible to look for Discourse(s) *and* examine how words are assembled and used (Miller, 1994).

Application to social work practice

There have been numerous attempts to portray the form and organization of social work and social work agencies as microcosms of particular types of society transmitted through Discourses. These shifts have variously been called 'postmodern' (McBeath and Webb, 1991; Parton, 1994a, 1994b), 'risk' (Parton, 1996; Webb, 2006) and 'information' (Parton, 2008) societies.

These analyses draw, in varying degrees, on poststructuralist ideas associated with Michel Foucault and others (as discussed elsewhere, such as in Chapter 4). Such analyses are usually very elegant, but, within these top-down frameworks, social workers can potentially be represented as the hapless victims of an unprecedented rate of social, or *Discursive*, change.

The inference that things happening at the level of individuals, families and groups can be properly explained by analysing changes in society itself is known as *downward reductionism*, which 'rests on the a priori assumption that the lower levels of analysis point to phenomena, which have no dynamics of their own, and can therefore be entirely explained in terms of regularities grasped at higher levels' (Mouzelis, 1991: 138). Thus, the identification of 'society' as the causal agent tends to ascribe a uniformity and predetermined quality to social workers' actions. They have very little 'wiggle room' (Erickson, 2004: 20). It is worth examining an early Foucauldian study in some detail to illustrate this point.

Notes on the 'form of knowledge'

Mark Philp (1979: 84) notes:

> [B]eneath the apparent freedom in social work there is a form, an underlying constitution to everything that is said. This form creates both the possibility of a certain form of knowledge for social work and also limits social workers to it.

Working from the above premise, Philp's influential (1979) paper advances a Foucauldian analysis of a specific 'form of knowledge' in social work. His analysis remains important and relevant because he identifies the relationship between social work and social science and suggests that the concepts of social science leak into social work but then take on a different form.

According to Philp, social workers eschew those parts of social scientific thought that attribute causation to factors *permanently* outside of individual control. Remedial work must be seen to be achievable through the ministering of the social worker – that is to say, the social worker routinely 'speaks for' clients, whatever their misdemeanours, by invoking their essential subjectivity, except in those situations where the actions or characteristics of individuals have somehow served to eradicate their very humanity.

The strengths and weaknesses of Philp's analysis represent two sides of the same coin. He places what is essentially a realist and humanist social work Discourse within its historical location and maps its boundaries with other Discourses. However, in so doing, he gives it 'a totalizing hegemony' (Law, 1994: 22) which is not adequate to explain the living contingencies of organizational life. For example, it 'can be argued that the social worker, like the doctor, the lawyer, the policeman, judge and psychiatrist, operates *in the control of discourse'* (Philp, 1979: 90, emphasis added).

Recently, Nigel Parton (2008) has returned to Philp's analysis to argue that, driven by rapid technological changes, social work has moved away from a social or relational to an informational modus operandi.

While their work is powerfully argued, neither Philp nor Parton undertakes a detailed analysis of ordinary talk and, as a result, inevitably glosses over some of the contradictions and resistances in social workers' talk. As Erickson (2004: 144) reminds us, 'no matter how totalizing, or sacralizing the institutional setting within which face-to-face interaction occurs, there is always room for secondary adjustments through mutterings, grumblings and snickerings and their written equivalents in graffiti'. Fundamentally, these contributions, while having due regard for the 'linguistic turn' in philosophy and social theory (and, hence, for social actors as vehicles for the reproduction of vocabularies), retain a degree of structural determinism.

So, what happens if we concentrate on discourses with a little 'd', as they are produced in everyday talk?

Rediscovering the 'actor': ethnomethodology and conversation analysis in social work

As outlined in Chapter 13, in his seminal works, Harold Garfinkel (in, for example, 1967) argued that traditional sociology paid insufficient attention to the social actor as free, purposeful and reasoning and able to order the world through the continual reaccomplishment of intersubjective understandings. The central assertion of Garfinkel's ethnomethodology is that members of society are equipped for practical reasoning, apparently qua members of society.

This signalled a break from structuralism and Parsonian functionalism. Garfinkel took the question 'how do subjects render their situations knowable?' and made it his problematic.

Conversation analysis (CA) grew from ethnomethodology's focus on the detail of what people actually do. The recognition that language was more than description and it was minutely sequentially organized to do complex social work led to a search for empirical methods to record and analyse talk. CA attends, inter alia, to the turns people take, the pauses in their talk and the ways new topics are introduced (see Sacks et al., 1974). CA uses detailed transcripts to represent as much of the real-time talk as possible, often using unconventional spellings to indicate regional accent. It records pauses, laughs, coughs, out breaths and non-lexical vocalizations (such as 'erm' or 'ahh') (see Hutchby and Wooffitt, 1998; West, 1996).

Its methods have facilitated the detailed analysis of particular types of encounters and been influential in DA. This has not always occurred without controversy, however – some of the fiercest methodological debates have taken place between conversation analysts and the wider discourse analytic academy.

Some exponents of CA argue that *all* 'order' must be produced anew *within* each encounter; if we cannot see it, observe it, and capture it in a transcript, it is simply, for all practical purposes, irrelevant. Claims such as this led to high-profile published disagreements in the late 1990s between Emanuel Schegloff, one of the founders of CA, and the psychologists Michael

Billig and Margaret Wetherell, who were interested in the analysis of discourse as a remedy for perceived individualistic, asocial deficiencies in cognitive psychology.

Schegloff (1997) took issue with some of the critical branches of DA, which, he argued, were in danger of imposing interpretations on the interaction by imposing analysts' categories at the expense of those of the 'members' (participants themselves). Thus, the analytic category 'gender' may impose meaning on an encounter that didn't exist for the participants. An analyst may be prone to overinterpret an interruption by a man of a woman's turn of talk, failing to recognize that overlapping turns are part of the sequential flow and unfolding of ordinary talk.

In response, Billig (1999a, 1999b) advanced an argument that stressed the intrinsically argumentative and rhetorical nature of everyday talk. Wetherell (1998) acknowledged the potential for analysts' categories to distort meaning, but argued that it was, nevertheless, necessary to consider the invocation by members of available repertoires derived from wider Discourses. Others have argued that the 'unsaid', or the 'could have been said if circumstances had been different', may sometimes be extremely significant (McHoul, 1994), reflecting, as the ethnomethodologists would accept, different dominant contextual expectations (or 'background expectancies') and wider Discourses (contemporary morality and dominant knowledges, or sets of ideas that originate outside the encounter; Jayyusi, 1991).

Thus, it is often argued that CA is strong on the analysis of talk in sequence, but weak on the critical analysis of the power of certain phrases or forms of thought that predate the encounter, as Pierre Bourdieu (1977: 81; see also Chapter 3) argues: '"interpersonal" relations are never, except in appearance, *individual to individual* relationships and ... the truth of the interaction is never entirely contained in the interaction'. CA's response to these alleged deficiencies has been largely shored up by (somewhat proprietorial) claims about the superiority and rigour of its methods and its focus on fine-grained analysis of turn-taking in talk-in-interaction (see Wooffitt, 2005: 159–85).

I have considerable sympathy for this methodological commitment on the grounds that I do not see social actors (or, for our purposes here, social workers) as trapped in an iron cage of Discourse. Yet, I am also persuaded by the arguments that we should be able to see, in the detail of what people actually say and do, what sorts of words and phrases appear to have an impact on the talk-in-interaction – what phrases *do* the social *work* in social work.

I concur with Robin Wooffitt (2005: 210) when he praises CA's capacity to 'offer an analysis of power relations, built upwards from real events, rather than an account deduced from theoretical arguments'. There are a number of studies, my own among them (such as White, 1998, 2002, 2003; see also Hall, 1997; Hall, Slembrouck and Sarangi, 2006), that make use of analytic devices derived from CA to examine the artfulness of social workers' talk and their use of storytelling and various forms of categorization to accomplish the 'social sorting' (see Bowker and Star, 2000) that is arguably their business. Crucially, these studies show how interactions between social workers and other professionals or social workers and clients involve moral work (see Taylor and White, 2000). Depictions and accusations, blameworthiness and creditworthiness are made and managed in everyday encounters. The same is true of the notions of risk so central to the working of contemporary social work. It will be helpful to illustrate this point with some data.

Practising discourse analysis: the pornographic videos

The following brief exchange is taken from a transcript of a weekly social work allocation meeting in which new cases were assigned to social workers in a children and families team in the UK in the late 1990s. The speakers, who have been made anonymous, are the team leader (TL), family resource worker (FRW) and two social workers (SW1 and SW2). The transcript makes some use of notations adapted from CA (see end of chapter for a key to their meanings).

Extract 1

TL: Right, moving on to pornographic videos, it makes a nice change, they are a family called (0.3) Thornton

FRW: Oh I don't know those .h.h((laughs)).

SW2: No I think you do know about pornographic videos and are pretending you *don't* h.h ((laughs))

TL: Right, basically the long and short of it is the obscene publication police- There's a nine- and a seven-year-old child in the family, obscene publications were given a tip that this man, the children's father, is distributing naughty videos. What is worrying is that when they went to the house and looked at the videos they were all stored along with the Postman Pats [children's TV series], which is worrying. They are in with the children's family videos, which is very worryi=

SW2: =They were in the lounge or?

TL: Yes in a box easily accessible with a number of catalogues containing sexually explicit pictures (0.7) erm you don't really need to know but they were nasty videos <right> Erm he's going to be formally interviewed and probably charged with it, but *he* said the children don't use the video recorder. The officer said that basically there was nothing to stop them and I don't know many nine-year-olds who don't switch on their family video I mean perso[nally= you what?]

SW2: [They know how to] work things better than us

TL: Well exactly. I just spoke with Peter Hampshire [sergeant, police child protection team] and they don't actually think there's a terrific lot to be gained from going in with a child *protection*, but what we need to do is ensure that this family *know* that this is obviously totally inappropriate very worrying and we will have to ring the children's school to check that they haven't got any concerns about the children ...

SW1: =Don't we need to check with them first, seek their permission?

TL: I don't know, it's a grey area really.

SW1: I mean when you said we're not saying you've hit your child. We're saying it's inappropriate to make videos available and I was saying it is a child protection issue

TL: =YES

SW1: = so therefore I think we should make some enquiries *beforehand*

TL: OK yeah, that's fine OK. I'm just desperately trying to work positively these days at the moment, that's fine.

SW1: I mean if the school said the children had sexualized behaviour we'd be thinking ooooh, do you know what I mean?

TL: Yeah, I mean it's too late to ask parents' permission and if they complain, well=

SW1: =I mean there's a police investigation

TL: Yeah that's fine, just check school and NSP[CC].

The transcript comprises a number of carefully constructed case narratives, delivered in such a way that 'concern' and 'worry' – about child welfare – are powerfully conveyed. These are potent identity claims in childcare social work and essential invocations for the team leader who is seeking to persuade a social worker to take the case. There are four utterances by the team leader of the words 'worry' or 'worrying' in this short extract. The stories are routinely interspersed with humour and semi-humorous (such as sarcastic) banter that could appear rather inappropriate in other circumstances. In the extract below, we can see an example of this (emphasis added):

TL: Right, moving on to pornographic videos, *it makes a nice change*, they are a family called (0.3) Thornton
FRW: *Oh I don't know those* .h.h((laughs)).
SW2:   *No I think you do know about pornographic videos and are pretending you don't* h.h((laughs))

Such humorous interludes are not only a routine feature of case talk in meetings but also form part of office chatter in social work generally. Cases with a sexual component are a routine matter for childcare social workers and here joking appears to facilitate the display of professional 'savvy' in relation to such cases.

There are numerous markers of deviance and opprobrium used by different speakers. For example:

We're saying it's inappropriate to make videos available and I was saying it is a child protection issue

Canny 'pull the other one' scepticism is displayed in that the parental account is quickly discredited by a commonsense proposition delivered in an ironic tone:

TL: … I don't know many nine-year-olds who don't switch on their family video I mean perso[nally= you what?]
SW1:   [They know how to] work things better than us

The specifically moral nature of social services' role (as distinct from that of the police) is defined as follows:

… what we need to do is ensure that this family *know* that this is obviously totally inappropriate and very worrying ….

For most of this exchange, the members can be seen to narrate the case together, each reinforcing the 'concern' and 'worry' of the other. However, in the extract below, one of the social workers opposes the team leader's assertion that, as the children have not been 'hit', this is not a child protection investigation *as such*. In drawing on *competing* maxims of everyday professional judgement in order to make their account persuasive, the team leader and social worker position themselves on the 'commonsense dilemmatic' (Billig et al., 1988), underscoring the argumentative and contested nature of mundane reasoning:

SW1:   I mean when you said we're not saying you've hit your child. We're saying it's inappropriate to make videos available and I was saying it is a child protection issue
TL: =YES

SW1:   = so therefore I think we should make some enquiries *beforehand*

TL: OK yeah, that's fine OK. I'm just desperately trying to work positively these days at the moment, that's fine.

The social worker's utterance is powerful and is readily accepted by the team leader whose statement about trying to 'work positively these days' is a reference to the 'refocusing debate', that was at its height when New Labour came into power in 1997. This was essentially concerned with trying to 'rebalance' the relationship between child protection and family support and work in stronger partnerships with parents. The team leader's statement 'OK yeah, that's fine OK. I'm just desperately trying to work positively these days at the moment, that's fine' can be read as a self-exonerative statement in response to the gentle rebuke from the social worker. The team leader makes reference to the imperative to 'work positively' in order to justify what appears to be a minor breach of the commonsense, culturally shared commitment to protecting children, which, in this case, involves seeking information from the school without parental consent.

Andrew Pithouse and Paul Atkinson (1988) use the term 'ethnopoetics' to depict social workers' case talk as skilful oratory and recital, accomplished in the moment-by-moment unfolding interaction that is, as mentioned, the analytic orientation of CA. Yet, we can see that the poetics draw on more widely circulating cultural phenomena, such as those derived from the contemporary policy debates, as well as ideas about what is normal and deviant, appropriate and inappropriate, and what 'damages' children. Clearly, all these potential relevancies must be made relevant again in *this* encounter, by *these* actors, but their status as *candidate* topics predates this meeting. It is because cultures can act as sustaining media for routinized action that the concept of 'reflexivity' is important, which brings me to the final section of this chapter.

Practising reflexivity

I noted, at the beginning of this chapter, that, for some commentators, reflexivity is 'an ordinary, unremarkable and unavoidable feature of [any social] action' (Lynch, 2000a: 26; see also Chapter 13). Clearly, this is so – for example, we all self-consciously reflect on our performance in meetings. However, there are aspects of our social life that become so routinized that we don't see them. Vocabularies are hedged in by cultural practices and sometimes we need help to shake language up a little. DA can do just this as it provides devices to analyse talk as text and look at how persuasive accounts are assembled and ambiguous signs, symptoms and competing accounts are interpreted and transformed in professionals' talk. These kinds of studies can assist in the processes of critical reflection and reflexivity in professional practice as part of professional education, supervision and development (see Taylor and White, 2000; White, 2006; White and Stancombe, 2003).

The production of audio and video recordings and verbatim transcripts of talk in various settings has the effect of slowing down the action and makes it possible for practitioners to make audible or visible phenomena that would not be available to us in real-time analyses.

Professional reflexivity requires that practitioners begin listening to themselves more carefully, attending to their rhetoric of persuasion and their own constituting practices – that is, listening with a critical ear to their sense- and knowledgemaking practices. If we are to develop the capacity of practitioners to evaluate whether or not they want to make changes to tacit aspects of their practice, we need techniques to help them make what is familiar strange. The analysis of talk and text can assist practitioners in the important business of being serious and playful at the same time so that they can rediscover the freedom of 'not knowing'

Study questions

1. Make a short audio recording of a professional discussion about a case. Students might consider recording themselves and their colleagues discussing a case study. The following are some suggestions for analysing transcripts.

   - What aspects of the case are constructed as 'fact'? Look for phrases such as 'it is', 'he confirmed'.
   - What aspects of the case are constructed as questionable? Look for phrases such as 'we think' and reported speech, such as 'they claimed' and 'they maintained'.
   - Try to generate alternative readings of the case.
   - Can you find instances of moral judgement?
   - Do the individuals concerned 'show their working' or is the judgement taken for granted?

2. Think about the stories you and your colleagues share about other professionals and the way they work. You could make an audio recording of a team meeting where these issues are discussed. What do these stories convey about the contribution you and you colleagues make to practice? Pay attention to the use of humour. What work is it doing? Students might think about the tales they tell each other about lecturing staff or pay particular attention to gossip in the group. What does it say about taken-for-granted norms and ideas?

3. Documents carry cultural assumptions and dominant vocabularies through time and space. Examine one of your recently completed sets of case notes, day-to-day records or completed forms. Look at how you have constructed 'facts' – that is, presented certainties. Who are the heroes, heroines and villains in your version of events? From what you remember, what is obscured in your record? What lines of enquiry are left unexplored? Students might think about their essays. Were there any arguments you avoided because your lecturer might disapprove? Did you provide arguments for which you felt little need to supply supporting evidence? An example I often encounter when teaching social workers is that they will criticize the 'medical model' without offering any supporting arguments. What does this say about the dominance of certain ideas within social work?

Glossary

Conversation analysis The analysis of detailed transcripts noting the sequential features of talk, such as the turns people take, the pauses, how topics are introduced and so forth.

Discourse Discourse with a capital 'D' refers to ways of thinking or bodies of knowledge about particular phenomena, such as gender, race, the family or mental health, and how they reflect particular historical, political or moral positions. Discourse with a lower-case 'd' refers to language used in talk or text, such as case notes or agency reports.

Discourse analysis A collection of research methods and analytical tools from diverse theoretical and disciplinary traditions that have a preference for 'naturally occurring' data, which are usually captured on audio recordings and transcribed using coding devices to retain as much detail as possible. Most important is the context in which the talk takes place or the audience for whom the accounts were written.

Foucauldian discourse analysis From the work of Michel Foucault, this is concerned with how ideas come to affect the way in which we see and understand phenomena. It focuses on 'knowledges' or 'discourses' (see above) about particular phenomena and how these reflect particular historical, political or moral positions.

Hegemonic discourse 'Hegemony' derives from the Ancient Greek, *hegeisthai* (to lead) and, with its adjective 'hegemonic', has been appropriated by social scientists, associated particularly with Antonio Gramsci. Hegemonic discourses are ideas and words propagated through institutions and processes that serve the interests of dominant groups.

Rhetoric and rhetorical Refers to powerful words and phrases deployed in talk and text.

Tacit knowledge Michael Polanyi's (1967) term for taken-for-granted knowledge. Tacit knowledge allows us to perform certain activities without consciously thinking about them.

Select bibliography

The commendable website http://bank.ugent.be/da/da.htm charts the multifarious genealogies of various branches of discourse analysis (Slembrouck, 2006). See also Taylor and White (2000) for exercises to practise reflexivity, White and Stancombe (2003), White (2006) and Wooffitt (2005).

Transcription symbols

[ ]	overlapping talk
( )	inaudible and, hence, untranscribed passage
(talk)	uncertainty about the transcription
((laughs))	contextual information not transcribed as actual sounds heard
(0.8)	pauses timed in tenths of second
(.)	audible, but very short pause
talk or talk	italics or underlining indicate emphasis
tal-	abrupt end to utterance
<slow>	noticeable slowing of tempo of talk
=	latching of utterances
.h	laughter (or, without a full-stop, an outbreath).

Evidence-based Practice

16

Debbie Plath

Introducing evidence-based practice

Pressure within health and social services to provide evidence that demonstrates the effectiveness of interventions has led to the adoption of evidence-based practice approaches in a range of disciplines, including social work. Informed by several theoretical perspectives, some of which are considered in this chapter, evidence-based practice has been supported, resisted and debated in social work. First, however, the nature, assumptions and principles associated with evidence-based practice are presented, along with some of the debates surrounding its application to social work.

Key ideas

With its origins in medicine, evidence-based practice has been defined as, 'the conscientious, explicit and judicious use of current best evidence in making decisions' (Sackett et al., 1997: 71). From a social work perspective it (Macdonald, 2001: xviii)

> indicates an approach to decision-making which is transparent, accountable and based on the careful consideration of the most compelling evidence we have about the effects of particular interventions on the welfare of individuals, groups and communities.

Arguments in favour of adopting an evidence-based approach in social work include an ethical responsibility to provide the most beneficial services to clients (Ainsworth and Hansen, 2005; Cheetham, 1992; Macdonald, 2001; Sheldon, 1986), enhancing the credibility of the profession (Cheetham, 1992; Gambrill, 1999; Gibbs and Gambrill, 2002; Macdonald, 2001; Macdonald and Sheldon, 1992; Sheldon, 1986; Witkin, 1991, 1996), increasing the body of practical, reliable information on interventions (Hausman, 2002; Newman, 2002; Newman and McNeish, 2005), promoting a critical approach to practice (Bilsker and Goldner, 2000; Macdonald, 2001) and supporting the development of a research culture (Cheetham, 1992, 1997; Mullen, 2002; Webb, 2002).

These arguments present evidence-based practice as an appealing prospect for advancing the quality, outcomes and status of social work. It is, however, interpreted in a range of different ways in social work (Dore, 2006; Gambrill, 2006; Rubin and Parrish, 2007; Smith, 2004a). Issues of contention arise when the assumptions and principles of evidence-based practice are examined from different theoretical perspectives.

Effectiveness research in social work

While the language of evidence has made an impact on social work only over the past decade, the issues and debates surrounding the demonstration of effectiveness are not new. Jill Gibbons (2001) traces the history of effectiveness research in social work back to the 1890s. Attention was focused on effectiveness research when Joel Fischer (1973) noted the paucity of research demonstrating that casework interventions had any positive effects for clients. These findings triggered ongoing division and debate between those advocating a rigorous application of experimental research designs and proponents of qualitative or interpretive evaluation of the nature and impact of social work (Cheetham 1992, 1997; Gibbons, 2001; Reid, 2001; Sheldon, 1986; Witkin, 1991). The evidence-based practice movement, however, has moved debates beyond evaluation and out of the academic realm into the practice arena, where social workers are expected by management and funding bodies to provide evidence demonstrating the effectiveness of their practice.

Domains of evidence-based practice

Evidence-based practice has been embraced not only as a basis for clinical decisionmaking but also as a model for organizational policymaking and community intervention. While many assume that clinical practitioners gather and critically review evidence in their daily decisionmaking, the application of evidence is also relevant at the organizational level (Gueron, 2007; Ohmer and Korr, 2006).

The growing interest in evidence-based decisionmaking by policymakers, managers and funding providers is reflected in recent work by Ray Pawson (2006), new journals such as *Evidence and Policy* and online resources such as *Evidence Network*. Indeed, funding bodies and policymakers are expected to make decisions about service implementation on the basis of evidence about the effectiveness of interventions in addressing social issues.

An evidence-based approach to policymaking thus has the potential to take decisions away from frontline practitioners, who become the implementers of 'evidence-based policies and practices' rather than critical appraisers of evidence in making decisions about appropriate practice responses. Edward Mullen et al. (2007) distinguish between top-down (organizational) and bottom-up (individual) approaches to evidence-based practice, showing that it impacts upon social workers engaged at all levels of intervention, including policy, management, community and clinical practice.

Assumptions and principles

The basic tenet of evidence-based practice is that social workers and policymakers use *evidence* regarding the *effectiveness* of *interventions* to inform practice. Presented below are some of the assumptions and principles that guide evidence-based practice.

Assumption 1:	*Evidence can be found to inform practice*
Principle 1:	Find the evidence
Assumption 2:	*Certain evidence is stronger or better than other evidence*
Principle 2:	Critically appraise the evidence
Assumption 3:	*Effectiveness of interventions can be established*
Principle 3:	Identify the most effective intervention
Assumption 4:	*Interventions can be replicated*
Principle 4:	Implement the most effective intervention

These assumptions and principles have been scrutinized and debated in social work to such an extent that implementing evidence-based practice is complex, contested and open to interpretation, as the following analysis shows.

Assumption 1: Evidence can be found to inform practice

Evidence-based practice has prompted the development of a number of organizations devoted to locating, reviewing and disseminating research findings to inform practice. The resources for identifying evidence for practice, along with the relative ease with which evidence can be disseminated to practitioners via the Internet, has facilitated access to research evidence via online databases where practitioners can locate systematic reviews of research relevant to their practice. The resources to conduct, then review and disseminate research are much less readily available.

Good-quality research is costly, time-consuming and resource-intensive, as is the process of reviewing and disseminating current, comprehensive and useful research. Contexts, issues and interventions in social work are dynamic and so keeping up to date with new research in the face of limited resources leads to delays in making research findings available to practitioners (Warburton and Black, 2002). Further, given the enormous variation in social work interventions, contexts and client groups, it is unrealistic to expect that relevant evidence will be available and, even when research findings are available, they might not apply to the diverse practice contexts encountered by social workers. The availability of relevant research studies is limited and there is a need more and better-quality social work research (Cheetham 1992, 1997; Gibbs and Gambrill, 2002; Gilgun, 2005; Macdonald and Sheldon, 1992; Mullen et al., 2005; Scott, 2002; Shaw, 2003; Sheldon, 1986). While certain types of practice may become well researched and abundant evidence made available, this will not be the case for new and innovative practices or the types of interventions that respond in multidimensional ways to emergent issues in practice.

Alongside efforts to increase investment in high-quality research, there needs to be acceptance that evidence for practice will not be full and complete. The lack of evidence for a particular practice may not be due to the inadequacy of the practice, but resulting from insufficient resources for research, the inadequacy of evaluation methods or uncertainty as to the nature of the social intervention.

For all these reasons, it is only reasonable to expect practitioners to produce evidence for their interventions if appropriate research is achievable and available. Even then, many social workers face challenges in accessing and using research evidence and many are reluctant to read and apply research to their practice (Reid, 2001; Webb, 2001, 2002). Practice research databases can be difficult to negotiate and incomplete (Gilgun, 2005; Newman, 2002). Locating relevant research can be frustrating for social workers when they discover that there is limited or inconclusive research evidence on the particular issue they are facing (Gilgun, 2005).

In conclusion, the current state of research in social work falls far short of the requirements of an evidence-based practice culture (Macdonald, 2001; Thyer, 2002).

Assumption 2: Certain evidence is stronger or better than other evidence

The critical appraisal of research is a central principle of evidence-based practice. Research findings cannot be taken at face value – the quality of the research methodology and the applicability of the findings to specific practice settings need to be critically reviewed.

In appraising the quality of evidence, social work has been strongly influenced by the positivist, scientific approach prevalent in medicine. This approach advocates a hierarchy of evidence with systematic reviews of randomized controlled trial studies as the gold standard and the only source of definitive answers about the impact and effectiveness of interventions (Gambrill, 1999; Gibbs and Gambrill, 2002; Howard et al., 2003; Macdonald, 2001; Macdonald and Sheldon, 1992; Mullen 2002; Reid, 2001; Sheldon, 1986; Thyer, 2002; Upshur et al., 2001). The methods of qualitative inquiry are at the bottom of the hierarchy, offering supportive insights rather than definitive answers. While evidence-based medicine has been influential, there is much debate, both within social work and the health disciplines, about what constitutes evidence (Gilgun, 2005; Morse, 2006; Rubin and Parrish, 2007).

Debates about the applicability of the scientific – positivist – approach to social work practice began long before the emergence of evidence-based practice. Due to its association with positivism, evidence-based practice is rejected by those social workers with a preference for interpretive research approaches. The experimental methods promoted by the positivist approach have been criticized in social work for reducing complex issues to limited, quantifiable variables and, consequently, providing findings that are of little use in practice (Epstein, 1996; Shaw, 1999a; Witkin, 1991, 1996). While the positivist approach to evidence-based practice remains strong, concern with the limitations of positivism has prompted several authors to develop a wider understanding of evidence that reflects the particular issues and requirements of social work practice (Dore, 2006; Gilgun, 2005; Hollway, 2001; Plath, 2006; Shaw, 1999a; Smith, 2004b; Webb, 2001, 2002). This understanding of the nature of evidence is still evolving in social work and may incorporate qualitative information, client values and what has broadly been referred to as 'practice wisdom' or 'professional judgement'.

Pawson (2006) provides a useful way of conceptualizing research evidence from a critical realist perspective. He proposes that research should not be incorporated into practice using positivist techniques and standards of evidence, but, rather, should be synthesized in a way that is both theory-driven and theory building. The purpose of reviewing research is, thus, to consider and question the extent to which theories facilitate understanding of the complex context of service provision. For social work, this entails the synthesis of a range of research and information, with particular attention to the applicability and usefulness of findings informing practice decisions. Research that utilizes a range of methods and integrates both qualitative and quantitative information on intervention outcomes and processes can be reviewed critically and integrated to inform future practice.

While some social work research using experimental designs *will* produce definitive evidence, generally social workers need to gather a range of evidence from different sources to guide and support practice judgements (Colgan and Cheers, 2002; Plath, 2006; Shaw and Shaw, 1997b; Webb, 2001). Supportive evidence comes from ethical frameworks, organizational and policy guidelines, critical reflection, prior experience, client feedback and mixed method research. All evidence is likely to be inadequate in some way, so it is up to the individual social worker or policymaker to gather, synthesize and critique it as it relates to the particular context when making practice decisions. Another challenge is reaching a common understanding of evidence when working in multidisciplinary areas of practice (Gould and Kendall, 2007).

Assumption 3: Effectiveness of interventions can be established

Evidence-based practice is sometimes reduced to notions of 'what works' or 'what works best'. While it may be reassuring for social workers, managers and policymakers to have answers to such questions, generally they are too simplistic for the types of practice dilemmas encountered in social work. It is more useful to ask 'What aspects worked well?', 'What aspects didn't work well?', 'Why?', 'For whom?', 'From whose perspective?', 'What were the relevant factors impacting on the situation?' and 'In what context did or didn't it work?'

It is easiest to determine the effectiveness of interventions in relation to specific and clearly defined objectives, such as achieving, changing or eliminating a behaviour, attitude or emotion (Gueron, 2007). Effective social work practice, however, also involves the application of ethical principles, such as promoting social justice and self-determination. While fundamental to social work practice, these principles are interpreted according to context and values. As such, they cannot be measured and so evaluation of their effectiveness is open to interpretation.

Social workers are concerned with the range of factors and conditions that impact the quality of life and well-being of clients and communities. Generally, multiple outcomes can emerge from social work interventions tailored in response to presenting issues. Just how effective these outcomes are depends on the values and perspective of the stakeholder making the assessment. For the client, it may be an intangible sense of feeling more positive about life. For the social worker it may be the degree to which goals established at the start of the intervention have been met. For the organization, effectiveness may be reflected in the proportion of clients returning to it with the same issue.

Thus, evaluation of the effectiveness of social work is a complex, interpretive and value-based process (Cheetham, 1992, 1997; Gibbs and Gambrill, 2002; Sheldon, 1986). What constitutes effectiveness is variable, open to interpretation and a matter of politics, with powerful voices controlling the effectiveness agenda. An organization preoccupied with costs and efficiency will define effectiveness in those terms (Dore, 2006). Practitioners with vested interests in the use of particular interventions might define effectiveness at the outset in a way that anticipates the types of outcomes they are likely to achieve. The experiences of clients can be ignored when the interests of more powerful voices determine the effectiveness agenda (Gibbs, 2001). When effectiveness is viewed in this kind of interpretive light, the gathering of evidence should also entail critical analysis of the context and background to the research. With adequate information and appropriate critical reflection, social workers and policymakers may be in a position to make informed judgements about the likely impacts of interventions.

Many do not agree that effectiveness is open to interpretation, however. Some argue that the assessment of effectiveness in social work should, as far as possible, be a technical, theory-free process where the strongest evidence is used to identify the best interventions (Howard et al., 2003).

There remains a tension in the literature between the theory-embedded (interpretive) and theory-free (technical) approaches to the evaluation of effectiveness.

Assumption 4: Interventions can be replicated

Evidence-based practice relies on reproducing interventions that have been found to be effective. This is possible when interventions are standardized and context-independent. Efforts are being made in some schools of social work to ensure that students are taught standard, manualized, evidence-based interventions that can be replicated in different contexts (Howard et al., 2003; Rubin and Parrish, 2007).

Much social work practice, however, does not entail discrete, standardized interventions. Social workers assess complex, contextual factors at the individual, group, organizational and societal levels before interventions are planned and adjusted to suit presenting issues. The goals and processes of social work interventions emerge through a collaborative relationship between social worker and client, group or community. Ethical principles, organizational requirements and theoretical frameworks guide this process. The practitioner's knowledge, experience, skill and critical reflection determine the most appropriate response to a presenting issue in practice.

Concerns have been expressed that evidence-based practice ignores the importance of the assessment, interaction and critically reflective processes by privileging standardized, treatment-orientated interventions suited to measurable outcome evaluation (Hausman, 2002; Hollway, 2001; Scott, 2002; Webb, 2001).

If social work is to continue to entail innovative, reflective responses to complex social and personal issues, then an overemphasis on discrete, standardized interventions should be avoided. While the replication of well-evidenced standard interventions is possible in some settings, this need not be at the expense of using ethical, theoretical and critical practice principles to guide responses to the unique, multidimensional situations encountered daily in most social work practice. These situations require multifaceted responses for which standardized treatment evaluations are generally inappropriate.

The implementation of evidence-based practice in social work entails more than replicating standardized interventions. Mullen et al. (2005) argue that, despite the potential of an evidence-based approach in social work, it is rarely seen in agency practice due to a range of conceptual and logistical challenges. The dissemination of information on evidence-based practices is unlikely to lead to changes in practice unless there is a broad change of approach within organizations supported by strategies addressing social work education, stakeholder participation, staff training and developmental work within an organization and the profession (Mullen et al., 2007).

Theoretical influences on evidence-based practice

Evidence-based practice can be approached from a number of theoretical perspectives, reflecting different values, principles and interpretations. Four theoretical perspectives on evidence-based practice are discussed below – *positivist, pragmatic, political* and *postmodern*.

These perspectives are presented as ideal types and, as such, particular authors or practitioners may not sit entirely within one theoretical perspective. A delineation of the different perspectives is helpful, however, in making sense of the varying ways in which evidence-based practice may be approached, both in the literature and in practice.

Positivist

The positivist approach is strongly influenced by the scientific paradigm and the physical sciences. The impact of social work is assessed in terms of measurable outcomes. The strongest evidence is sought to provide definitive answers on the most effective interventions. The emphasis is on identifying and facilitating 'gold standard' experimental research – that is, large, randomized, controlled trials that examine the outcomes of standardized interventions as the only type of research that can provide definitive answers about the effectiveness of interventions. Other types of evidence are used to enrich or support these research findings. Systematic reviews provide meta-analyses of research experiments as the strongest form of evidence for practice.

Social work authors who favour a positivist approach to evidence-based practice include Geraldine Macdonald (2001), Brian Sheldon (2001), Bruce Thyer (2002), Matthew Howard et al. (2003) and Aaron McNeece and Bruce Thyer (2004).

Pragmatic

The pragmatic approach is strongly influenced by the realities of professional social work practice. The emphasis is on identifying useful evidence for social workers needing to make informed judgements in practice.

Research and information from a range of sources are gathered and critically evaluated in terms of their strengths, limitations and applicability to the practice setting. There is recognition that the findings of randomized, controlled trials are context-dependent and not necessarily relevant to the particular practice context and issues being faced. Thus, the relevance of the research is regarded as being of greater importance than the particular methodological approach used. Research must be accessible and integrated with practice. Practitioners require skills in synthesizing and critically evaluating research and other information gleaned from practice in order to make informed judgements, rather than definitive claims about their own practice.

A pragmatic approach to evidence-based practice is evident in the work of Ian Shaw (1999a, 2003), Tony Newman and Di McNeish (2005), Debbie Plath (2006) and David Smith (2004b).

Political

A political approach recognizes that there are differences in the power and influence of groups in society. As with all social life, the processes involved in gathering and presenting evidence for particular interventions reflect these power differences. Political decisions will affect the funding of research, the particular interventions evaluated, the research methods employed, access to research findings, the 'social issues' identified, how 'effectiveness' is defined and the value given to different types of evidence.

Practitioners engage in evidence-based practice when they use evidence strategically to obtain resources and advance their own and their clients' causes as well as those of their profession and employing organizations.

A political analysis also recognizes that the voices of less powerful groups, such as service users, are not influential in debates about evidence.

Some authors who have integrated a political analysis in writing about evidence-based practice are Ian Dore (2006), Janice Morse (2006), Ray Pawson (2006) and Debbie Plath (2006).

Postmodern

A postmodern approach asserts that the social world is open to interpretation and meaning is created through the use of language and discourse. This approach does not fit naturally with the evidence-based practice movement's emphasis on effective outcomes. A postmodern influence is nonetheless evident in writing on evidence-based practice that acknowledges the role of interpretation and meaning in identifying and examining evidence (Shaw, 1999a, 2003; Smith, 2004b; Webb, 2002).

A postmodern perspective can assist in understanding how the language of evidence is used to support the status of the social work profession and the position of particular interventions in the practice of social work. From a postmodern perspective, 'intervention', 'success', 'effectiveness' and 'best evidence' are not objective or measurable but open to interpretation. The meanings of these terms are established through discourse among those engaged in social work.

Table 16.1 provides a summary of these theoretical perspectives in terms of the type of evidence sought, the processes employed to gather and use evidence, and the relationship between research and practice.

Table 16.1   Four theoretical influences on evidence-based practice

Positivist	Pragmatic	Political	Postmodern
Type of evidence sought			
Strong evidence	Useful evidence	Influential evidence	Evidence as discourse
Definitive answers about effectiveness	Relevant information to assist practice decision making	Information that can be used strategically to obtain resources and further causes	Information used to enhance particular meanings and interpretations of practice and its impact
Processes employed			
Experimental designs	Research synthesis – range of methods	Strategically negotiated evidence in contested domains.	Discourse to establish common meaning and interpretation of experi-ences in the profession, organizations, and other social groupings
Systematic reviews of literature and meta-analyses	Critical reflection on limitations and applicability of research to practice	Advocacy and lobbying	
Relationship between research and practice			
Research directs practice	Symbiotic relationship between research and practice	Research is a tool to achieve professional practice goals	Research and practice both contribute to enhancing meaning and status of social work

Application to social work practice

When discussing the methodological applications to social work, the following case example is useful to illustrate how each of the theoretical perspectives outlined above might guide social workers when responding to an issue encountered in practice.

The issue: The Sunshine Community Centre provides individual and group programmes for parents and children. Faced with a growing waiting list, management has requested that the social workers examine their practices and identify evidence-based strategies to address this issue.

Positivist social worker 1: Using several Internet databases, the social worker engages in a thorough review of the literature on parenting programmes, focusing particularly on meta-analyses of randomized, controlled trials that examine the effectiveness of standardized interventions.

Based on the strongest international evidence, a recommendation is made that the Sunshine Community Centre focuses its resources on the provision of the parenting programme that has been found to achieve the most effective outcomes for clients.

Pragmatic social worker 2: This social worker talks with colleagues in other organizations about ideas for dealing with growing waiting lists and identifies single session and group programmes as interventions that could provide services to clients more efficiently.

Using an Internet practice research database, the social worker finds a number of articles on the implementation of these strategies, critically reviews them and finds a few that are applicable to the current context.

It appears that single-session interventions have been useful in reducing waiting lists in a number of settings while also offering clients a satisfactory service.

A trial period and internal evaluation process are recommended to management.

Political social worker 3: This skilled narrative therapist is a member of the Narrative Social Workers group. In the social worker's professional experience, the effectiveness of narrative work with particular groups of disadvantaged clients has been demonstrated.

Armed with a number of illustrative case studies and a convincingly argued academic article, the social worker meets with management to explain the nature of the intervention and how effective it can be in practice.

A recommendation for additional ongoing resources for this work is made and followed up with a letter of support from the Narrative Social Workers group.

Postmodern social worker 4: This social worker is not strongly committed to any particular intervention, believing that, through discussions, a way forward will emerge.

Sceptical about whether the effectiveness of practice can really be determined by research, the social worker prefers to focus on experiences and the meanings derived from these.

Through discussions about the issues and possible strategies, the social work group will strengthen their common understanding of the nature and role of their work. This social worker does not make a recommendation to management.

Social work literature on evidence-based practice is replete with tensions between differing ideological stances. Despite these differences, the focus on evidence-based practice has resulted in a heightened awareness of the role that research can play in informing social work practice. Evidence-based practice is influencing social workers to seek out and utilize research findings that both question and justify their practices. The literature and debates surrounding evidence-based practice have raised awareness about the importance of critically questioning standard practices and the impact of interventions. Debates about the nature of evidence that is appropriate for social work and the limitations of an evidence-based approach continue. Such debates have strengthened the profession by encouraging the use of research to identify social work practices that are valued by clients, management, funding bodies and social workers.

Regardless of how broadly 'research' is defined, research evidence is a necessary, but insufficient requirement for quality social work practice. There is wide recognition, even among those who support the scientific paradigm for evidence most strongly, that practitioners' skills and expertise determine the implementation of effective interventions. For social work practice to be effective, therefore, an evidence-based approach should be combined with a strong ethical and moral framework (Gambrill, 2006; Gray and McDonald, 2006), a client-centred approach (Gilgun, 2005), theoretical analysis, critical reflection and questioning (Fook, 2004; Gambrill, 2006; Gilgun, 2005; Plath, 2006) and an innovative, creative approach to practice (Pollio, 2006). For practice to be evidence-based, social workers require skills in the critical appraisal and synthesis of research and the ability to usefully apply findings to make decisions about future practice. At the organizational level, resources need to be directed into research and the findings made accessible to social workers so that there is a realistic potential for research to be integrated into practice.

Study questions

1. Describe your understanding of evidence-based practice. How does this relate to the four theoretical perspectives described in this chapter? What part does evidence-based practice play in the overall quality of social work practice?
2. What are the benefits of adopting an evidence-based practice approach? What are the challenges for social work practitioners, managers, funding bodies and policymakers?
3. Choose a social work practice or policy question that you have encountered. What sources of evidence could be drawn on to inform practice in relation to this question? Use the web-based practice research databases given in the select bibliography at the end of this chapter to locate research that could inform your practice question.

Glossary

Critical reflection The process of analysing one's own practice in the context of personal history, values, prejudices and knowledge and understanding social oppression.

Experimental design Research method that looks for causes and impacts by varying one or more independent variable. A true experiment entails random allocation to groups, whereas a quasi-experimental design does not.

Interpretive approach An explanation and understanding of social phenomena are regarded as being shaped by the meanings and perspectives of individuals or groups.

Intervention A purposeful activity undertaken by a social worker with, or on behalf of, an individual client, couple, family, group or community.

Political Concerned with the nature and processes of power and influence.

Positivist approach The social world, like the physical world, is regarded as real and tangible. As such, an understanding and explanation of social phenomena are sought by systematic observation and measurement.

Pragmatic approach Concerned with practical consequences and outcomes; accounting for the range of contextual factors that impact on a situation.

Scientific The systematic study of patterns and general laws through deduction and inference based on observations and measurements.

Select bibliography

Besides Gambrill (2006), Pawson (2006) and Smith (2004b), the following are useful web-based resources on evidence-based practice:

- *The Cochrane collaboration*: www.cochrane.org/index.htm
- *The Campbell collaboration*: www.campbellcollaboration.org
- *The Evidence for Policy and Practice Information and Co-ordinating Centre (EPPI-Centre)*: http://eppi.ioe.ac.uk/cms
- *Evidence Network, Centre for Evidence Based Policy and Practice:* www.evidencenetwork.org
- *Research in Practice*: www.rip.org.uk
- *Research in Practice For Adults.* www.ripfa.org.uk
- *Social Care Institute for Excellence:* www.scie.org.uk
- *Social Care Online:* www.scie-socialcareonline.org.uk

Ways of Knowing

17

Ian Shaw

Introduction

My aim in this final chapter is to help readers gain competence – and confidence – in asking tricky questions about knowledge for social work practice and research. Knowing how and when to ask the right questions and gain an appropriate disposition towards social work knowledge are hard won and more easily lost. Once lost, there is a danger of wrenching the 'doing' apart from the 'knowing' so that no one recognizes the importance of the question, 'How do I know when I have got it right?' Much of this book will be more readily understood and assessed if we undertake some preliminary groundclearing.

I am not a philosopher and would have little plausibility were I to claim expertise in philosophical work on knowledge and reality. Perhaps I should have declined the invitation to write. I don't know. As philosophers might remind us, though, 'I don't know' may be an acknowledgement of ignorance but it can also be a philosophical position.

Thinking about ways of knowing in social work takes us immediately to epistemology[1] – that branch of philosophy concerned with the theory of knowledge, its origin and nature, compared with, for example, 'belief' or 'opinion':

---

[1]I have included definitions of key terms in the chapter.

Epistemology, or the theory of knowledge, is driven by two main questions: 'What is knowledge?' and 'What can we know?' If we think we can know something, as nearly everyone does, then a third main question arises: 'How do we know what we do know?' (Greco, 1998, 2007, unpaginated)

The three questions are closely related as it is unlikely that someone will address one of them without addressing the others or, at least, assuming something about the others.

The first part of this chapter picks up the questions of what knowledge is and how we know. The second moves on to consider how the social work community has responded to questions of how we can know what we know and, in particular, asks if it makes helpful sense to think about social work knowledge as socially constructed. I conclude with a brief reflection on scepticism and advocate that a moderate Socratic scepticism is essential for social work knowledge based on evidence, understanding and justice. I refer quite frequently to arguments about evidence-based practice in social work (see Chapter 16). However, this chapter is not meant to smuggle in either a critique or defence of evidence-based practice (see Shaw, 2006), but exploring a strong version of evidence-based practice is a helpful way of making some of the issues stand out.

Forms of knowledge in social work

Requirements for the accreditation of social work training programmes have much to say regarding knowledge. Skills for Care for social work programmes in England, for example, include the requirement that:

In your specific area of practice, you must understand, critically analyse, evaluate and apply the following knowledge:

1. The legal, social, economic and ecological context of social work practice.
2. The context of social work practice for this area.
3. Values and ethics.
4. Social work theories, models and methods for working with individuals, families, carers, groups and communities. (www.topssengland.net)

Each element is spelt out in detail. The relevant point for our purposes is that there are different kinds of knowledge and understanding in this list. To understand and apply social work theories or the legal context of work in a given area of practice is not the same as to understand and apply values or methods of working. To express this differently, knowing that something is the case is not the same as knowing *how* to do something.

Furthermore, knowledge clearly entails more than being right. Take the following simple hypothetical example from social work practice. You are convinced that a task-centred intervention will prove effective in applying a cognitive behavioural intervention with a young person who has serious school refusal problems. Let us suppose that there is research evidence somewhere – but unbeknown to you – that yields plausible evidence that your belief is correct. Does your correct belief count as knowledge? While hypothetical, it seems likely that this scenario may be quite common in social work practice.

The classic answer from Socrates is that 'someone who can't give and receive an account of something isn't knowledgeable about that thing' (Plato, *Theaetetus*)[2]. I have knowledge about something if I believe it, my belief is justified and it is true. According to this reading, knowledge is justified true belief.

What is entailed in justifying or giving a good enough account of something is not straightforward. Perhaps we should say that the person with knowledge believes something in a good way – perhaps as an act of intellectual virtue – whereas the person with mere opinion assents to the merits of task-centred intervention in a way that lacks intellectual merit. What exactly counts as a good way of believing, though, is not easy to agree on.

Let us take a different example to illustrate this difficulty. There has been much – welcome – attention given to diverse arguments for reflective learning and practice in social work (such as Jan Fook, 1996; Nick Gould and Imogen Taylor, 1996; Helen Martyn, 2000; Donald Schön, 1983). While Schön (1983) has little to say explicitly about social work, his distinction between reflecting *on* action and reflecting *in* action has entered the vocabulary of social work students. We can call this a strong version of the 'internalist' approaches to giving an account of a belief. From this perspective, we assume that we can find out what we are justified in believing primarily by a process of learned reflection, that this process is internal to our mind, at least to a significant degree, and it is a process we can consciously access.

Tacit knowledge

None of these assumptions is without controversy. Taking the third assumption, *can* we always access our reflective processes?

Commonsense knowledge, for example, is often tacit knowledge. When we think of tacit knowledge in professional work, it can be defined as knowledge or abilities that can be passed between experts by personal contact, but cannot be or has not been set out or passed on in formal statements, diagrams, verbal descriptions or instructions for action (Collins, 2000). There are actions, judgements and recognitions that we accomplish spontaneously. We do not have to think about them prior to performance. We are often unaware of having learned to do them. While we may remember once being aware of the understanding necessary for the action, we typically are now unable to describe the knowing that our actions reveal. It has become 'thinking as usual' knowledge: 'Tacit knowledge exists in that time when action is taken that is not understood, when understanding is offered without articulation, and when conclusions are apprehended without an argument' (Altheide and Johnson, 1994: 492).

There is nothing intrinsically wrong with an implicit, unarticulated theory: 'Reality is what we choose not to question at the moment ... [and] the better shape science is in, more the positions are implicit' (Baker, 1993: 220). Equally 'When we watch new scientific consensus emerging we are watching the growth of new bodies of tacit knowledge' (Collins, 2001: 111).

Tacit knowledge is not limited to what goes on in an individual's mind. For example, sociologists of knowledge in practice have explored ways that practice is a social form: 'People

---

[2]Socrates does not, in fact, find this argument convincing.

in different social groups take different things to be certain knowledge but they are not aware of the social basis of their certainties'. (Collins, 2001: 110)[3].

A consequence of prioritizing reflective practice in social work ought to be that different kinds of tacit knowledge will be recognized. The significance of personal contact and the sharing of practical knowledge between social work practitioners will be brought out and sources of trust and mistrust between social workers made clear. This is a big agenda and one that social work has only begun to tackle.

Is tacitness inherent in our knowledge? Is it a part of how we are or is it a 'God of the gaps' kind of explanation, where we might conceivably be able to render our knowledge explicit? This question 'matters' when we are engaged in identifying the different forms of knowledge that are part of professional work. For example, in a recent helpful example of such an attempt in the case of social care knowledge, Ray Pawson et al. (2003) devote effort to suggesting how tacit practitioner knowledge can be rendered explicit. The aspiration may be wise, if only to avoid the alchemy of intuitionism and appeals to 'personal style' that beset some professional practice, so long as we do not deceive ourselves that the goal is fully achievable.

The question arises as to whether or not tacit, implicit understanding is in tension with more explicit, planned research-based practice. Evaluation writers Stake and Trumbull may seem to suggest as much when they argue that, 'For practitioners ... formal knowledge is not necessarily a stepping stone to improved practice ... We maintain that practice is guided far more by personal knowings' (1982: 5).

There is a frequent tension in social work between 'internalist' and 'externalist' ways of justifying what we believe. Reflective practice is clearly a different approach from evidence-based practice (EBP), as we saw in Chapter 16. EBP is strongly externalist, and rests on the view that we can only find a sufficient basis for knowledge for practice from empirical evidence external to ourselves.

Practical knowledge

We discover the same tension within the social work research community when social work researchers talk about appropriate criteria for judging the quality of research (Shaw and Norton, 2007). Needless to say, knowledge from reasoning or from experience does not exhaust kinds of knowledge. Thomas Schwandt (1997) distinguishes theoretical knowledge ('knowing that'), craft or skill knowledge ('knowing how'), and practical–moral knowledge ('knowing from').

For Schwandt, when we talk about 'application', something more is intended than the instrumental sense of practicality (as though a social work model of intervention or a finding about effectiveness could be applied like a 'tool') – that is, the more fundamental sense of making something relevant to oneself. This involves a particular kind of knowledge – 'knowing from within or practical–moral knowledge', which 'requires not cleverness in application but

---

[3]For an engaging review of major controversies in the history of science and an exemplification of how scientific certainties do not come from experimental method, but from the way ambiguous evidence is interpreted, see Collins and Pinch (1998).

understanding' (Schwandt, 1997: 76). 'Practical–moral knowledge aims to actually move people, not simply give them good ideas' (Schwandt, 1997: 81).

If being practical means having an impact, then 'practical' per se is neutral rather than a good thing. We can have bad as well as good practical research. We cannot predefine whether or not social work will be practical. Its practicality is created.

How do we acquire knowledge that is not observed?[4]

To begin with, we do so empirically. There is a major field of study in the sociology of science that has extensively explored the issues arising from this statement.

As part of acquiring an empirical understanding of epistemology within social work, we should not ignore the commonsense ways in which practitioners endeavour to make evaluative sense of their practical activities (Shaw and Shaw, 1997a, 1997b). In a similar way, recognizing the role of informal logic means that we also need to discover how researchers draw conclusions about evidence. For example, Stuart Kirk and William Reid (2002) argued that we know little of the everyday epistemologies of practitioners.

There is a problem with this kind of research, however. While we may learn what social workers believe, do these beliefs constitute knowledge? We face a logical problem – the relationship between 'evidence' and the 'conclusion': 'These empirical investigations may enable us to describe the ways in which people arrive at *beliefs* about unobserved facts, but they leave open the question of whether beliefs arrived at in this way actually constitute *knowledge*' (Salmon, 1967, 2007: 252).

Philosophically, this is the problem of inductive evidence. 'Evidence-based-practice' has been criticized partly because it appears to some that the relationship between evidence and the conclusion is treated too straightforwardly – as if the evidence spoke unambiguously and the inferences for practice were indisputable and obvious.

There are two sorts of inference. A *demonstrative* inference is one where, logically speaking, the conclusion says no more than was in the premises. A *non-demonstrative* inference, however, is one where the premises do not necessitate the conclusion – they could be true while the conclusion is false.

The critique of 'evidence-based-practice'[5] I have in mind can be expressed as saying that some advocates present the argument for evidence-based practice as if the inference were demonstrative, whereas it is indubitably non-demonstrative. The social work version of this problem can be observed in other fields, such as, evaluation: 'Everyone agrees that information somehow informs decisions, but the relationship is not direct, not simple. Often the more important the decision, the more obscure the relationship seems to be'(House, 1980: 68).

Ernest House goes so far as to say that, 'subjected to serious scrutiny, evaluations always appear equivocal' (1980: 72), concluding that evaluations can be no more than acts of persuasion:

---

[4]This problem is associated with the work of Scottish philosopher David Hume.
[5]I have hyphenated the phrase in this passage as an indication of the assumption that inference and conclusion are demonstrative and inseparable. I have placed it in inverted commas because I do not accept the assumption.

'Evaluation persuades rather than convinces, argues rather than demonstrates, is credible rather than certain, is variably accepted rather than compelling' (1980: 73). When, as social workers or evaluators, we underplay the role of judgement and, hence, of argumentation, this results in an unduly technical, methods-orientated analysis, an overconfidence in quantification and a tendency to represent knowledge in an impersonal, objectified form. Those who fail to accept the 'compelling' conclusions drawn from the evaluation are dismissed as irrational. If results were unequivocal, then those who failed to accept them would be 'wrong'.

The pervasiveness of non-demonstrative inferences in identifying and making use of knowledge in social work makes practice more demanding. There have been several attempts to take a different approach to thinking through the reasoning process involved in constructing justified evaluative arguments (Fournier, 1995; Fournier and Smith, 1993; Scriven, 1997). These emphasize the complex connection between evidence and conclusions and commence from the differences between formal and informal reasoning.

Whereas formal reasoning assumes a tight fit between the premises and conclusions within an argument, informal logic 'deals with ordinary, everyday language, where rules of inference are less precise and more contextual' (Fournier and Smith, 1993: 317). Stephen Toulmin's *The Uses of Argument* (1958) has been perhaps the most influential text in this area. In explicating the connection between claims and evidence, he gives a central role to 'warrants', which provide the grounds for explaining how we get from evidence to a claim – he argues that a warrant legitimizes the inference we make.

So far we have seen that social work knowledge calls for more than simply having an opinion or even being correct – it needs some kind of justifying account. We have seen that some accounts are 'externalist' (such as evidence-based practice) and some are 'internalist' (such as reflective practice) and there are perhaps unavoidable tensions between the two – albeit we should remember that the tensions are logical and philosophical and may not always be pragmatic (we return to this point in the next section). We have also seen that the relationship between evidence and practice inferences is rarely self-evident or demonstrative. Finally, we have reminded ourselves of Schwandt's point that knowledge includes 'knowing from' – practical–moral knowledge – as well as 'knowing that' and 'knowing how'.

Experience and knowledge

Two final distinctions are in order. First, knowledge by acquaintance – what we derive from our senses – is distinct from knowledge by description. This distinction is shaky, however. When we express knowledge by acquaintance in language, it becomes knowledge by description. The face-to-face interview between client and social worker entails knowledge by acquaintance on both sides, but, as soon as the social worker refers to that interview verbally or in writing (in a record, e-mail or report), it becomes knowledge by description. Likewise with a research article or report: 'It is a deep question how we learn to name objects of common experience ... from our private knowledge by acquaintance' (Gregory, 1987: 412).

While the distinction is not absolute, I am not sure that it is well enough observed. Take a recent influential and interesting account of the kinds of knowledge in social work and social care mentioned earlier. Pawson et al. (2003) helpfully invite us to distinguish between knowledge held by practitioners, the policy community, service users and carers, researchers and organizations and that set out to develop provisional criteria for assessing knowledge through a common framework of quality criteria.

One of the difficulties of this scheme is that there may be as much diversity of knowledge by acquaintance and description *within* each of these as there is *between* them. However, the acquaintance/description distinction has limited purchase in practical terms, in that it is now widely accepted that there is description within perception and experience – evident, for example, in understandings of the world as being (socially) constructed.

Robert Stake and Thomas Schwandt (2006) have explored a different, though related, distinction – that between experience-far and experience-near knowledge. This is the second of our two final distinctions. In their discussion of discerning quality in evaluation, they distinguish between 'quality-as-measured' and 'quality-as-experienced' (we might say 'knowledge' rather than 'quality').

In the first case, quality is regarded as measurable and judging quality takes on the characteristic of 'thinking criterially', through explicit comparison of the research in question to a set of standards for it – is it reliable, valid, free from bias and so on. Judging quality criterially is more or less an 'experience-distant' undertaking. 'Quality-as-experienced' starts from the view that quality is a phenomenon we personally experience and only later make technical, if need be:

> This view emphasizes grasping quality in experience-near understandings, that is, in the language and embodied action of those who actually are undergoing the experience of a program or policy. Criterial thinking is important but it is rooted in interpretation of personal experience. (Stake and Schwandt, 2006: 408)

The importance of experience is closely related to another question addressed in several places in this book – the relation between knowledge and power.

Class, gender, race and education are factors that indelibly shape who is accepted as having knowledge. Feminist work illustrates this powerfully. Although there are important variations on questions of epistemology within feminism, all feminist positions start from the proposition that social workers must ask questions that make sense within women's experience and for women (Hawkesworth, 1989). While most feminists would now reject the idea that there is one single woman's experience, they would also reject a relativist position (see Chapter 6).

Perhaps the strongest form anti-relativism takes is feminist 'standpoint' theory, which has its origins in Marxist and Hegelian arguments that reality is obscured to people from certain backgrounds because of the effects of ideology:

> Standpoint theory builds on the assertion that the less powerful members of society experience a different reality as a consequence of their oppression ... To survive they must have knowledge, awareness and sensitivity of both the dominant group's view of society and their own – the potential for 'double vision' or consciousness and thus the potential for a more complete view of social reality (Swigonski, 1993: 173).

This theory makes two linked assertions: the double vision of the oppressed and the partial vision of the more powerful – 'privilege and its invisibility to those who hold it' (Swigonski, 1993: 174). My own position is that a strong standpoint approach is hard to sustain, but a moderate one is persuasive (Shaw, 1996: 117–120; Shaw and Gould, 2001: 172–173).

Ideas about knowledge by acquaintance, experience-near research, power and social construction take us to the remaining discussion regarding social constructivism and scepticism.

Realism and constructivism

Can we know the world as it really is or are we restricted to knowing it as shaped by our thoughts and experience? Can our knowledge be objective or is it 'only' made up from subjective perspectives? Discussions in social work about this issue are often presented in the form of a question: is social work 'positivist' or 'postmodern'? I do not intend to address this issue, primarily because I believe it is often ill-conceived, presented in an unduly polarized form (see Shaw, 1999a: Chapter 3; 1999b) and rarely illuminating.

There are different understandings of what may be meant by 'objective' (Greco, 1998, 2007, for example). I find myself drawn to a moderate realism, taking the view that what is represented by at least some of our beliefs, is objective – that is, logically and causally independent of how we conceive of that thing. Such a position is not easy to defend, nor is it easy to show that it does not beg relevant questions in an arbitrary way. It follows that an appropriate humility about human reasoning is warranted.

An important driver of such diffidence about human reasoning is the realization that critical, emancipatory approaches to social work and research conceptualize problems as part of the social, political and cultural contexts in which social work is formed. Hence, the basic logic is not preoccupied solely with the formal organization of argument, 'but also particular forms of reasoning that give focus to scepticism towards social institutions' (Popkewitz, 1990: 49). Hence, critical knowledge derived from social work is never neutral (Comstock, 1982: 374): 'It is always for some particular subject'. For many, this involves an obligation to pursue political commitments through active participation in political movements. Before we say anything more about realism, however, it is worth pausing to recognize that, for many practitioners and researchers, the pathway of pragmatism is more attractive: 'What should count is not the favoured method of a particular group, but rather how well we answer the question or achieve the purpose ... it matters little which perspective or purpose has been adopted' (Chelimsky, 1997: 109).

Howard Becker (1993), writing of epistemological issues, notes: 'I think it is fruitless to try to settle them ... These are simply the commonplaces, in the rhetorical sense, of scientific talk in the social sciences, the framework in which the debate goes on' (1993: 219). He believes that we should take an empirical perspective on such matters, treating them as 'a topic rather than an aggravation' (1993: 222). We should also beware the paralysing effect of too much methodological discussion, however: 'We still have to do theoretical work, but we needn't think we are being especially virtuous when we do' (1993: 221). Rather than regard such theoretical work as the responsibility of all, he is content to view it as a specialism – the profession of 'philosophical and methodological worry'! (1993: 226)

We should distinguish between *methodological* and *philosophical* pragmatism. Methodological pragmatism rests on impatience with philosophy and an emphasis on real-world evaluation and practice; it claims that methods can be separated from the epistemology out of which they have emerged. The emphasis, thus, is on practical utility and the credibility of the methods used. Most of the pleas for pragmatism referred to above are of this kind. Thus, in complaining about the 'philosophically besotted' (1997: 478), Michael Scriven says 'it is better to build on what might conceivably be sand ... than not to build at all ... It is a waste of time to try to solve the problems of epistemology without getting on with the job' (1997: 479). William Reid (1994) argues to similar effect, if more temperately, for social work: 'Irreconcilable conflicts may indeed exist in the discourse of philosophers, but their perspectives are not essential to the task of resolving differences and building consensus in the practical worlds of social work' (1994: 478). Despite its disclaimer, this is, of course, a philosophical position and one that seems to assume a fairly strong acceptance of a realist position. Holding to a realist position does not necessarily entail either positivism or even strong confidence in objective knowledge. Sociologist Herbert Blumer (1969) argued that a view of knowledge as socially constructed:

> does not shift 'reality', as so many conclude, from the empirical world to the realm of imagery and conception ... [The] empirical world can 'talk back' to our picture of it or assertions about it – talk back in the sense of challenging and resisting, or not bending to, our images or conceptions of it. This resistance gives the empirical world an obdurate character that is the mark of reality. (1969: 22)

Constructivism of this kind is thus not incompatible with realism. On this view of things, we can maintain belief in the existence of phenomena independent of our claims about them and in their knowability, 'without assuming that we can know with certainty whether our knowledge of them is valid or invalid' (Hammersley, 1992: 50). 'The essence of this position is that, although a real world, driven by real natural causes, exists, it is impossible for humans truly to perceive it with their imperfect sensory and intellective mechanism' (Cook and Campbell, 1979: 29).

There is a wide range of positions within this broad approach. My own is that, while some version of objectivity remains as a 'regulatory ideal' (Phillips, 1990: 43), social work processes and results are always significantly jeopardized by interests, the social location of the practitioner and agency, powerful stakeholders and, in Egon Guba's (1990) surprisingly realist phrase, 'nature's propensity to confound' (1990: 19).

Such epistemological modesty does not necessarily lead to modest aspirations for social change. For example, from within social work, Reid (1988) has asked, 'Is it better to make limited but well-documented progress or to work toward more important goals with less certainty of what we have attained?' (1988: 45) Yet, fallible realist social work practitioners and researchers are less likely to pronounce confidently that they have got it right. They are likely to concur with Denis Phillips (1990) when he admits that 'the objectivity of an inquiry does not guarantee its truth ... *nothing* can guarantee that we have reached the truth' (1990: 43).

We have taken constructivism too much for granted. Suppose a given intervention, X, is found to be effective in working with young people who have challenging behaviour problems. Assume that for someone this can be stated as, 'It is a fact that X is effective in working with young people who have challenging behaviour problems'. Is this a fact for everyone? Not in the sense that all social workers believe it to be a fact (a trivial case of 'not a fact for everyone'). Is it possible, then, to say, 'It holds true for you but not for me'? Is it true independently of what I believe or how society is organized?

A social constructionist would respond by saying that:

- facts are social constructions rather than objects;
- it is constitutive of a given fact that it is so constructed;
- the construction is contingent and not universal.

The interest lies in exposing constructions where none is thought to exist, 'where something constitutively social had come to masquerade as natural' (Boghossian, 2006: 18). To 'de-construct' is then thought to be potentially liberating.[6]

This is a strong version of social constructionism. The classical philosophical view is that it is sometimes possible for the evidence alone to explain why we come to believe something. Task-centred social work may be considered a case in point. The original experiment, *Brief and Extended Casework* (Reid and Shyne, 1969), was carried out with the assumption that open-ended casework would prove most effective, given ideal circumstances. When the contrary was supported by the evidence, it led to a prolonged programme of research to develop and test the effectiveness of the model. A strong version of constructionism would respond by asserting the *descriptive dependence of the facts* in this experiment. A moderate constructionist would respond by asserting the weaker position of the *social relativity of descriptions*. However, even if we go for the weaker position, making judgements about evidence still remains a demanding task. If we accept that there are some mind-independent facts, 'This argument ... does not tell us all by itself which facts obtain and which ones don't; nor does it tell us, of the facts that do obtain, which ones are mind-independent and which ones aren't' (Boghossian, 2006: 57).

Judicious scepticism

'I don't know' might, as I suggested at the beginning of this chapter, be a philosophical position. Is evidence-based practice the right way to improve quality of services? I do not know.

The philosopher most associated with scepticism is perhaps René Descartes. To provide a firm ground for knowledge, he began by 'doubting all that could be doubted' (Grau, 2005, 2007: 195) by, for example, asking what if he were only dreaming. Contemporary films explore this idea via speculations about technology (such as *The Matrix*). Hume saw no way out of Descartes' problem and thought that we have to live with it, on the grounds that we can be philosophical sceptics yet sustain a practical belief in reason.

---

[6]There is a philosophical problem in the deconstruction project as it seems to require an assumption that the 'deconstructor' is able to see through the construct. This risks the accusation being made of 'ontological' gerrymandering' (Woolgar and Pawluch, 1985).

Does (moderate) scepticism lead to paralysed inaction? Not necessarily. It is possible to be philosophically sceptical yet practically committed to action.[7] This tension between philosophy and practice is perhaps inescapable. Jennifer Greene (1996) talks of qualitative evaluators, but her remarks will stand for social work practitioners and probably also researchers:

> Many qualitative practitioners struggle with the dissonance invoked by the assumed mind-dependence of all social knowledge claims in the face of the contextual (as well as personal, ego-related) demands to *'get it right'*, to *'find out what's really going on in this setting'*. (1996: 280)

Study questions

1. In this chapter, I have illustrated 'external' and 'internal' ways of knowing from evidence-based practice and reflective practice. On the basis of what you have read, what do you think are the strengths and limitations of each of these?
2. Read Chapter 11 on postmodernism and Chapter 16 on evidence-based practice. How do the issues discussed in this chapter help you critically assess and compare those two chapters?
3. Make brief notes on something about which you hold strong beliefs. What do you know in support of this belief? How do you know it?

Select bibliography

I recommend, Collins and Pinch (1998), Kirk and Reid (2002), Pawson et al. (2003), Shaw (1999b) and Stake and Schwandt (2006).

---

[7]Off-stage, as it were, I would also argue that such skepticism is not incompatible with a strong faith-based position.

References

Aarre, K. (1998) 'The child welfare debate in Portugal: A case study of a children's home', in I.R. Edgar and A. Russell (eds), *The Anthropology of Welfare*. London: Routledge.

Abu-Laban, Y. (2002) 'Liberalism, multiculturalism, and the problem of essentialism', *Citizenship Studies*, 6 (4): 459–82.

Adams, R., Dominelli, L. and Payne, M. (eds) (2002) *Critical Practice in Social Work*. Basingstoke: Palgrave Macmillan.

Agar, M. (1996) *The Professional Stranger: An informal introduction to ethnography*. London: Academic Press.

Agger, B. (1998) *Critical Social Theories: An introduction*. Boulder, CO: Westview Press.

Ainsworth, F. and Hansen, P. (2005) Evidence based social work practice: A reachable goal? in A. Bilson (ed.), *Evidence-based Practice in Social Work*. London: Whiting & Birch.

Al-Krenawi, A. and Graham, J. (eds) (2003) *Multicultural Social Working in Canada: Working with diverse ethno-racial communities*. Don Mills, ON: Oxford University Press.

Allan, G. (1983) 'Informal networks of care: issues raised by Barclay', *British Journal of Social Work*, 13 (1): 417–33.

Allan, J., Pease, B. and Briskman, L. (eds) (2003) *Critical Social Work: An introduction to theories and practice*. Sydney: Allen & Unwin.

Almack, J.C. (1922) 'The influence of intelligence on the selection of associates', *School and Society*, 16: 529–30.

Altheide, D. and Johnson, J. (1994) 'Criteria for assessing interpretive validity in qualitative research', in N. Denzin and Y. Lincoln (eds), *Handbook of Qualitative Methods*. Thousand Oaks, CA: Sage.

Alverson, H., Alverson, M. and Drake, R.E. (2001) 'An ethnographic study of the longitudinal course of substance abuse among people with severe mental illness', *Community Mental Health Journal*, 36 (6): 557–69.

Alverson, H., Carpenter, E. and Drake, R.E. (2006) 'An ethnographic study of job seeking among people with severe mental illness', *Psychiatric Rehabilitation Journal*, 30 (1): 15–22.

Antaki, C. (2006) 'Mental-health practitioners' use of idiomatic expressions in summarising clients' accounts', *Journal of Pragmatics*, 39: 527–41.

Antaki, C., Barnes, R. and Leudar, I. (2005) 'Self-disclosure as a situated interactional practice', *British Journal of Social Psychology*, 44: 181–99.

Arminen, I. (2004) 'Second stories: The salience of interpersonal communication for mutual help in Alcoholics Anonymous', *Journal of Pragmatics*, 36: 319–47.

Ashenden, S. (2004) *Governing Child Sexual Abuse: Negotiating the boundaries of public and private, law and science*. London: Routledge.

Austin, J.L. (1962) *How to do Things with Words*. Oxford: Clarendon.

Baccus, M.D. (1986) 'Multipiece truck wheel accidents and their regulations', in H. Garfinkel (ed.), *Ethnomethodological Studies of Work*. London: Routledge & Kegan Paul. pp. 20–59.

Bailey, R. and Brake, M. (1975) *Radical Social Work*. New York: Pantheon Books.

Baines, C., Evans, P. and Neysmith, S. (eds) (1998) *Women's Caring: Feminist perspectives on social welfare*. Toronto, ON: Oxford University Press.

Baldwin, D.M. (1998) 'Staff models and practice: managing 'trouble' in a community-based programme for chronically mentally ill adults in the USA', in I.R. Edgar and A. Russell (eds), *The Anthropology of Welfare*. London: Routledge.

Balloch, S. (1997) 'Gender and occupational attainment in the social services', *Making a Difference: Women and career progression in social services*. Social Work Research Centre, Stirling University: National Institute of Social Work.

Bannerji, H. (2000) *The Dark Side of the Nation: Essays on multiculturalism, nationalism, and gender*. Toronto, ON: Canadian Scholar's Press.

Barnes, J.A. (1972) *Social Networks*. Reading, MA: Addison-Wesley Modular Publications, Module No. 26: 1–29.

Batagelj, V. and Mrvar, A. (2003) 'PAJEK: Program for large network analysis' at www.insna.org software

Bauman, Z. (1992) *Intimations of Postmodernity*. London: Routledge.

Bauman, Z. (2000) 'Am I my brother's keeper?', *European Journal of Social Work*, 3 (1): 5–11.

Beck, U. (1992) *Risk Society: Towards a new modernity*. London: Sage.

Beck, U. (2000) 'Zombie categories', in J. Rutherford (ed.), *The Art of Life*. London: Lawrence & Wishart.

Beck, U. and Beck-Gernsheim, E. (2002) *Individualization*. London: Sage.

Becker, H. (1993) 'Theory: The necessary evil', in D. Flinders and G. Mills (eds), *Theory and Concepts in Qualitative Research: Perspectives from the field*. New York: Teachers College Press.

Beckett, S. (1938) *Murphy*. London: Routledge.

Beckett, S. (1965) *Three Novels: Molloy, Malone Dies, The Unnamable*. New York: Grove Press.

Bedard, G. (2000) 'Deconstructing whiteness: Pedagogical implications for anti-racism education', in A.M. Calliste and G.J. Dei (eds), *Power, Knowledge, and Anti-racism education: A critical reader*. Halifax, NS: Fernwood Publishing. pp. 41–56.

Begam, R. (1996) *Samuel Beckett and the End of Modernity*. Palo Alto, CA: Stanford University Press.

Bell, M. (2007) 'Community-based parenting programmes: An exploration of the interplay between environmental and organizational factors in a Webster Stratton project', *British Journal of Social Work*, 37 (1): 55–72.

Bell, V. (1999) 'On speech, race and melancholia: An interview with Judith Butler', *Theory, Culture and Society*, 16 (2): 163–74.

Benhabib, S. (1986) *Critique, Norm and Utopia: A study of the foundations of critical theory*. New York: Columbia University Press.

Benhabib, S. (1995) 'Feminism and postmodernism', in L. Nicholson (ed.), *Feminist Contentions: A philosophical exchange*. London: Routledge.

Benhabib, S., Butler, J., Cornell, D. and Fraser, N. (1995) *Feminist Contentions: A philosophical exchange*. London: Routledge.

Beresford, P. (2000) 'Service users' knowledges and social work theory: Conflict or collaboration?', *British Journal of Social Work*, 30: 489–503.

Beresford, P. and Croft, S. (2004) 'Service users and practitioners reunited: The key component for social work reform', *British Journal of Social Work*, 34: 53–68.

Beringer, A., Fletcher, M.E. and Taket, A.R. (2006) 'Rules and resources: A structuration approach to understanding the coordination of children's inpatient health care', *Journal of Advanced Nursing*, 56 (3): 325–335.

Bernard, R.H. (2002) *Research Methods in Anthropology: Qualitative and quantitative approaches* (3rd edn). Walnut Creek, CA: AltaMira.

Bernstein, R.J. (1991) *The New Constellation*. Cambridge: Polity Press.

Best, S. and Kellner, D. (1992) *Postmodern Theory: Critical interrogations*. Basingstoke: Macmillan.

Best, S. and Kellner, D. (1997) *The Postmodern Turn*. New York: Guilford Press.

Bhabha, H. (1994) *The Location of Culture*. London: Routledge.

Billig, M. (1999a) 'Whose terms?: Whose ordinariness? Rhetoric and ideology in conversation analysis', *Discourse and Society*, 10 (4): 543–58.

Billig, M. (1999b) 'Conversation analysis and claims of naivety', *Discourse and Society*, 10 (4): 572–6.

Billig, M., Condor, S., Edwards, D., Grane, M., Middleton, D. and Radley, A. (1988) *Ideological Dilemmas: A social psychology of everyday thinking*. London: Sage.

Bilsker, D. and Goldner, E.M. (2000) 'Teaching evidence based practice in mental health', *Research on Social Work Practice*, 10 (5): 664–9.

Bishop, A. (1994) *Becoming an Ally: Breaking the cycle of oppression*. Halifax, NS: Fernwood Publishing.

Bissoondath, N. (1994) *Selling Illusions: The cult of multiculturalism in Canada*. Toronto, ON: Penguin Books.

Bittner, E. (1967a) 'The police on skid row: A study of peace keeping', *American Sociological Review*, 32: 699–715.

Bittner, E. (1967b) 'Police discretion in emergency apprehension of mentally ill persons', *Social Problems*, 14 (3): 278–92.

Bittner, E. (1976) 'Policing juveniles: The social bases of common practice', in M. Rosenheim (ed.), *Pursuing Justice for the Child*. Chicago, IL: University of Chicago Press.

Blaug, R. (1995) 'Distortion of the face to face: Communicative reason and social work practice', *British Journal of Social Work*, 25: 423–39.

Blumer, H. (1969) *Symbolic Interactionism: Perspective and method*. Englewood Cliffs, NJ: Prentice Hall.

Boghossian, P. (2006) *Fear of Knowledge*. New York: Oxford University Press.

Bohannan, P. and Van der Elst, D. (1998) *Asking and Listening: Ethnography as personal adaptation*. Prospect Heights, IL: Waveland Press.

Boland, T. and Fowler, A. (2002) 'A systems perspective of performance management in public sector organisations', *International Journal of Public Sector Management*, 13 (5): 417–46.

Borgatti, S.P., Everett, M.G. and Freeman, L.C. (2006) 'UCINET 6 Social network analysis software' at: www.insna.org software

Bott, H. (1928) 'Observations of play activities in a nursery school', *Genetic Psychology Monographs*, 4: 44–88.

Bourdieu, P. (1977) *Outline of a Theory of Practice*. Cambridge: Cambridge University Press.

Bourdieu, P. (1991) *Language and Symbolic Power*. Cambridge: Polity Press.

Bourdieu, P. (1994) *In Other Words*. Cambridge: Polity Press .

Bourdieu, P. (1998) *On Television and Journalism*. London: Pluto.

Bourdieu, P. (2001) *Acts of Resistance: Against the new myths of our time* (2nd reprint). Cambridge: Polity Press.

Bourdieu, P. (2002a) 'Social space and symbolic power', in M. Haugaard (ed.), *Power: A reader*. Manchester: Manchester University Press. pp. 229–45.

Bourdieu, P. (2002b) 'Habitus', in J. Hillier and E. Rooksby (eds), *Habitus: A sense of place*. Aldershot: Ashgate. pp. 27–34.

Bourdieu, P. (2003a) *Outline of a Theory of Practice* (17th printing, 1st English translation 1977). Cambridge: Cambridge University Press.

Bourdieu, P. (2003b) *Firing Back*. London: Verso.

Bourdieu, P. (2003c) *Pascalian Meditations* (1st English translation 2000). Cambridge: Polity.

Bourdieu, P. (2004, 1979) *Distinction* (10th reprint, 1st English translation 1984). London: Routledge.

Bourdieu, P., Accardo, A., Balazas, G., Beaud, S., Bonvin, F., Bourdieu, E., Bourgois, P., Broccolichi, S., Champagne, P., Christin, R., Faguer, J.P., Garcia, S., Lenoir, R., Oeuvrard, F., Pialoux, M., Pinto, L., Podalydes, D., Sayad, A., Soulie, C. and Wacquant, J.D. (2002) *The Weight of the World: Social suffering in contemporary society* (1st reprint, 1st English translation 1999). Cambridge: Polity Press.

Bourdieu, P. and Eagleton, T. (1994) 'Doxa and the common life: An interview', in S. Zizek (ed.), *Mapping ideology*. London: Verso.

Bourdieu, P. and Wacquant, L. (1999) 'On the cunning of imperialist reason', *Theory, Culture & Society*, 16 (1): 41–59.

Bourdieu, P. and Wacquant, L. (2001) 'NewLiberalSpeak: Notes on the new planetary vulgate', *Radical Philosophy*, 105: 2–6.

Bourdieu, P. and Wacquant, L.J.D. (2004) *An Invitation to Reflexive Sociology* (2nd reprint, 1st English translation 1992). Cambridge: Polity Press.

Bourgois, P. (2002) *In search of Respect: Selling crack in El Barrio* (2nd edn). Cambridge: Cambridge University Press.

Bowker, G.C. and Star, S.L. (2000) *Sorting Things Out: Classification and its consequences*. Cambridge, MA: MIT Press.

Bracken, P. and Thomas, P. (2005) *Postpsychiatry: Mental health in a postmodern world*. Oxford: Oxford University Press.

Braithwaite, A. (2002) 'The personal, the political, third wave and post feminism', *Feminist Theory*, 3 (2): 335–44.

Brake, M. and Bailey, R. (1980) *Radical Social Work and Practice*. London: Edward Arnold.

Braye, S. and Preston-Shoot, M. (1995) *Empowering Practice in Social Care*. Buckingham: Open University Press.

Bridge, G. (2004) 'Pierre Bourdieu', in P. Hubbard, R. Kitchin and G. Valentine (eds), *Key Thinkers on Space and Place*. London: Sage.

Brugha, T.S. (ed.) (1995) *Social Support and Psychiatric Disorder: Research findings and guidelines for clinical practice*. Cambridge: Cambridge University Press.

Bryant, C. (1989) 'Review: Towards post-empiricist sociological thinking', *British Journal of Sociology*, 40 (2): 319–27.

Bryant, C. and Jarry, D. (eds) (2001) *Giddens' Theory of Structuration*. London: Routledge.

Bryson, V. (1999) *Feminist Debates: Issues of theory and political practice*. Basingstoke: Macmillan.

Buchanan, James, M. and Tullock, G. (1962) *The Calculus of Consent: Logical foundations of constitutional democracy*. Ann Arbor, MI: University of Michigan Press.

Burawoy, M. (1991) *Ethnography Unbound: Power and resistance in the modern metropolis*. Berkeley, CA: University of California Press.

Burchell, G., Gordon, C. and Miller, P. (eds) (1991) *The Foucault Effect*. Hemel Hempstead: Harvester Wheatsheaf.

Butler, J. (1987) *Subjects of Desire: Hegelian reflections in twentieth-century France*. New York: Columbia University Press.

Butler, J. (1990) *Gender Trouble: Feminism and the subversion of identity*. London: Routledge.

Butler, J. (1993) *Bodies that Matter: On the discursive limits of 'sex'*. London: Routledge.

Butler, J. (1995) 'Contingent foundations', in L. Nicholson (ed.), *Feminist Contentions: A philosophical exchange*. London: Routledge.

Butler, J. (1997a) *Excitable Speech: A politics of the performative*. London: Routledge.

Butler, J. (1997b) *The Psychic Life of Power: Theories in subjection*. Palo Alto, CA: Stanford University Press.

Butler, J. (2000) *Antigone's Claim: Kinship between life and death*. New York: Columbia University Press.

Butler, J. (2002) 'Is kinship always already heterosexual?', *Differences: A Journal of Feminist Cultural Studies*, 15 (1): 14–44.

Butler, J. (2003) 'No it's not anti-Semitic', *London Review of Books*, 21 August.

Butler, J. (2004a) *Precarious Life: The powers of mourning and violence*. London: Verso.

Butler, J. (2004b) *Undoing Gender*. London: Routledge.

Butler, J. (2005) *Giving an Account of Oneself*. New York: Fordham University Press.

Buxton, W. (1985) *Talcott Parsons and the Capitalist Nation-state: Political sociology as a strategic vocation*. Toronto, ON: University of Toronto Press.

Callincos, A. (1989) *Against Postmodernism: A Marxist critique*. Cambridge: Polity Press.

Callinicos, A. (1999) *Social Theory: A historical introduction*. Oxford: Blackwell.

Callinicos, A. (2000) 'Impossible anti-capitalism?', *New Left Review*, 2: 117–25.

Calliste, A. and Dei, G. (2000) *Power, Knowledge, and Anti-racism Education: A critical reader*. Halifax, NS: Fernwood Publishing.

Cameron, A. and Palan, R. (2004) *The Imagined Economies of Globalization*. London: Sage.

Campbell, K.E. and Lee, B.A. (1991) 'Name generators in surveys of personal networks', *Social Networks*, 13: 203–21.

Cantley, C. and Smith, G. (1983) 'Social work and a relatives support group in a psychogeriatric day hospital: A research note', *British Journal of Social Work*, 13 (1): 663–70.

Carabine, J. (1996) 'Heterosexuality and social policy', in D. Richardson (ed.), *Theorizing Heterosexuality*. Buckingham: Open University Press. pp. 55–74.

Carniol, B. (1992) 'Structural social work: Maurice Moreau's challenge to social work practice', *Journal of Progressive Human Services*, 3 (1): 1–20.

Carniol, B. (2005a) 'Structural social work (Canada)', in J.M. Herrick and P.H Stuart (eds), *Encyclopedia of Social Welfare History in North America*. Thousand Oaks, CA: Sage Publications.

Carniol, B. (2005b) *Case Critical: Social services & social justice in Canada* (5th edn). Toronto, ON: Between the Lines.

Carniol, B. (2005c) 'Analysis of social location and change: Practice implications', in S. Hick, J. Fook and R. Pozzuto (eds), *Social Work: A critical turn*. Toronto, ON: Thompson Educational Press.

Carniol, B. (2007) Personal email correspondence with Steven Hick, 18 March 2007.

Carr, E.S. (2006) '"Secrets keep you sick": Metalinguistic labor in a drug treatment program for homeless women', *Language in Society*, 35 (5): 631–55.

Cavanagh, K. and Cree, V. (eds) (1996) *Working with Men: Feminism and social work*. London: Routledge.

Chambon, A., Irving, A. and Epstein, L. (eds) (1999) *Reading Foucault for Social Work*. New York: Columbia University Press.

Cheetham, J. (1992) 'Evaluating social work effectiveness', *Research on Social Work Practice*, 2 (3): 265–87.

Cheetham, J. (1997) 'Evaluating social work: Progress and prospects', *Research on Social Work Practice*, 7 (3): 291–310.

Chelimsky, E. (1997) 'Thoughts for a new evaluation society', *Evaluation*, 3 (1): 97–118.

Choi, H. (2002) 'Understanding adolescent depression in ethnocultural context', *Advances in Nursing Research*, 25 (2): 71–85.

Christensen, P., Hockey, J. and James, A. (1998) '"You just get on with it": Questioning models of welfare dependency in a rural community', in I.R. Edgar and A. Russell (eds), *The Anthropology of Welfare*. London: Routledge.

Christie, A. (ed.) (2001) *Men and Social Work: Theories and practices*. Basingstoke: Palgrave Macmillan.

Christie, A. (2006) 'Negotiating the uncomfortable intersections between gender and professional identities to social work', *Critical Social Policy*, 26 (2): 390–411.

Cixous, H. (1988) *Writing Differences: Readings from the seminar of Hélène Cixous*. Buckingham: Open University Press.

Clarke, J. (1996) 'After social work', in N. Parton (ed.), *Social Theory, Social Change and Social Work*. London: Routledge.

Clarke, J. (2004a) *Changing Welfare, Changing States: New directions in social policy*. London: Sage.

Clarke, J. (2004b) 'Dissolving the public realm?', The logics and limits of neo-liberalism', *Journal of Social Policy*, 33 (1): 27–48.

Clifford, J. and Marcus, G.E. (eds) (1986) *Writing Culture: The poetics of politics of ethnography*. Berkeley, CA: University of California Press.

Cohen, M. and Mullender, A. (eds) (2003) *Gender and Groupwork*. London: Routledge.

Colarossi, L.G. (2001) 'Adolescent gender differences in social support: Structure, function, and provider type', *Social Work Research*, 25 (4): 233–41.

Coleman, J., Katz, E. and Menzel, H. (1957) 'The diffusion of an innovation among physicians', *Sociometry*, 20: 253–70.

Colgan, C. and Cheers, B. (2002) 'The problem of justification in social work', *Australian Social Work*, 55 (2): 109–18.

Collins, B.G. (1986) 'Defining feminist social work', *Social Work*, 31 (3): 214–19.

Collins, H. (2000) *Tacit Knowledge, Trust and the Q of Sapphire*, Working Paper 1(2000) at: www.cf.ac.uk/socsi/research/publications/workingpapers/paper-1.html (subsequently published (2001) in *Social Studies of Science*, 31 (1): 71–85). Cardiff: Cardiff University School of Social Sciences.

Collins, H. (2001) 'What is tacit knowledge?', in T. Schatzki, K. Cetina and E. von Savigny (eds), *The Practice Turn in Contemporary Theory*. London: Routledge.

Collins, H. and Pinch, T. (1998) *The Golem: What you should know about science*. Cambridge: Cambridge University Press.

Collins, R. (1988) *Theoretical Sociology*. San Diego, CA: Harcourt Brace Jovanovich.

Comstock, D. (1982) 'A method for critical research', in F. Bredo and W. Feinburg (eds), *Knowledge and Values in Educational Research*. Philadelphia, PA: Temple University Press.

Connections (1977) *Connections*, 1 (1): 1–30.

Connell, R.W. (1994) *Gender and Power*. Cambridge: Polity Press.

Connolly, D.R. (2000) *Homeless Mothers: Face to face with women and poverty*. Minneapolis, MN: University of Minnesota Press.

Cook, T. and Campbell, D. (1979) *Quasi-experimentation*. Chicago, IL: Rand McNally.

Corrigan, P. and Leonard, P. (1978) *Social Work under Capitalism: A Marxist approach*. London: Macmillan.

Coulshed, U. and Orme, J. (2006) *Social Work Practice*. Basingstoke Palgrave Macmillan.

Creswell, J. (1994) *Research Design: Qualitative and quantitative approaches*. Thousand Oaks, CA: Sage.

Crinall, K. (1999) 'Offending mothers: Theorising in a feminist minefield', in B. Pease and J. Fook (eds), *Transforming Social Work Practice: Postmodern critical perspectives*. London: Routledge.

Curtis, R., Friedman, A., Neaigus, B., Goldstein, M. and Ildefonso, G. (1995) 'Street-level drug markets: Network structure and HIV risk', *Social Networks*, 17 (3–4): 229–49.

Dale, J. and Foster, P. (1986) *Feminists and State Welfare*. London: Routledge & Kegan Paul.

Dalley, G. (1988) *Ideologies of Caring*. Basingstoke: Macmillan.

Dalrymple, J. and Horan, H. (2007) 'Best practice in child advocacy: Matty's story', in K. Jones, B. Cooper and H. Ferguson (eds), *Best Practice in Social Work: Critical perspectives*. Basingstoke: Palgrave Macmillan.

Daly, M. (1990) *Gyn/Ecology: The metaethics of radical feminism*. Boston, MA: Beacon Press.

Davies, C.A. (1998) 'Caring communities or effective networks? Community care and people with learning difficulties in South Wales', in I.R. Edgar and A. Russell (eds), *The Anthropology of Welfare*. London: Routledge.

Davis, A. (1991) 'A structural approach to social work', in J. Lishman (ed.), *Handbook of Theory for Practice Teachers in Social Work*. London: Jessica Kingsley.

Davis, A. and Garrett, P.M. (2004) 'Progressive practice for tough times: Social work, poverty and division in the 21st century', in M. Lymbery and S. Butler (eds), *Social Work Ideals and Practice Realities*. London: Palgrave.

D'Cruz, H., Gillingham, P. and Melendez, S. (2007) 'Reflexivity, its meanings and relevance for social work: A critical review of the literature', *British Journal of Social Work*, 37 (1): 73–90.

de Beauvoir, S. (1972) *The Coming of Age*. New York: GP Putnam's Sons.

de Beauvoir, S. (1993, 1949) *The Second Sex*. London: Everyman.

de Botton, A. (2002) *The Art of Travel*. London: Penguin.

de Montigny, G. (1995) *Social Working: An ethnography of front-line practice*. Toronto, ON: University of Toronto Press.

de Montigny, G. (2007) 'Ethnomethodology for social work', *Qualitative Social Work*, 6 (1): 95–120.

de Saussure, F. (1974, 1916) *Course in General Linguistics*. London: Fontana.

de Saussure, F. (R. Harris trans.) (1983) *Course in General Linguistics*. La Salle, IL: Open Court.

Deacon, A. and Mann, K. (1999) 'Agency, modernity and social policy', *Journal of Social Policy*, 28: 413–35.

Dean, R. (2001) 'The myth of cross-cultural competence', *Families in Society*, 82 (6): 623–30.

Dei, G. (1996) *Theory and Practice: Anti-racism education*. Halifax, NS: Fernwood Publishing.

Dei, G., Karumanchery, L. and Karumanchery-Luik, N. (2004) *Playing the Race Card: Exposing white power and privilege*. New York: Peter Lang.

Delenze, G. (S. Hand trans. and ed.) (1988) *Foucault*. Minneapolis, MN: University of Minnesota Press.

Delgado, R. (ed.) (1995) *Critical Race Theory: The cutting edge*. Philadelphia, PA: Temple University Press.

Derrida, J. (A. Bass trans.) (1978) *Writing and Difference*. Chicago, IL: University of Chicago Press.

Desjarlais, R. (1997) *Shelter Blues: Sanity and selfhood among the homeless*. Philadelphia, PA: University of Pennsylvania Press.

Dewey, J. (1910) *How we Think*. Lexington, MA: D.C. Heath.

Dewing, M. and Leman, M. (2006) *Canadian Multiculturalism*. Ottawa, ON: Political and Social Affairs Division, Parliamentary Information and Service, Research Library of Parliament.

Dickens, D.R. and Fontana, A. (1994) *Postmodernism and Social Enquiry*. London: UCL Press.

Disch, L. (1999) 'Review essay: Judith Butler and the politics of the performative', *Political Theory*, 27 (4): 545–59.

Di Stefano, C. (1990) 'Dilemmas of difference: feminism, modernity, and postmodernism', in L. Nicholson (ed.), *Feminism/Postmodernism*. London: Routledge.

Dolowitz, D.P., with Hulme, R., Nellis, M. and O'Neill, F. (eds) (2000) *Policy Transfer and British Social Policy*. Buckingham: Open University Press.

Dominelli, L. (1997a) *Sociology for Social Work*. London: Macmillan.

Dominelli, L. (1997b) *Anti-racist Social Work* (2nd edn). London: Macmillan.

Dominelli, L. (2002a) *Anti-oppressive Social Work Theory and Practice*. New York: Palgrave Macmillan.

Dominelli, L. (2002b) *Feminist Social Work: Theory and practice*. Basingstoke: Palgrave Macmillan.

Dominelli, L. and McCleod, E. (1989) *Feminist Social Work*. Basingstoke: Palgrave Macmillan.

Donoghue, J. (2008) 'Antisocial Behaviour Orders (ASBOs) in Britain: Contextualising risk and reflexive modernization', *Sociology*, 42: 337–55.

Donovan, M. (2003) 'Family therapy beyond postmodernism: Some considerations on the ethical orientation of contemporary practice', *Journal of Family Therapy*, 25: 285–306.

Dore, I.J. (2006) 'Evidence focused social care: On target or off-side?', *Social Work and Society*, 4 (2) at: www.socwork.net/2006/2/articles/dore.

Dreyfus, H. and Rabinow, P. (1982) *Michel Foucault: Beyond structuralism and hermeneutics*. Hemel Hempstead: Harvester.

Dworkin, A. (1981) *Pornography: Men possessing women*. London: The Women's Press.

Edgar, I.R. and Russell, A. (eds) (1998) *The Anthropology of Welfare*. London: Routledge.

Elden, S. (2001) *Mapping the Present: Heidegger, Foucault and the project of a spatial history*. London: Continuum.

Epstein, I. (1996) 'In quest of a research-based model for clinical practice: Or, why can't a social worker be more like a researcher?', *Social Work Research*, 20 (2): 97–100.

Eribon, D. (B. Wing trans.) (1991) *Michel Foucault*. Cambridge, MA: Harvard University Press.

Erickson, F. (2004) *Talk and Social Theory: Ecologies of speaking and listening in everyday life*. Cambridge: Polity Press.

Estroff, S.E. (1981) *Making it Crazy: An ethnography of psychiatric clients in an American community*. Los Angeles, CA: University of California Press.

Eyrich, K.M., Pollio, D.E. and North, C.S. (2003) 'An exploration of alienation and replacement theories of social support in homelessness', *Social Work Research*, 27 (4): 222–31.

Fairclough, N. (2005) 'Peripheral vision: Discourse analysis in organization studies: the case for critical realism', *Organization Studies*, 26: 915–39.

Fawcett, B. (2000) *Feminist Perspectives on Disability*. Harlow: Prentice Hall.

Fawcett, B. (2007) 'Women and violence', in B. Fawcett and F. Waugh (eds), *Addressing Violence, Abuse and Oppression: Debates and challenges*. London: Routledge.

Fawcett, B. and Featherstone, B. (1998) 'Quality assurance and evaluation in social work in a postmodern era', in J. Carter (ed.), *Postmodernity and the Fragmentation of Welfare*. London: Routledge.

Fawcett, B., Featherstone, B., Fook, J. and Rossiter, A. (eds) (2000) *Practice and Research in Social Work: Postmodern feminist perspectives*. London: Routledge.

Fawcett, B., Featherstone, B. and Goddard, J. (2004) *Contemporary Child Care Policy and Practice*. Basingstoke: Palgrave Macmillan.

Fawcett, B., Featherstone, B., Heam, J. and Toft, C. (eds) (1996) *Violence and Gender Relations: Theory and Interventions*. London: Sage.

Fawcett, B., Featherstone, B. and Karban, K. (2005) *Contemporary Mental Health: Theory, policy and practice*. London: Routledge.

Featherstone, B. (2004) *Family Life and Family Support: A feminist analysis*. Basingstoke: Palgrave Macmillan.

Featherstone, B. and Fawcett, B. (1995a) 'Feminism and child abuse: Opening up some possibilities', *Critical Social Policy*, 42: 61–80.

Featherstone, B. and Fawcett, B. (1995b) 'Oh No! Not more isms: Feminism, postmodernism, poststructuralism and social work education', *Social Work Education*, 14 (3): 25–43.

Featherstone, B., Rivett, M. and Scourfield, J. (2007) *Working with Men in Health and Social Care*. London: Sage.

Ferguson, H. (1997) 'Protecting children in new times: Child protection and the risk society', *Child and Family Social Work*, 2 (4): 221–34.

Ferguson, H. (2001) 'Social work, individualisation and life politics', *British Journal of Social Work*, 31 (1): 41–56.

Ferguson, H. (2003a) 'In defence (and celebration) of life politics in social work', *British Journal of Social Work*, 33 (5): 699–707.

Ferguson, H. (2003b) 'Welfare, social exclusion and reflexivity: The case of child and woman protection', *Journal of Social Policy*, 32 (2): 199–216.

Ferguson, H. (2003c) 'Outline of a critical best practice perspective on social work and social care', *British Journal of Social Work*, 33: 1005–24.

Ferguson, H. (2004) *Protecting Children in Time: Child abuse, child protection and the consequences of modernity*. Basingstoke: Palgrave Macmillan.

Ferguson, H. (2008) 'Best practice in family support and child protection: Promoting child safety and democratic families', in K. Jones., B. Cooper and H. Ferguson (eds), *Best Practice in Social Work: Critical perspectives*. Basingstoke: Palgrave Macmillan.

Ferguson, H., Jones, K. and Cooper, B. (eds) (2008) *Best Practice in Social Work: Critical perspectives.* Basingstoke: Palgrave Macmillan.

Ferguson, H. and Hogan, F. (2004) *Strengthening Families through Fathers: Developing policy and practice in relation to vulnerable fathers and their families.* Dublin: Department of Social and Family Affairs.

Ferguson, H. and O'Reilly, M. (2001) *Keeping Children Safe: Child abuse, child protection and the promotion of welfare.* Dublin: A & A Farmar.

Ferguson, I. (2007) *Reclaiming Social Work: Challenging neoliberalism and promoting social justice.* London: Sage.

Firestone, S. (1971) *The Dialectic of Sex.* London: Jonathan Cape.

Fischer, C.S. (1982) *To Dwell Among Friends: Personal networks in town and city.* Berkeley, CA: University of California Press.

Fischer, J. (1973) 'Is casework effective?: A review', *Social Work,* 18 (1): 5–20.

Fisher, M. (1994) 'Man-made care: Community care and older male carers', *British Journal of Social Work,* 24: 659–80.

Flax, J. (1990) *Thinking Fragments: Psychoanalysis, feminism and postmodernism in the contemporary west.* Berkeley, CA: University of California Press.

Floersch, J. (2000) 'Reading the case record: The oral and written narratives of social workers', *Social Service Review,* 74 (2): 169–91.

Floersch, J. (2002) *Meds, Money, and Manners: The case management of severe mental illness.* New York: Columbia University Press.

Floersch, J. (2004a) 'Ethnography: A case study of invented clinical knowledge', in D.K. Padgett (ed.), *The Qualitative Research Experience.* Belmont, CA: Wadsworth/Thomson Learning.

Floersch, J. (2004b) 'A method for investigating practitioner use of theory in practice', *Qualitative Social Work,* 3 (2): 161–77.

Fook, J. (1993) *Radical Casework: A theory for practice.* St Leonards, NSW: Allen & Unwin.

Fook, J. (1996) *The Reflective Researcher: Social work theories of practice and research.* St Leonards, NSW: Allen & Unwin.

Fook, J. (2002) *Social Work: Critical theory and practice.* London: Sage.

Fook, J. (2004) 'What professionals need from research: Beyond evidence-based practice', in D. Smith (ed.), *Social Work and Evidence-based Practice.* London: Jessica Kingsley Publishers. pp. 29–46.

Forrester, M. and Reason, D. (2006) 'Conversation analysis and psychoanalytic psychotherapy research: Questions, issues, problems and challenges', *Psychoanalytic Psychotherapy,* 20: 40–64.

Forsberg, H. and Vagli, A. (2006) 'The social construction of emotions in child protection case-talk', *Qualitative Social Work,* 5 (1): 9–31.

Foucault, M. (A.M. Sheridan Smith trans.) (1972) *The Archaeology of Knowledge.* New York: Pantheon Books.

Foucault, M. (1973) *The Order of things: An archaeology of the human sciences.* New York: Vintage Books.

Foucault, M. (Alan Sheridan trans.) (1979) *Discipline and Punish: The birth of the prison.* New York: Vintage.

Foucault, M. (Robert Hurley trans.) (1980a) *The History of Sexuality, Volume 1: An introduction.* New York: Vintage Books.

Foucault, M. (Colin Gordon ed.) (1980b) *Power/Knowledge: Selected interviews and other writings, 1972–1977.* New York: Pantheon Books.

Foucault, M. (1983) 'Afterword: The subject and power', in H.L. Dreyfus and P. Rabinow (eds), *Michel Foucault: Beyond structuralism and hermeneutics* (2nd edn) Chicago, IL: University of Chicago Press. pp. 208–26.

Foucault, M. (Robert Hurley trans.) (1985) *The History of Sexuality, Volume 2: The use of pleasure.* New York: Pantheon Books.

Foucault, M. (Alan Sheridan trans.) (1987) *Mental Illness and Psychology.* Berkeley, CA: University of California Press.

Foucault, M. (Richard Howard trans.) (1988) *Madness and Civilization: A history of insanity in the age of reason*. New York: Vintage Books.

Foucault, M. (1990) *Politics, Philosophy, Culture: Interviews and other writings, 1977–1984*. New York: Routledge.

Foucault, M. (Paul Rabinov ed.) (1997) *Essential Works of Foucault, 1954–1984, Volume 1: Ethics, subjectivity and truth*. New York: The New Press.

Foucault, M. (James Faubion ed.) (1998) *Essential Works of Foucault, 1954–1984, Volume 2: Aesthetics, method, and epistemology*. New York: The New Press.

Foucault, M. (James Faubion ed.) (2000) *Essential Works of Foucault, 1954–1984, Volume 3: Power*. New York: The New Press.

Foucault, M. (David Macey trans.) (2003) *Society must be Defended: Lectures at the College de France, 1975–1976*. New York: Picador.

Foucault, M., Donald, F., Bouchard and Sherry Simon trans. (1977) *Language, Counter-memory, Practice: Selected essays and interviews*. Ithaca, NY: Cornell University Press.

Fournier, D. (ed.) (1995) *Reasoning in Evaluation: Inferential links and leaps*. San Francisco, CA: American Evaluation Association/Jossey-Bass.

Fournier, D. and Smith, N. (1993) 'Clarifying the merits of argument in evaluation practice', *Evaluation and Program Planning*, 16 (4): 315–23.

Fowler, B. (1997) *Pierre Bourdieu and Cultural Theory: Critical investigations*. London: Sage.

Fowler, B. (2003) 'Reading Pierre Bourdieu's *Masculine Domination*: Notes towards an intersectional analysis of gender, culture and class', *Cultural Studies*, 17 (3/4): 468–94.

Frankenberg, R. (ed.) (1993) *White Women, Race Matters: The social construction of whiteness*. Minneapolis, MN: University of Minnesota Press.

Fraser, N. (1989) *Unruly Practices: Power, discourse and gender in contemporary social theory*. Cambridge: Polity Press.

Fraser, N. and Nicholson, L. (1993) 'Social criticism without philosophy: An encounter between feminism and postmodernism', in M. Docherty (ed.), *Postmodernism: A reader*. Hemel Hempstead: Harvester Wheatsheaf.

Freeman, L.C. (2000a) 'See you in the funny papers: Cartoons and social networks', *Connections*, 23 (1): 32–42.

Freeman, L.C. (2000b) 'Visualizing social networks', *Journal of Social Structure*, 1 (1): 1–21.

Freeman, L.C. (2004) *The Development of Social Network Analysis: A study in the sociology of science*. Vancouver: Empirical Press.

Freire, P. (1970) *Pedagogy of the Oppressed*. New York: Continuum International Publishing Group.

Friedan, B. (1986) *The Feminine Mystique*. Harmondsworth: Penguin.

Friedman, M. and Friedman, R. (1980) *Free to Choose*. London: Secker & Warburg.

Gabardi, W. (2001) *Negotiating Postmodernism*. Minneapolis, MN: University of Minnesota Press.

Galper, J. (1975) *The Politics of Social Services*. Englewood Cliffs, NJ: Prentice Hall.

Galper, J. (1980) *Social Work Practice*. Englewood Cliffs, NJ: Prentice Hall.

Gambrill, E. (1999) 'Evidence-based practice: An alternative to authority-based practice', *Families in Society*, 80 (4): 341–50.

Gambrill, E. (2006) 'Evidence-based practice and policy: Choices ahead', *Research on Social Work Practice*, 16 (3): 338–57.

Garfinkel, H. (1967) *Studies in Ethnomethodology*. Cambridge: Polity Press.

Garfinkel, H. (1991) 'Respecification: Evidence for locally produced, naturally accountable phenomena of order, logic, reason, meaning, method, etc. in and as of the essential haecceity of immortal ordinary society (I): An announcement of studies', in G. Button (ed.), *Ethnomethodology and the Human Sciences*. Cambridge: Cambridge University Press. pp. 10–19.

Garfinkel, H. (2002) *Ethnomethodology's Program: Working out Durkheim's aphorism*. Lantham, MD: Rowman & Littlefield.

Garfinkel, H. (A.W. Rawls ed.) (2006) *Seeing Sociologically: The routine grounds of social action*. Boulder, CO: Paradigm.

Garfinkel, H., Lynch, M. and Livingston, E. (1981) 'The work of a discovering science construed with materials from the optically discovered pulsar', *Philosophy of the Social Sciences*, 11 (2): 131–58.

Garfinkel, H. and Sacks, H. (1970) 'On formal structures of practical actions', in J.C. McKinney and E.A. Tiryakian (eds), *Theoretical Sociology Perspectives and Developments*. New York: Appleton-Century Crofts. pp. 337–66.

Garrett, P.M. (2003a) *Remaking Social Work with Children and Families*. London: Routledge.

Garrett, P.M. (2003b) 'The trouble with Harry: Why the new agenda of life politics fails to convince', *British Journal of Social Work*, 33: 381–97.

Garrett, P.M. (2004a) 'More trouble with Harry: A rejoinder in the "life politics" debate', *British Journal of Social Work*, 34 (4): 577–89.

Garrett, P.M. (2004b) *Social Work and Irish People in Britain: Historical and contemporary responses to Irish children and families*. Bristol: Policy Press.

Garrett, P.M. (2004c) 'Talking child protection: The police and social workers "working together"', *Journal of Social Work*, 4 (1): 77–79.

Garrett, P.M. (2004d) 'The electronic eye: Emerging surveillant practices in social work with children and families', *European Journal of Social*, 17 (1): 57–71.

Garrett, P.M. (2005) 'Social work's "electronic turn": Notes on the deployment of information and communication technologies in social work with children and families', *Critical Social Policy*, 25 (4): 529–54.

Garrett, P.M. (2007a) 'Making social work more Bourdieusian: Why the social professions should critically engage with the work of Pierre Bourdieu', *European Journal of Social Work*, 10 (2): 225–43.

Garrett, P.M. (2007b) 'The relevance of Bourdieu for social work: A reflection on obstacles and omissions', *Journal of Social Work*, 7 (3): 357–81.

Garrett, P.M. (2008a) 'Helping Labour to Win Again? Anothony Giddens' programme for the new Prime Minister', *Critical Social Policy*, 28 (2): 235–45.

Garrett, P.M. (2008b) 'How to be modern: New Labour's neoliberal modernity and the Change for Children programme', *British Journal of Social Work*, 38 (2): 270–89.

Garrett, P.M. (forthcoming) 'Thinking with the Sardinian: Antonio Gramsci and social work', *European Journal of Social Work*.

Garrison, J. and Werfel, S. (1977) 'A network approach to clinical social work', *Clinical Social Work Journal*, 5 (2): 108–17.

Gee, J.P. (1990) *Social Linguistics and Literacies: Ideology in discourses*. London: Falmer.

George, P. and Marlowe, S. (2005) 'Structural social work in action: Experiences from Rural India', *Journal of Progressive Human Services*, 16 (1): 5–24.

Gibbons, J. (2001) 'Effective practice: Social work's long history of concern about outcomes', *Australian Social Work*, 54 (3): 3–13.

Gibbs, A. (2001) 'The changing nature and context of social work research', *British Journal of Social Work*, 31: 687–704.

Gibbs, L. and Gambrill, E. (2002) 'Evidence-based practice: Counterarguments to objections', *Research on Social Work Practice*, 12 (3): 452–76.

Giddens, A. (1971) *Capitalism and Modern Social Theory*. Cambridge: Cambridge University Press.

Giddens, A. (1976) *New Rules of Sociological Method*. London: Hutchinson.

Giddens, A. (1979) *Central Problems in Social Theory*. London: Macmillan.

Giddens, A. (1981) *A Contemporary Critique of Historical Materialism, Volume 1*. London: Macmillan.

206 Social Work Theories and Methods

Giddens, A. (1984) *The Constitution of Society*. Cambridge: Polity Press.

Giddens, A. (1985) *The Nation State and Violence: Volume 2 of a contemporary critique of historical materialism*. Cambridge: Polity Press.

Giddens, A. (1990) *The Consequences of Modernity*. Cambridge: Polity Press.

Giddens, A. (1991) *Modernity and Self-identity: Self and society in the late modern age*. Cambridge: Polity Press.

Giddens, A. (1992) *The Transformation of Intimacy*. Cambridge: Polity Press.

Giddens, A. (1993) *Sociology*. Cambridge: Polity Press.

Giddens, A. (1994a) *Beyond Left and Right: The future of radical politics*. Cambridge: Polity Press.

Giddens, A. (1994b) 'Living in a post-traditional society', in U. Beck, A. Giddens and S. Lash, *Reflexive Modernization*. Cambridge: Polity Press.

Giddens, A. (1998) *The Third Way: The renewal of social democracy*. Cambridge: Polity Press.

Giddens, A. (1999) *Runaway World: How globalization is reshaping our lives*. London: Profile.

Giddens, A. (2000) *The Third Way and its Critics*. Cambridge: Polity Press.

Giddens, A. (ed.) (2001) *The Global Third Way Debate*. Cambridge: Polity Press.

Giddens, A. (ed.) (2003) *The Progressive Manifesto: New ideas for the Centre-Left*. Cambridge: Polity Press.

Giddens, A. (ed.) (2005) *The New Egalitarianism*. Cambridge: Polity Press.

Giddens, A. (2007a) *Europe in the Global Age*. Cambridge: Polity Press.

Giddens, A. (2007b) *Over to You, Mr Brown: How Labour can win again*. Cambridge: Polity Press.

Gilgun, J.F. (2005) 'The four cornerstones of evidence-based practice in social work', *Research on Social Work Practice*, 15 (1): 52–61.

Gilligan, C. (1983) *In a Different Voice*. Cambridge, MA: Harvard University Press.

Girton, G.D. (1986) 'Kung Fu: Toward a praxiological hermeneutic of the martial arts', in H. Garfinkel (ed.), *Ethnomethodological Studies of Work*. London: Routledge & Kegan Paul. pp. 60–91

Goffman, E. (1981) *Forms of Talk*. Oxford: Oxford University Press.

Gontarski, S.E. (1995) 'Introduction', in *Samuel Beckett: The complete short prose: 1929–1989*. New York: Grove Press. pp. xi–xxxii.

Gordon, L. (1989) *Heroes of their Own Lives: The politics and history of family violence: Boston 1870–1960*. London: Virago.

Gould, N. and Kendall, T. (2007) 'Developing NICE/SCIE guidelines for dementia care: The challenges of enhancing the evidence base for social health care', *British Journal of Social Work*, 37 (3): 475–90.

Gould, N. and Taylor, I. (1996) *Reflective Learning for Social Work*. Aldershot: Ashgate.

Granovetter, M. (1973) 'The strength of weak ties', *American Journal of Sociology*, 78 (4): 1360–80.

Granovetter, M. (1974) *Getting a Job: A study of contacts and careers*. Cambridge, MA: Harvard University Press.

Grass, G. and Bourdieu, P. (2002) 'The "progressive" restoration', *New Left Review*, 14: 63–79.

Grau, C. (2005, 2007) 'Bad dreams, evil demons and the experience machine: Philosophy and *The Matrix*', in J. Perry, M. Bratman and J.M. Fischer (eds), *Introduction to Philosophy: Classical and contemporary readings*. New York: Oxford University Press.

Gray, M. (2008) 'Viewing spirituality in social work through the lens of contemporary social theory', *British Journal of Social Work*, 38 (1): 175–96.

Gray, M., Coates, J. and Yellow Bird, M. (2008) *Indigenous Social Work around the World: Towards culturally relevant social work education and practice*. Aldershot: Ashgate.

Gray, M. and Lovat, T. (2006) 'The shaky high moral ground of postmodern "ethics"', *Social Work/ Maatskaplike*, 42: 201–12.

Gray, M. and McDonald, C. (2006) 'Pursuing good practice?: The limits of evidence-based practice', *Journal of Social Work*, 4 (6): 7–20.

Greco, J. (1998, 2007) 'Introduction: What is epistemology?', in J. Greco and E. Sosa (eds), *The Blackwell Guide to Epistemology*. Oxford: Blackwell Publishing.

Greene, D.G. (1987) *Medicines in the Marketplace*. Health Unit Paper No.1. London: Institute for Economic Affairs (IEA).

Greene, J. (1996) 'Qualitative evaluation and scientific citizenship', *Evaluation*, 2 (3): 277–89.

Gregory, R.L. (ed.) (1987) *The Oxford Companion to the Mind*. Oxford: Oxford University Press.

Guba, E. (1990) 'The alternative paradigm dialog', in E. Guba (ed.), *The Paradigm Dialog*. Newbury Park, CA: Sage.

Gueron, J.M. (2007) 'Building evidence: What it takes and what it yields', *Research on Social Work Practice*, 17 (1): 134–42.

Gurwitsch, A. (1964) *The Field of Consciousness*. Pittsburgh, PA: Duquesne University Press.

Gurwitsch, A. (1966) *Studies in Phenomenology and Psychology*. Evanston, IL: Northwestern University Press.

Gutmann, A. (1994) 'Introduction', in C. Taylor and A. Gutmann (eds), *Multiculturalism*. Princeton, NJ: Princeton University Press. pp. 3–24.

Habermas, J. (1968) *Knowledge and Human Interests*. London: Heinemann.

Habermas, J. (1979) *Communication and the Evolution of Society*. Boston, MA: Beacon Press.

Habermas, J. (1987) *The Theory of Communicative Action*, Volume 2. Cambridge: Polity Press.

Habermas, J. (1996) *Between Facts and Norms*. Cambridge: Polity Press.

Hage, G. (2000) *White Nation: Fantasies of white supremacy in a multicultural society*. Riverwood, NSW: Pluto Press.

Hak, T. (1995) 'Ethnomethodology and the institutional context', *Human Studies*, 18 (2–3): 109–37.

Hall, C. (1997) *Social Work as Narrative*. Aldershot: Ashgate.

Hall, C., Jokinen, A. and Suoninen, E. (2003) 'Legitimating the rejecting of your child in a social work meeting', in C. Hall, K. Juhila, N. Parton and T. Pösö (eds), *Constructing Clienthood in Social Work and Human Services: Interaction, identities and practices*. London: Jessica Kingsley. pp. 27–44.

Hall, C., Slembrouck, S. and Sarangi, S. (2006) *Language Practices in Social Work: Categorisation and accountability in child welfare*. London: Routledge.

Hall, T. (2003) *Better Times than This: Youth homelessness in Britain*. London: Pluto Press.

Hama, H. (1999) 'Ethnomethodology and the Rashomon problem', *Human Studies*, 22: 183–92.

Hammersley, M. (1992) *What's Wrong with Ethnography?* London: Routledge.

Hammersley, M. and Atkinson, P. (1995) *Ethnography: Principles in practice* (2nd edn). London: Routledge.

Hanmer, J. and Statham, D. (eds) (1988) *Women and Social Work: Towards a women-centred practice*. Basingstoke: Palgrave Macmillan.

Hardiman, E.R. (2004) 'Networks of caring: A qualitative study of social support in consumer-run mental health agencies', *Qualitative Social Work*, 3 (4): 431–48.

Harding, S. (1987) *Feminism and Methodology*. Buckingham: Open University Press.

Harlow, E. (2004) 'Why don't women want to be social workers anymore? New managerialism, postfeminism and the shortage of social workers in Social Services Departments in England and Wales', *European Journal of Social Work*, 7 (2): 167–79.

Hare, I. (2004) 'Defining social work for the 21st century: The International Federation of Social Workers' revised definition of social work', *International Social Work*, 47 (3): 407–27.

Harris, R. and Seldon, A. (1979) *Over-ruled on Welfare: The increasing desire for choice in education and medicine and its frustration by 'representative' government*, Hobart Paper No. 13. London: Institute for Economic Affairs.

Hartley, J. and Pike, A. (eds) (2005) *Managing to Improve Public Services: A report by the Advanced Institute of Management Research Public Service Fellows*. London: EPSRC/ESRC.

Harvey, D. (2005) *A Brief History of Neoliberalism*. Oxford: Oxford University Press.

Harvey, D. (2006) *Spaces of Global Capitalism: Towards a theory of uneven geographical development*. London: Verso.

Harvey, L. (1992) *Critical Social Research*. London: Unwin Hyman.

Hausman, A.J. (2002) 'Implications of evidence-based practice for community health', *American Journal of Community Psychology*, 30 (3): 149–66.

Hawkesworth, M. (1989) 'Knowers, knowing, known: Feminist theory and claims of truth', *Signs: Journal of Women in Culture and Society*, 14 (3): 533–57.

Hayek, F. (1952) *The Sensory Order: An inquiry into the foundations of theoretical psychology*. London: Routledge & Kegan Paul.

Hayek, F. (1959) *The Constitution of Liberty*. London: Routledge & Kegan Paul.

Hayek, F. (1979) *The Counter-revolution of Science*. London: Routledge & Kegan Paul.

Hayek, F. (1982) *The Political Order of a Free People*, Volume 3, *Law, Legislation and Liberty: A new statement of the liberal principles of justice and political economy*. London: Routledge & Kegan Paul.

Healy, K. (2000) *Social Work Practices: Contemporary perspectives on change*. London: Sage.

Healy, K. (2005) *Social Work Theories in Context: Creating frameworks for practice*. Basingstoke: Palgrave Macmillan.

Hearn, J. and Morgan, D. (eds) (1990) *Men, Masculinities and Social Theory*. London: Unwin Hyman.

Held, V. (ed.) (1995) *Justice and Care: Essential readings in feminist ethics*. Oxford: Westview Press.

Henderson, M. and Argyle, M. (1985) 'Source and nature of social support given to women at divorce/separation', *British Journal of Social Work*, 15 (1): 57–65.

Henkel, M. (1995) 'Conceptions of knowledge and social work education', in M. Yelloly and M. Henkel (eds), *Learning and Teaching in Social Work: Towards reflective practice*. London: Jessica Kingsley.

Henry, F., Tator, C., Mattis, W. and Rees, T. (2006) *The Colour of Democracy: Racism in Canadian society* (2nd edn). Toronto, ON: Harcourt Canada.

Heritage, J. (1984) *Garfinkel and Ethnomethodology*. Cambridge: Polity Press.

Hesch, K. (1998) 'Wraparound: Linking formal and informal supports', *Journal of Leisurability*, 25 (4): 1–6.

Hesse, M. (1980) *Revolutions and Reconstructions in the Philosophy of Science*. Brighton: Harvester.

Hester, M., Kelly, L. and Radford, J. (eds) (1996) *Women, Violence and Male Power*. Buckingham: Open University Press.

Hick, S. (1997) 'Participatory research: An approach for structural social workers', *Journal of Progressive Human Services*, 8 (2): 63–78.

Hick, S. (1998) *Elements of Structural Social Work*. Module 16: Structural Social Work, click on 'contents' at: www.socialpolicy.ca/52100

Hick, S. (2002) 'Introduction: Anti-oppressive practice: Challenges for social work', *Critical Social Work*, 2 (2): 5.

Hick, S. (2005) 'Reconceptualizing critical social work', in S. Hick, J. Fook and R. Pozzuto (eds), *Social Work: A critical turn*. Toronto, ON: Thompson Educational Publishing.

Hick, S. (2006) *Social Work in Canada: An introduction* (2nd edn). Toronto, ON: Thompson Educational Publishing.

Hick, S. (2007) *Social Welfare in Canada: Understanding income security* (2nd edn). Toronto, ON: Thompson Educational Publishing.

Hick, S., Fook, J. and Pozzuto, R. (eds) (2005) *Social Work: A critical turn*. Toronto, ON: Thompson Educational Publishing.

Hiebert, D. (2003) 'Are immigrants welcome?: Introducing the Vancouver Community Studies Survey', *Research on Immigration and Integration in the Metropolis*, Working Paper Series, 03–06: 1–69. Vancouver: Vancouver Centre of Excellence.

Hilbert, R.A. (1992) *The Classical Roots of Ethnomethodology: Durkheim, Weber, and Garfinkel*. Chapel Hill, NC: University of North Carolina Press.

Hilbert, R.A. (1995) 'Garfinkel's recovery of themes in classical sociology', *Human Studies*, 18: 157–75.

Himmelfarb, G. (2004) *The Roads to Modernity: The British, French, and American Enlightenments*. New York: Knopf.

Hobbes, T. (1958, 1651) *Leviathan*. Harmondsworth: Penguin.

Hoggett, P. (2001) 'Agency, rationality and social policy', *Journal of Social Policy*, 30 (1): 37–56.

Holland, S., Scourfield, J., O'Neill, S. and Pithouse, A. (2005) 'Democratising the family and the State?: The case of family group conferences in child welfare', *Journal of Social Policy*, 34 (1): 59–77.

Hollway, W. (2001) 'The psycho-social subject in "evidence based practice"', *Journal of Social Work Practice*, 15 (1): 10–21.

Hollway, W. (2006) *The Capacity to Care: Gender and ethical subjectivity*. London: Routledge.

Hollway, W. and Featherstone, B. (eds) (1997) *Mothering and Ambivalence*. London: Routledge.

Honneth, A. (2002) 'Recognition or redistribution? Changing perspectives on the moral order of society', in S. Lash and M. Featherstone (eds), *Recognition and Difference: Politics, identity and multiculture*. London: Sage. pp. 43–55.

hooks, b. (1984) 'Feminism: A movement to end sexist oppression', in A. Phillips (ed.), *Feminism and Equality*. Oxford: Blackwell.

Horkheimer, M. (1937) 'Traditionelle und kritische theorie', *Zeitschrift fuer Sozialforschung*, 6 (2): 245–74.

House, E. (1980) *Evaluating with Validity*. Beverley Hills, CA: Sage.

Houston, S. (2002a) 'Reflecting on habitus, field and capital: Towards a culturally sensitive social work', *Journal of Social Work*, 2 (2): 149–67.

Houston, S. (2002b) 'Re-thinking a systemic approach to child welfare: A critical response to the framework for the assessment of children in need and their families', *European Journal of Social Work*, 5: 301–12.

Houston, S. (2003) 'A method from the "lifeworld": Some possibilities for person centred planning for children in care', *Children & Society*, 17: 57–70.

Houston, S. (2004) 'Garrett contra Ferguson: A meta-theoretical appraisal of the "rumble in the jungle"', *British Journal of Social Work*, 34: 261–7.

Howard, M.O., McMillen, C.J. and Pollio, D.E. (2003) 'Teaching evidence-based practice: Toward a new paradigm for social work education', *Research on Social Work Practice*, 13 (2): 234–59.

Howe, D. (1986) 'The segregation of women and their work in the personal social services', *Critical Social Policy*, 15: 21–35.

Howe, D. (1994) 'Modernity, postmodernity and social work', *British Journal of Social Work*, 24: 513–32.

Hugman, R. (2001) 'Post-welfare social work? Reconsidering post-modernism, post-Fordism and social work education', *Social Work Education*, 20 (3): 321–33.

Humm, M. (ed.) (1992) *Feminisms: A reader*. London: Harvester Wheatsheaf.

Hummon, N.P. and Carley, K. (1993) 'Social networks as normal science', *Social Networks*, 15 (1): 71–106.

Husserl, E. (W.R. Boyce Gibson trans.) (1962) *Ideas: General introduction to pure phenomenology*. New York: Collier.

Husserl, E. (David Carr trans.) (1970) *The Crisis of European Sciences and Transcendental Phenomenology: An introduction to phenomenological philosophy*. Evanston, IL: Northwestern University Press.

Hutchby, I. (2005) '"Active listening": Formulations and the elicitation of feelings-talk in child counselling', *Research on Language and Social Interaction*, 38 (3): 303–29.

Hutchby, I. and Wooffitt, R. (1998) *Conversation Analysis*. Cambridge: Polity Press.

Huyssen, A. (1990) 'Mapping the postmodern', in L. Nicholson (ed.), *Feminism/Postmodernism*. London: Routledge.

Ife, J. (1997) *Rethinking Social Work: Towards critical practice*. Melbourne: Longman.

Ife, J. (2001) *Human Rights and Social Work: Towards rights-based practice*. Cambridge: Cambridge University Press.

Ignatieff, M. (1984) *The Needs of Strangers*. London: Chatto & Windus.

Ixer, G. (1999) 'There is no such thing as reflection', *British Journal of Social Work*, 29 (4): 513–28.

Jackson, S. (1992) 'The amazing deconstructing woman', *Trouble and Strife*, 25: 25–31.

James, C. (2003) *Seeing Ourselves: Exploring race, ethnicity, and culture* (3rd edn). Toronto, ON: Thompson Educational Publishing.

Jamieson, L. (1998) *Intimacy: Personal relationships in modern society*. Cambridge: Polity Press.

Jansen, C. (2005) 'Canadian multiculturalism', in C. James (ed.), *Possibilities and Limitations: Multicultural policies and programs in Canada*. Halfax, NS: Fernwood Publishing. pp. 21–33.

Jayyusi, L. (1991) 'Values and moral judgement', in G. Button (ed.), *Ethnomethodology and the Human Sciences*. Cambridge: Cambridge University Press. pp. 227–51.

Jefferson, G. and Lee, J.R.E. (1981) 'The rejection of advice: Managing the problematic convergence of a "troubles-telling" and a "service encounter"', *Journal of Pragmatics*, 5 (5): 399–422.

Jones, C. (1983) *State Social Work and the Working Class*. London: Macmillan.

Jones, C. (2001) 'Voices from the front line: State social workers and New Labour', *British Journal of Social Work*, 31: 547–62.

Kadushin, C. (2004) 'Too much investment in social capital?', *Social Networks*, 26 (1): 75–90.

Karakayali, N. (2004) 'Reading Bourdieu with Adorno: The limits of critical theory and reflexive sociology', *Sociology*, 38 (2): 351–68.

Keenan, E. (2004) 'From sociocultural categories to socially located relations: Using critical theory in social work practice', *Families in Society*, 85 (4): 539–47.

Khan, S. (2000) *Aversion and Desire: Negotiating Muslim female identity in the diaspora*. Toronto, ON: The Women's Press.

Kirk, S.A. and Reid, W.J. (2002) *Science and Social Work: A critical appraisal*. New York: Columbia University Press.

Kirke, D.M. (1995) 'Teenage peer networks in the community as sources of social problems: a sociological perspective', in T.S. Brugha (ed.), *Social Support and Psychiatric Disorder: Research findings and guidelines for clinical practice*. Cambridge: Cambridge University Press. pp. 174–94.

Kirke, D.M. (1996) 'Collecting peer data and delineating peer networks in a complete network', *Social Networks*, 18 (4): 333–46.

Kirke, D.M. (2004) 'Chain reactions in adolescents' cigarette, alcohol and drug use: similarity through peer influence or the patterning of ties in peer networks?', *Social Networks*, 26 (1): 3–28.

Kirke, D.M. (2006) *Teenagers and Substance Use: Social networks and peer influence*. Basingstoke and New York: Palgrave Macmillan.

Kivisto, P. (2002) *Multiculturalism in a Global Society*. Oxford: Blackwell.

Kleinman, A. (1988) *The Illness Narratives: Suffering, healing, and the human condition*. New York: Basic Books.

Knoke, D. and Kuklinski, J.H. (1982) *Network Analysis*. Sage University Paper Series on Quantitative Applications in the Social Sciences. Series No. 07–028. Beverley Hills, CA, and London: Sage.

Kobayashi, A. (2005) 'Employment equity in Canada: The paradox of tolerance and denial', in C. James (ed.), *Possibilities and Limitations: Multicultural policies and programs in Canada*. Halifax, NS: Fernwood Publishing. pp. 154–62.

Koehn, D. (1998) *Rethinking Feminist Ethics: Care, trust and empathy*. London: Routledge.

Kohlberg, L. (1981) *The Philosophy of Moral Development: Moral stages and the idea of justice*. London: Harper & Row.

Kurri, K. and Whalström, J. (2005) 'Placement of responsibility and moral reasoning in couple therapy', *Journal of Family Therapy*, 27: 352–69.

Kymlicka, W. (1995) *Multicultural Citizenship*. New York: Oxford University Press.

LaCapra, D. (2000) *History and Reading: Tocqueville, Foucault, French Studies*. Toronto, ON: University of Toronto Press.

Ladson-Billings, G. (1998) 'Just what is critical race theory and what's it doing in a nice field like education?', *Qualitative Studies in Education*, 11 (1): 7–24.

Lane, J. (2000) *Pierre Bourdieu: A critical introduction*. London: Pluto.

Langan, M. and Lee, P. (eds) (1989) *Radial Social Work Today*. London: Unwin.

Lash, S. (1994) *Reflexive Modernization*. Cambridge: Polity Press.

Lash, S. and Urry, J. (1994) *Economies of Signs and Space*, London: Sage.

Law, J. (1994) *Organizing Modernity*. Oxford: Blackwell.

Layder, D. (1995) *Understanding Social Theory*. London: Sage.

Lecompte, R. (1990) 'Connecting private troubles and public issues in social work education', in B. Wharf (ed.), *Social Change and Social Work in Canada*. Toronto, ON: McClelland Stewart.

Lee, E. (2005) 'Marital conflict and social support of Korean immigrants in the United States', *International Social Work*, 48 (3): 313–24.

Lemert, C. (2000) 'The clothes have no emperor: Bourdieu on American imperialism', *Theory, Culture & Society*, 17 (1): 97–106.

Leonard, P. (1995) 'Postmodernism, socialism and social welfare', *Journal of Progressive Human Services*, 6 (2): 3–19.

Leonard, P. (1997) *Postmodern Welfare: Reconstructing an emancipatory project*. London: Sage.

Leonard, P. (2001) 'The future of critical social work in uncertain conditions', *Critical Social Work Online*, 2 (1): unpaginated.

Lessa, I. (2006) 'Discursive struggles within social welfare: Restaging teen motherhood', *British Journal of Social Work*, 36: 283–98.

Lewis, G. and Neal, S. (2005) 'Introduction: Contemporary political contexts, changing terrains and revisited discourses', *Ethnic and Racial Studies*, 28 (3): 423–44.

Li, P. (1991) 'Race and ethnic relations', in L. Tepperman and R. Richardson (eds), *An Introduction to Sociology: The social world* (2nd edn). Toronto, ON: McGraw-Hill Ryerson. pp. 257–86.

Lin, N. (2001) *Social Capital: A theory of social structure and action*. New York: Cambridge University Press.

Lin, N., Cook, K.S. and Burt, R.S. (2001) *Social Capital: Theory and research*. New York: Aldine de Gruyter.

Lincoln, Y. and Guba, E. (1985) *Naturalistic Inquiry*. Beverley Hills, CA: Sage.

Lister, R. (1997) *Citizenship: Feminist perspectives*. Basingstoke: Macmillan.

Loesberg, J. (2005) *A Return to Aesthetics: Autonomy, indifference, and postmodernism*. Palo Alto, CA: Stanford University Press.

Longhofer, J. and Floersch, J. (2004) 'The phenomenological practice gap: The role of qualitative research in studies of practice guidelines, evaluation, and clinical judgement', *Qualitative Social Work*, 3 (4): 483–6.

Lorenz, W. (2006) '*Social work with vulnerable children in Europe today: The impact of neo-liberal social policies on practice*', presentation in Copenhagen, 24 August.

Lovell, T. (2003) 'Resisting with authority: Historical specificity, agency and the performative self', *Theory, Culture and Society*, 20 (1): 1–17.

Luhrmann, T.M. (2000) *Of Two Minds: The growing disorder in American psychiatry*. New York: Knopf.

Lum, D. (1999) *Culturally Competent Practice: A framework for growth and action*. Pacific Grove, CA: Brooks/Cole.

Lundy, C. (2004) *Social Work and Social Justice: A structural approach to practice*. Toronto, ON: Broadview Press.

Lynch, M. (1993) *Scientific Practice and Ordinary Action: Ethnomethodology and social studies of science*. Cambridge: Cambridge University Press.

Lynch, M. (2000a) 'Against reflexivity as an academic virtue and source of privileged knowledge', *Theory, Culture & Society*, 17 (3): 26–54.

Lynch, M. (2000b) 'The ethnomethodological foundations of conversation analysis', *Text*, 20 (4): 517–32.

Lyotard, J.F. (1994, 1979) *The Postmodern Condition: A report on knowledge*. Manchester: Manchester University Press.

Macdonald, G. (2001) *Effective Interventions for Child abuse and Neglect: An evidence-based approach to planning and evaluating interventions*. Chichester: Wiley.

Macdonald, G. (2002) 'The evidence-based perspective', in M. Davies (ed.), *The Blackwell Companion to Social Work*, Oxford: Blackwell. pp. 424–30.

Macdonald, G. and Sheldon, B. (1992) 'Contemporary studies of the effectiveness of social work', *British Journal of Social Work*, 22 (6): 615–43.

Macey, O. (1994) *The Lives of Michel Foucault*. New York: Pantheon.

Mannheim, K. (1952) 'On the interpretation of "Weltanschauung"', in P. Kecskemeti (ed.), *Essays on the Sociology of Knowledge*. New York: Oxford University Press. pp. 33–83.

Margolin, L. (1997) *Under the Cover of Kindness: The invention of social work*. Charlottesville, VA: University Press of Virginia.

Marris, P. (1996) *The Politics of Uncertainty: Attachment in private and public life*. London: Routledge.

Martin, R. (1988) 'Truth, power, self: An interview with Michel Foucault', in L.H. Martin, H. Gutman and P.H. Hutton (eds), *Technologies of the Self: A seminar with Michel Foucault*. Amherst, MA: University of Massachusetts Press.

Martin, S.J. and Davies, H. (2001) 'What works and for whom?: The competing rationalities of "best value"', *Policy and Politics*, 29 (4): 465–75.

Martyn, H. (2000) *Developing Reflective Practice*. Bristol: Policy Press.

Maynard, D. and Heritage, J. (2005) 'Conversation analysis, doctor–patient interaction and medical communication', *Medical Education*, 39: 428–35.

Mayo, M. (1977) *Women in the Community*. London: Routledge.

McBeath, G.B. and Webb, S.A. (1991) 'Social work, modernity and postmodernity', *The Sociological Review*, 39: 171–92.

McBeath, G.B. and Webb, S.A. (2005) '"Post-critical social work analytics" in social work: A critical perspective', in S. Hick, J. Fook and R. Pozzuto (eds), *Social Work: A critical turn*. Toronto, ON: Thompson Educational Publishing.

McCourt, C. (1998) 'Concepts of community in changing health care: A study of change in midwifery practice', in I.R. Edgar and A. Russell (eds), *The Anthropology of Welfare*. London: Routledge.

McDonald, C. (2006) 'Institutional transformation: The impact of performance measurement on professional practice in social work', *Social Work & Society*, 4 (1) at: www.socwork.net/2006/1/series/professionalism/mcdonald

McDowell, T. (2004) 'Exploring the racial experience of therapists in training: A critical race theory perspective', *The American Journal of Family Therapy*, 32 (4): 305–24.

McHoul, A. (1994) 'Towards a critical ethnomethodology', *Theory, Culture and Society*, 11: 105–26.

McKinnon, C. (1992) 'Feminism, Marxism, method, and the state: An agenda for theory', in M. Humm (ed.), *Feminisms: A reader*. London: Harvester Wheatsheaf.

McLaren, P. (1994) 'White terror and oppositional agency: Towards a critical multiculturalism', in D.T. Goldberg (ed.), *Multiculturalism: A critical reader*. Oxford: Blackwell. pp. 45–74.

McNay, L. (1992) *Foucault and Feminism*. Cambridge: Polity Press.

McNeece, C.A. and Thyer, B.A. (2004) 'Evidence-based practice and social work', *Journal of Evidence-Based Social Work*, 1 (1): 7–25.

McPherson, J.M., Smith-Lovin, L. and Cook, J.M. (2001) 'Birds of a feather: Homophily in social networks', *Annual Review of Sociology*, 27: 415–44.

McRobbie, A. (2006) 'Vulnerability, violence and (cosmopolitan) ethics: Butler's precarious life', *The British Journal of Sociology*, 57 (1): 69–86.

Mead, G.H. (1934, 1962) *Mind, Self, and Society*. Chicago, IL: University of Chicago Press.

Megill, A. (1985) *Prophets of Extremity: Nietzsche, Heidegger, Foucault, Derrida*. Berkeley, CA: University of California Press.

Middleman, R.R. and Goldberg, G. (1974) *Social Service Delivery: A structural approach to social work practice*. New York: Columbia University Press.

Milchman, A. and Rosenberg, A. (eds) (2003) *Foucault and Heidegger: Critical encounters*. Minneapolis, MN: University of Minnesota Press.

Miller, G. (1994) 'Toward ethnographies of institutional discourse: Proposal and suggestions', *Journal of Contemporary Ethnography*, 23 (3): 280–306.

Miller, G. and Silverman, D. (1995) 'Troubles talk and counseling discourse: A comparative study', *The Sociological Quarterly*, 36 (4): 725–47.

Miller, J. (1993) *The Passion of Michel Foucault*. New York: Simon & Schuster.

Milner, J. (2001) *Women and Social Work: Narrative approaches*. Basingstoke: Palgrave Macmillan.

Milton, M. and Friedman, R. (1980) *Free to Choose: A personal statement*. San Diego, CA: Harcourt.

Mitchell, D. (1999) *Governmentality: Power and rule in modern society*. Cambridge: Cambridge University Press.

Mitchell, J. (1974) *Psychoanalysis and Feminism*. London: Allen Lane.

Mitchell, J. and Oakley, A. (eds) (1986) *What is Feminism?* Oxford: Blackwell.

Modood, T. (1997) 'Introduction', in T. Modood and P. Werbner (eds), *The Politics of Multiculturalism in the New Europe*. London: Zed Books. pp. 1–25.

Moffatt, K. (2001) *A Poetics of Social Work: Personal agency and social transformation in Canada, 1920–1939*. Toronto, ON: University of Toronto Press.

Moi, T. (1991) 'Appropriating Bourdieu: Feminist theory and Pierre Bourdieu's sociology of culture', *New Literary History*, 22: 1017–49.

Moreau, M. (1979) 'A structural approach to social work practice', *Canadian Journal of Social Work Education*, 5 (1): 78–94.

Moreau, M. and Frosst, S. (1993) *Empowerment II: Snapshots of the structural approach in action*. Ottawa, ON: Carleton University Press.

Moreau, M. with Leonard, L. (1989) *Empowerment through a Structural Approach to Social Work: A report from practice*. Ottawa, ON: Carleton University.

Moreno, J.L. (1932) *Applications of the Group Method to Classification*. New York: National Committee on Prisons and Prison Labor.

Moreno, J.L. (1934) *Who Shall Survive?* Washington, DC: Nervous and Mental Disease Publishing Company.

Morris, J. (1993) 'Feminism and disability', *Feminist Review*, 43: 57–70.

Morris, J. (1996) *Encounters with Strangers: Feminism and disability*. London: The Women's Press.

Morse, J.M. (2006) 'The politics of evidence', *Qualitative Health Research*, 16 (3): 395–404.

Mouzelis, N. (1991) *Back to Sociological Theory: The social construction of social orders*. London: Macmillan.

Mouzelis, N. (2001) 'Reflexive modernization and the Third Way: The impasses of Giddens' social-democratic politics', *Sociological Review*, 49 (3): 436–56.

Mullaly, B. (1993) *Structural Social Work: Ideology, theory and practice*. Toronto, ON: McLelland and Stewart.

Mullaly, B. (1997) *Structural Social Work* (2nd edn). Oxford: Oxford University Press.

Mullaly, B. (2002) *Challenging Oppression: A critical social work approach*. Don Mills, ON: Oxford University Press.

Mullaly, B. (2007) *The New Structural Social work* (3rd edn). Don Mills, ON: Oxford University Press.

Mullen, E.J. (2002) 'Evidence-based social work theory and practice: Historical and reflective perspective', 4th International Conference on Evaluation for Practice, University of Tampere, Finland, 4–6 July.

Mullen, E.J., Bledsoe, S.E. and Bellamy, J.L. (2007) 'Implementing evidence-based social work practice', *Research on Social Work Practice*. Advance Access 12 June doi:10.1177/1049731506297827.

Mullen, E.J., Shlonsky, A., Bledsoe, S.E. and Bellamy, J.L. (2005) 'From concept to implementation: Challenges facing evidence-based social work', *Evidence & Policy*, 1 (1): 61–84.

Murty, S.A. and Gillespie, D.F. (1995) 'Introducing network analysis into the social work curriculum', *The Journal of Applied Social Sciences*, 19 (2): 107–19.

Napier, L. and Fook, J. (eds) (2000) *Breakthroughs in Practice: Social workers theorise critical moments in practice*. London: Whiting & Birch.

Narayan, N. (2005) 'An ordinary love', *Social Identities*, 11 (4): 395–412.

Nash, R. (1999) 'Bourdieu, "habitus", and educational research: Is it all worth the candle?', *British Journal of Sociology of Education*, 20 (2): 175–88.

Nehamas, A. (1985) *Nietzsche: Life as literature*. Cambridge, MA: Harvard University Press.

Newman, T. (2002) *Developing Evidence Based Practice in Social Care: Locating, appraising and using research findings on effectiveness*. Exeter: Barnardo's Centre for Evidence-Based Social Services, University of Exeter.

Newman, T. and McNeish, D. (2005) 'Promoting evidence-based practice in a child care charity: The Barnardo's experience', in A. Bilson (ed.), *Evidence-based Practice in Social Work*. London: Whiting & Birch.

Nicholson, L. (ed.) (1990) *Feminism/Postmodernism*. London: Routledge.

Nietzsche, F. (W. Kaufman and R.J. Hollingdale trans.) (1968) *The Will to Power*. New York: Vintage.

Nietzsche, F. (R.J. Hollingdale trans.) (1997, 1876) *Untimely Meditations*. New York: Cambridge University Press.

Niskanen, W.A. (1987) 'Bureaucracy', in C.K. Rowley (ed.), *Democracy and Public Choice*. Oxford: Blackwell.

Noble, G. and Watkins, M. (2003) 'So, how did Bourdieu learn to play tennis?: Habitus, consciousness and habituation', *Cultural Studies*, 17 (3/4): 520–38.

Nylund, D. (2006) 'Critical multiculturalism, whiteness, and social work: Towards a more radical view of cultural competence', *Journal of Progressive Human Services*, 17 (2): 27–42.

Oakley, A. (1972) *Sex, Gender and Society*. London: Temple Smith.

Oakley, A. (1994) 'Who cares for health?: Social relations, gender, and public health', *Journal of Epidemiology and Community Health*, 48: 427–34.

Oakley, A. (2005) 'Science, gender and women's liberation', *The Ann Oakley Reader*. Bristol: Policy Press.

O'Brien, C.A. (1994) 'The social organization of lesbian, gay, and bisexual youth in group homes and youth shelters', *Canadian Review of Social Policy*, 34: 37–57.

O'Brien, M. (2007) *A Crisis of Waste: Understanding the rubbish society*. Abingdon: Routledge.

O'Brien, M. and Penna, S. (1998) *Theorising Welfare: Enlightenment and modern society*. London: Sage. Chapter 3.

O'Brien, M., Penna, S. and Hay, C. (1998) *Theorising Modernity: Reflexivity, environment and identity in Gidden's social theory*. London: Longman.

O'Brien, M. and Yar, M. (2008) *Criminology: The key concepts*. Abingdon: Routledge

Ochocka, J. and Lord, J. (1998) 'Support clusters: A social network approach for people with complex needs', *Journal of Leisurability*, 25 (4): 14–22.

Odem, M. (1995) *Delinquent Daughters: Protecting and policing adolescent female sexuality in the United States, 1885–1920*. Chapel Hill, NC: University of North Carolina.

Ohmer, M.L. and Korr, W.S. (2006) 'The effectiveness of community practice interventions: A review of the literature', *Research on Social Work Practice*, 16 (2): 132–45.

Oliver, M. and Sapey, B. (2006) *Social Work with Disabled People*. Basingstoke: Palgrave Macmillan.

O'Reilly, M. (2005) '"Active noising": The use of noises in talk, the case of onomatopoeia, abstract sounds, and the functions they serve in therapy', *Text*, 25 (6): 745–62.

Orme, J. (1994) 'Violent women', in C. Lupton and T. Gillespie (eds), *Working with Violence*. Basingstoke: Macmillan.

Orme, J. (2001) *Gender and Community Care: Social work and social care perspectives*. Basingstoke: Palgrave Macmillan.

Orme, J. (2002a) 'Feminist social work', in R. Adams, L. Dominelli and M. Payne (eds), *Social Work: Themes, issues and critical debates*. Basingstoke: Palgrave Macmillan.

Orme, J. (2002b) 'Social work: Gender, care and justice', *British Journal of Social Work*, 32: 799–814.

Orme, J. (2003) '"It's feminist because I say so!"': Feminism, social work and critical practice, *Qualitative Social Work*, 2 (2): 131–53.

Orme, J., Dominelli, L. and Mullender, A. (2000) 'Domestic violence: Working with men from a feminist perspective', *International Social Work*, 43 (1): 69–105.

Osvaldsson, K. (2004) 'On laughter and disagreement in multiparty assessment talk', *Text*, 24 (4): 517–45.

Ovenden, K. (2000) 'The politics of protest', *Socialist Review*, 242, at: http://pubs.socialistreview index.org.uk/sr242/ovenden.htm

Park, Y. (2005) 'Culture as deficit: A critical discourse analysis of the concept of culture in contemporary social work discourse', *Journal of Sociology and Social Welfare*, 32 (3): 11–33.

Parsons, T. (1937) *The Structure of Social Action: A study in social theory with special reference to a group of recent European writers*, Volumes 1 and 2. New York: The Free Press.

Parton, N. (1994a) 'Problematics of government: (Post) modernity and social work', *British Journal of Social Work*, 24: 9–32.

Parton, N. (1994b) 'The nature of social work under conditions of (post)modernity', *Social Work and Social Sciences Review*, 5 (2): 93–112.

Parton, N. (1996) 'Social work, risk and "the blaming system"', in N. Parton (ed.), *Social Theory, Social Change and Social Work*. London: Routledge.

Parton, N. (2003) 'Rethinking professional practice: The contribution of social constructionism and the feminist "ethic of care"', *British Journal of Social Work*, 33: 1–16.

Parton, N. (2008) 'Changes in the form of knowledge in social work: From the "social" to the "informational"', *British Journal of Social Work*, 38 (2): 253–69.

Parton, N. and O'Byrne, P. (2000) *Constructive Social Work*. Basingstoke: Palgrave Macmillan.

Pateman, C. (1987) 'Critiques of the public/private dichotomy', in A. Phillips (ed.), *Feminism and Equality*. Oxford: Blackwell.

Pawson, R. (2006) *Evidence-based Policy: A realist perspective*. London: Sage.

Pawson, R., Boaz, A., Grayson, L., Long, A. and Barnes, C. (2003) *Types and Quality of Knowledge in Social Care*. London: Social Care Institute for Excellence.

Payne, M. (1996) *What is Professional Social Work?* Birmingham: Venture Press.

Payne, M. (2005) *Modern Social Work Theory*. Basingstoke: Palgrave Macmillan.

Pease, B. and Fook, J. (eds) (1999) *Transforming Social Work Practice: Postmodern critical perspectives*. London: Routledge.

Peillon, M. (1998) 'Bourdieu's field and the sociology of welfare', *Journal of Social Policy*, 27 (2): 213–29.

Penna, S. and O'Brien, M. (2006) 'What price health and social care?: Commodities, competition and consumers', *Social Work & Society*, 4 (2), at: www.socwork.net/2006/2/articles/pennaobrien

Peräkylä, A. (1998) 'Authority and accountability: The delivery of diagnosis in primary health care', *Social Psychology Quarterly*, 61 (4): 301–20.

Phillips, D. (1990) 'Postpositivistic science: Myths and realities', in E. Guba (ed.), *The Paradigm Dialog*. Newbury Park, CA: Sage.

Phillips, J. (2005) *The Marquis De Sade: A very short introduction*. Oxford: Oxford University Press.

Philp, M. (1979) 'Notes on the form of knowledge in social work', *Sociological Review*, 27 (1): 83–111.

Phillips, D. (1990) 'Postpositivistic science: Myths and realities', in E. Guba (ed.), *The Paradigm Dialog*. Newbury Park, CA: Sage.

Phillips, J. (2005) *The Marquis De Sade: A very short introduction*. Oxford: Oxford University Press.

Pileggi, M.S. and Patton, C. (2003) 'Bourdieu and cultural studies', *Cultural Studies*, 17 (3/4): 313–25.

Pincus, F.L. (2006) *Understanding Diversity: An introduction to class, race, gender, and sexual orientation*. Boulder, CO: Lynne Rienner Publishers.

Pithouse, A. and Atkinson, P. (1988) 'Telling the case: Occupational narrative in a social work office', in N. Coupland (ed.), *Styles of Discourse* Beckenham: Croom Helm.

Plant, R. (1973) *Social and Moral Theory in Casework*. London: Routledge & Kegan Paul.

Plath, D. (2006) 'Evidence-based practice: Current issues and future directions', *Australian Social Work*, 59 (1): 56–72.

Polansky, N.A., Ammons, P.W. and Weathersby, B.L. (1983) 'Is there an American standard of child care?', *Social Work*, 23 (5): 341–7.

Polanyi, M. (1967) *The Tacit Dimension*. New York: Doubleday.

Pollio, D.E. (2006) 'The art of evidence based practice', *Research on Social Work Practice*, 16 (2): 224–32.

Pollner, M. (1974) 'Mundane reasoning', *Philosophy of the Social Sciences*, 4: 35–54.

Popkewitz, T. (1990) 'Whose future?: Whose past?', in E. Guba (ed.), *The Paradigm Dialog*. Newbury Park, CA: Sage.

Pozzuto, R. (2000) 'Notes on a possible critical social work', *Critical Social Work*, 1 (1), at: www.criticalso cialwork.com (click on Volume, Volume 1, No.1).

Psathas, G. (1995) *Conversation Analysis: The study of talk-in-interaction*. Thousand Oaks, CA: Sage.

Putnam, R.D. (2000) *Bowling Alone: The collapse and revival of American community*. New York: Simon & Schuster.

Rasmussen, M.L. (2006) '*Play School*, melancholia and the politics of recognition', *British Journal of Sociology of Education*, 27 (4): 473–87.

Rattansi, A. (2004) 'Dialogues on difference: Cosmopolitans, locals, and "Others" in a post-national age', *Sociology*, 38 (3): 613–21.

Rawls, A.W. (2006) 'Respecifying the study of social order: Garfinkel's transition from theoretical conceptualization to practices in details', in H. Garfinkel (ed.), *Seeing Sociologically: The routine grounds of social action*, Boulder, CO: Paradigm Publishers. pp. 1–97.

Razack, N. and Jeffrey, D. (2002) 'Critical race discourse and tenets for social work', *Canadian Social Work Review*, 19 (2): 257–71.

Reid, W.J. (1988) 'Service effectiveness and the social agency', in R. Patti, J. Poertner, and C. Rapp (eds), *Managing for Effectiveness in Social Welfare Organizations*. New York: Haworth.

Reid, W.J. (1994) 'Reframing the epistemological debate', in E. Sherman and W.J. Reid (eds), *Qualitative Research in Social Work*. New York: Columbia University Press.

Reid, W.J. (2001) 'The role of science in social work: The perennial debate', *Journal of Social Work*, 1 (3): 273–93.

Reid, W.J. and Shyne, A. (1969) *Brief and Extended Casework*. New York: Columbia University Press.

Reisch, M. and Andrews, J. (2002) *The Road not Taken: A history of radical social work in the United States*. New York: Brunner-Routledge.

Rhodes, L. (1991) *Emptying the Beds: The work of an emergency psychiatric unit*. Berkeley, CA: University of California Press.

Richardson, D. (1996) 'Heterosexuality and social theory', in D. Richardson (ed.), *Theorizing Heterosexuality*. Buckingham: Open University Press. pp. 1–20.

Robinson, V. (1949) *Dynamics of Supervision under Functional Controls: A professional process in social casework*. Philadelphia, PA: University of Pennsylvania Press.

Rorty, R. (1989) *Contingency, Irony and Solidarity*. Cambridge: Cambridge University Press.

Rossiter, A. (1996) 'A perspective on critical social work', *Journal of Progressive Human Services*, 7 (2): 23–41.

Rossiter, A. (2000) 'The postmodern feminist condition: New conditions for social work', in B. Fawcett, B. Featherstone, J. Fook and A. Rossiter (eds), *Practice Research in Social Work: Postmodern feminist perspectives*. London: Routledge.

Rowbotham, S. (1983) *Dreams and Dilemmas: Collected writings*. London: Virago

Rowbotham, S. (1992, 1973) 'Women's consciousness: Man's world', in M. Humm (ed.), *Feminisms: A reader*. London: Harvester Wheatsheaf.

Ruan, D., Freeman, L.C., Dai, X., Pan, Y. and Zhang, W. (1997) 'On the changing structure of social networks in urban China', *Social Networks*, 19: 75–89.

Rubin, A. and Parrish, D. (2007) 'Views on evidence-based practice', *Research on Social Work Practice*, 17 (1): 110–22.

Sabia, D.R. and Wallulis, J. (1983) *Changing Social Science: Critical theory and other critical perspectives*. Albany, NT: State University of New York Press.

Sackett, D.L., Richardson, W.S., Rosenberg, W. and Haynes, R.B. (1997) *Evidence-based Medicine: How to practice and teach EBM*. New York: Churchill Livingstone.

Sacks, H. (G. Jefferson ed. and Introduction by E.A. Schegloff) (1995) *Lectures on Conversation*, Volumes I and II. Cambridge, MA: Blackwell.

Sacks, H., Schegloff, E.A. and Jefferson, G. (1974) 'A simplest systematics for the organization of turn-taking for conversation', *Language*, 50: 696–735.

Said, E.W. (2003) *Orientalism*. London: Penguin Books.

Saleebey, D. (ed.) (2002) *The Strengths Perspective in Social Work Practice* (3rd edn). Boston, MA: Allyn & Bacon.

Salih, S. (2004) 'Introduction', in S. Salih and J. Butler (eds), *The Judith Butler Reader*. Oxford: Blackwell.

Salmon, W.C. (2007, 1967) 'The problem of induction', in J. Perry, M. Bratman and J.M. Fischer (eds), *Introduction to Philosophy: Classical and contemporary readings*. New York: Oxford University Press.

Sands, R. and Nuccio, K. (1992) 'Postmodern feminist theory and social work', *Social Work*, 37 (6): 481–576.

Sarup, M. (1993) *An Introductory Guide to Post-structuralism and Postmodernism*. Hemel Hempstead: Prentice Hall/Harvester Wheatsheaf.

Satzewich, V. (ed.) (1998) *Racism & Social Inequality in Canada: Concepts, controversies & strategies of resistance*. Toronto, ON: Thompson Educational Publishing.

Sawyer, K. (2002) 'A discourse on discourse: An archeological history of an intellectual concept', *Cultural Studies*, 16 (3): 433–56.

Schaeffer, N. (1999) *The Marquis de Sade: A life*. New York: Knopf.

Schegloff, E.A. (1992) 'On talk and its institutional occasions', in P. Drew and J. Heritage (eds), *Talk at Work: Interaction in institutional settings*. Cambridge: Cambridge University Press. pp. 101–34.

Schegloff, E.A. (1997) 'Whose text?: Whose context?', *Discourse and Society*, 9 (3): 457–60.

Schegloff, E.A. (2007) *Sequence Organization in Interaction: A primer in conversation analysis*, Volume 1. Cambridge: Cambridge University Press.

Schegloff, E.A., Jefferson, G. and Sacks, H. (1977) 'The preference for self-correction in the organization of repair in conversation', *Language*, 53: 361–82.

Schinkel, W. (2003) 'Pierre Bourdieu's political turn?', *Theory, Culture and Society*, 20 (6): 69–93.

Schön, D. (1983) *The Reflective Practitioner: How professionals think in action*. New York: Basic Books.

Schulz, A. (2005) *Goya's Caprichos: Aesthetics, perception and the body*. New York: Cambridge University Press.

Schuster, L. and Solomos, J. (2002) 'Rights and wrongs across European borders: Migrants, minorities, and citizenship', *Citizenship Studies*, 6 (1): 37–54.

Schütz, A. (1962a, b, c) *Collected Papers I, II, III: The problem of social reality*. The Hague: Martinus Nijhoff.

Schütz, A. (1973) 'Multiple realities', in M. Natanson (ed.), *Alfred Schütz Collected Papers I: The problem of social reality*. The Hague: Martinus Nijhoff. pp. 207–59.

Schwandt, T. (1997) 'Evaluation as practical hermeneutics', *Evaluation*, 3 (1): 69–83.

Schwartz, H. (1976) 'On recognizing mistakes: A case of practical reasoning in psychotherapy', *Philosophy of the Social Sciences*, 6: 55–73.

Scott, D. (2002) 'Adding meaning to measurement: The value of qualitative methods in practice research', *British Journal of Social Work*, 32: 923–30

Scott, J. (1988) 'Trend report social network analysis', *Sociology*, 22 (1): 109–27.

Scott, J. (1991) *Social Network Analysis: A handbook*. London: Sage.

Scourfield, J. (2002) *Gender and Child Protection*. Basingstoke: Palgrave Macmillan.

Scourfield, J. and Welsh, I. (2003) 'Risk, reflexivity and social control in child protection: New times or same old story?', *Critical Social Policy*, 23 (3): 398–420.

Scriven, M. (1997) 'Truth and objectivity in evaluation', in E. Chelimsky and W. Shadish (eds), *Evaluation for the 21st Century*. Thousand Oaks, CA: Sage.

Seed, P. (1987) *Applied Social Network Analysis: A set of tools for social services research and practice: Information pack*. Tunbridge Wells: Costello Publishers.

Seed, P. (1990) *Introducing Network Analysis in Social Work*. London: Jessica Kingsley.

Segal, L. (1987) *Is the Future Female?* London: Virago.

Segal, L. (1990) *Slow Motion: Changing masculinities and changing men*. London: Virago.

Selman, R.L. (1980) *The Growth of Interpersonal Understanding*. New York: Academic Press.

Sewpaul, V. (2004) 'Ethics and deconstruction', *Social Work*, 40: 218–31.

Sharrock, W. (2000) 'Where the simplest systematics fits: A response to Michael Lynch's "The ethnomethodological foundations of conversation analysis"', *Text*, 20 (4): 533–9

Sharrock, W. and Button, G. (1991) 'The social actor: Social action in real time', in G. Button (ed.), *Ethnomethodology and the Human Sciences*. Cambridge: Cambridge University Press.

Shaw, I. (1996) *Evaluating in Practice*. Aldershot: Ashgate.

Shaw, I. (1999a) 'Evidence for practice', in I. Shaw and J. Lishman (eds), *Evaluation and Social Work Practice*. London: Sage. pp.14–40.

Shaw, I. (1999b) *Qualitative Evaluation*. London: Sage.

Shaw, I (1999c) 'Seeing the trees for the wood: The politics of evaluating in practice', in B. Broad (ed.), *The Politics of Research and Evaluation*. Birmingham: Venture Press.

Shaw, I. (2003) 'Cutting edge issues in social work research', *British Journal of Social Work*, 33: 107–20.

Shaw, I. (2006) 'The human services', in I. Shaw, J. Greene and M. Mark (eds), *Sage Handbook of Evaluation*. London: Sage.

Shaw, I. and Gould, N. (2001) *Qualitative Research in Social Work*. London: Sage.

Shaw, I. and Norton, M. (2007) *Kinds and Quality of Social Work Research*. London: Social Care Institute for Excellence.

Shaw, I. and Shaw, A. (1997a) 'Keeping social work honest: Evaluating as profession and practice', *British Journal of Social Work*, 27 (6): 847–69.

Shaw, I. and Shaw, A. (1997b) 'Game plans, buzzes and sheer luck: Doing well in social work', *Social Work Research*, 21 (2): 69–79.

Sheldon, B. (1986) 'Social work effectiveness experiments: Review and implications', *British Journal of Social Work*, 6: 223–42.

Sheldon, B. (2001) 'The validity of evidence-based practice in social work: A reply to Stephen Webb', *British Journal of Social Work*, 31 (6): 801–9.

Shildrick, M. and Price, J. (1996) 'Breaking the boundaries of the broken body', *Body and Society*, 2 (4): 93–113.

Singer, J. (2005) 'Understanding racism through the eyes of African American male student-athletes', *Race, Ethnicity, and Education*, 8 (4): 365–86.

Silverman, D. (1998) *Harvey Sacks: social science and conversation analysis*. New York: Oxford University Press.

Sinclair, T. (2005) 'Mad, bad or sad? Ideology, distorted communication and child abuse prevention', *Journal of Sociology*, 41: 227–46.

Skerrett, D. (2000) 'Social work: A shifting paradigm', *Journal of Social Work Practice*, 14: 63–73.

Skoll, G. (1992) *Walk the Walk and Talk the Talk: Ethnography of a drug abuse treatment center facility*. Philadelphia, PA: Temple University Press.

Slembrouck, S. (2006) 'What is meant by "discourse analysis"' at: http://bank.ugent.be/da/da.htm

Slembrouck, S. and Hall, C. (2003) 'Caring but not coping: Fashioning a legitimate parent identity', in C. Hall, K. Juhila, N. Parton and T. Pösö (eds), *Constructing Clienthood in Social Work and Human Services: Interaction, identities and practices*. London: Jessica Kingsley. pp. 44–61.

Sluga, H. (2005) 'Foucault's encounter with Heidegger and Nietzsche', in G. Gutting (ed.), *The Cambridge Companion to Foucault* (2nd edn). New York: Cambridge University Press. pp. 210–39.

Smalley, R. (1967) *Theory for Social Work Practice*. New York: Columbia University Press.

Smart, C. (2007) *Personal Life: New directions in sociological thinking*. Cambridge: Polity Press.

Smart, C. and Neale, B. (1999) *Family Fragments?* Cambridge: Polity Press.

Smart, C. and Shipman, B. (2004) 'Visions in monochrome: Families, marriage and the individualization thesis', *The British Journal of Sociology*, 55 (4): 491–509.

Smith, C. (2001) 'Trust and confidence: Possibilities for social work in "high modernity"', *British Journal of Social Work*, 31: 287–305.

Smith, C. and White, S. (1997) 'Parton, Howe and postmodernity: A critical comment on mistaken identity', *British Journal of Social Work*. 27: 275–95.

Smith, D. (1987) *The Everyday World as Problematic: A feminist sociology*. Toronto, ON: University of Toronto Press.

Smith, D. (1990) *The Conceptual Practices of Power: A feminist sociology of knowledge*. Toronto, ON: University of Toronto Press.

Smith, D. (2004a) 'Introduction: Some versions of evidence-based practice', in D. Smith (ed.), *Social Work and Evidence-based Practice*. London: Jessica Kingsley. pp. 7–27.

Smith, D. (ed.) (2004b) *Social Work and Evidence-based Practice*. London: Jessica Kingsley.

Snijders, T.A.B., Steglich, C.E.G., Schweinberger, M. and Huisman, M. (2005) *Manual for SIENA version 2.1*. Groningen: ICS, Department of Sociology. Also at: http://stat.gamma.rug.nl/snijders/siena.html

Solas, J. (2002) 'The poverty of postmodern human services', *Australian Social Work*, 55 (2): 128–35.

Soroka, S., Johnston, R. and Banting, K. (2007) 'Ties that bind? Social cohesion and diversity in Canada', in K. Banting, T. Courchene and L. Seidle (eds), *Belonging?: Diversity, recognition and shared citizenship in Canada*. Montreal, QC: Institute for Research on Public Policy. pp. 561–600.

Spratt, T. and Houston, S. (1999) 'Developing critical social work in theory and practice: Child protection and communicative reason', *Child and Family Social Work*, 4: 1–10.

Stabile, C.A. and Morooka, J. (2003) 'Between two evils, I refuse to choose the lesser evil', *Cultural Studies*, 17 (3/4): 326–48.

Stake, R. and Schwandt, T.A. (2006) 'On discerning quality in evaluation', in I. Shaw, J. Greene and M. Mark (eds), *Sage Handbook of Evaluation*. London: Sage. Chapter 18.

Stake, R. and Trumbull, D. (1982) 'Naturalistic generalizations', *Review Journal of Philosophy and Social Science*, 7: 1–12.

Stanley, L. and Wise, S. (eds) (1990) *Feminist Praxis: Research, theory and epistemology*. London: Routledge.

Stanley, L. and Wise, S. (2000) 'But the empress has no clothes!: Some awkward questions about the "missing revolution" in feminist theory', *Feminist Theory*, 1 (3): 261–89.

Stocker, S.S. (2001) 'Problems of embodiment and problematic embodiment (significance for disability studies)', *Hypatia*, 16 (3): 30.

Stone, H. (2006) *Tables of Knowledge: Descartes in Vermeer's studio*. Ithaca, NY: Cornell University Press.

Stones, R. (2005) *Structuration Theory*. Basingstoke: Palgrave.

Swigonski, M. (1993) 'Feminist standpoint theory and questions of social work research', *Affilia*, 8 (2): 171–83.

Taft, J. (1944) *Functional Approach to Family Casework*. Philadelphia, PA: University of Pennsylvania Press.

Taylor, C. (1994) 'The politics of recognition', in C. Taylor and A. Gutmann (eds), *Multiculturalism*. Princeton, NJ: Princeton University Press. pp. 25–74.

Taylor, C. (2006) 'Narrating significant experience: Reflective accounts and the production of (self) knowledge', *British Journal of Social Work*, 36 (2): 189–206.

Taylor, C. and Gutmann, A. (eds) (1997) *Multiculturalism*. Princeton, NJ: Princeton University Press. pp. 3–24.

Taylor, C. and White, S. (2000) *Practising Reflexivity in Health and Welfare: Making knowledge*. Buckingham: Open University Press.

ten Have, P. (1999) *Doing Conversation Analysis: A practical guide*. Thousand Oaks, CA: Sage.

Thyer, B.A. (2002) 'Evidence-based practice and clinical social work', *Evidence Based Mental Health*, 5: 6–7.

Timms, E. (1983) 'On the relevance of informal social networks to social work intervention', *British Journal of Social Work*, 13 (1): 405–15.

Tomlinson, J.A. (1992) *Goya in the Twilight of Enlightenment*. New Haven, CT: Yale University Press.

Toulmin, S. (1958) *The Uses of Argument*. Cambridge: Cambridge University Press.

Townsend, E. (1998) *Good Intentions Overruled: A critique of empowerment in the routine organization of mental health services*. Toronto, ON: University of Toronto Press.

Trevillion, S. and Green, D. (1998) 'The co-operation concept in a team of Swedish social workers: Applying grid and group to studies of community care', in I.R. Edgar and A. Russell (eds), *The Anthropology of Welfare*. London: Routledge.

Tsang, A. and George, U. (1998) 'Towards an integrated framework for cross-cultural social work practice', *Canadian Social Work Review*, 15 (1): 73–93.

Tullock, G. (1989) *The Economics of Special Privilege and Rent-seeking*. Boston, MA, and Dordrecht, Netherlands: Kluwer Academic Publishers.

Turner, J. (1988) *A Theory of Social Interaction*. Cambridge: Polity Press.

Turner, R. (1972) 'Some formal properties of therapy talk', in D. Sudnow (ed.), *Studies in Social Interaction*. New York: The Free Press. pp. 367–96.

UK Department of Health (1999) *The National Service Framework for Mental Health*. London: TSO.

Ungerson, C. (1987) *Policy is Personal: Sex, gender and informal care*. London: Tavistock.

Unrau, Y.A., Gabor, P.A. and Grinnell, R.M. (2007) *Evaluation in Social Work: The art and science of practice*. New York: Oxford University Press.

Upshur, R.E.G., Van Den Kerkhof, E.G. and Goel, V. (2001) 'Meaning and measurement: An inclusive model of evidence in health care', *Journal of Evaluation in Clinical Practice*, 7 (2): 91–9.

Valente, T.W. (1995) *Network Models of the Diffusion of Innovations*. Cresskill, NJ: Hampton Press.

Valente, T.W. (1996) 'Social network thresholds in the diffusion of innovations', *Social Networks*, 18 (1): 69–89.

van der Poel, M.G.M. (1993) 'Delineating personal support networks', *Social Networks*, 15 (1): 49–70.

Vehviläinen, A. (2003) 'Avoiding providing solutions: Orienting to the ideal of students' self-directedness in counselling interaction', *Discourse Studies*, 5 (3): 389–414.

Wacquant, L.J.D. (1998) 'Pierre Bourdieu', in R. Stones (ed.), *Key Sociological Thinkers*. Houndsmill: Palgrave.

Wagner, D. (1993) *Checkerboard Square: Culture and resistance in a homeless community*. Boulder, CO: Westview Press.

Warburton, B. and Black, M. (2002) 'Evaluating processes for evidence-based health care in the National Health Service', *British Journal of Clinical Governance*, 7 (3): 158–64.

Walsh, J. (1994) 'Gender differences in social networks of persons with severe mental illnesses', *Affilia*, 9 (3): 247–68.

Ware, N.C., Tugenberg, T., Dickey, B. and McHorney, C.A. (1999) 'An ethnographic study of the meaning of continuity of care in mental health services', *Psychiatric Services*, 50 (3): 395–400.

Warren, L. (1998) 'Considering the culture of community care: Anthropological accounts of the experiences of frontline carers, older people and a researcher', in I.R. Edgar and A. Russell (eds), *The Anthropology of Welfare*. London: Routledge.

Wasserman, S. and Faust, K. (1994) *Social Network Analysis: Methods and applications*. Cambridge: Cambridge University Press.

Watson, D.R. (1981) 'Conversational and organisational uses of proper names: an aspect of counsellor-client interaction', in P. Atkinson and C. Heath (eds), *Medical Work: Realities and routines*. Farnborough: Gower. pp. 91–106.

Wearing, B. (ed.) (1986) *Gender Reclaimed: Feminist theory and social work*. Sydney: Hale & Iremonger.

Webb, S.A. (2001) 'Some considerations on the validity of evidence-based practice in social work', *British Journal of Social Work*, 31: 57–79.

Webb, S.A. (2002) 'Evidence-based practice and decision analysis in social work: An implementation model', *Journal of Social Work*, 2 (1): 45–63.

Webb, S.A. (2006) *Social Work in a Risk Society*. Basingstoke: Palgrave Macmillan.

Weedon, C. (1999) *Feminism, Theory and the Politics of Difference*. Oxford: Blackwell.

Weinberg, D. (2005) *Of Others Inside: Insanity, addiction and belonging in America*. Philadelphia, PA: Temple University Press.

Wellman, B. (1926) 'The school child's choice of companions', *Journal of Educational Research*, 14: 126–32.

Wellman, B. (1979) 'The community question: The intimate networks of East Yorkers', *American Journal of Sociology*, 84: 1201–31.

Wellman, B. (1988) 'Structural analysis: From method and metaphor to theory and substance', in B. Wellman and S.D. Berkowitz (eds), *Social Structures: A network approach*. Cambridge: Cambridge University Press.

Wellman, B. and Berkowitz, S.D. (eds), *Social Structures: A network approach*. Cambridge: Cambridge University Press.

Wellman, B. and Wortley, S. (1990) 'Different strokes from different folks: Community ties and social support', *American Journal of Sociology*, 96: 558–88.

Wendell, S. (1996) *The Rejected Body: Feminist philosophical reflections on disability*. New York: Routledge.

West, C. (1996) 'Ethnography and orthography: A modest methodological proposal', *Journal of Contemporary Ethnography*, 25 (3): 327–52.

Wetherell, M. (1998) 'Positioning and interpretive repertoires: Conversation analysis and post-structuralism in dialogue', *Discourse and Society*, 9 (3): 387–412.

Whelehan, I. (1995) *Modern Feminist Thought: From second wave to 'post-feminism'*. Edinburgh: Edinburgh University Press.

White, P. (2003) 'Sex education; or, how the blind became heterosexual', *GLQ: A Journal of Lesbian and Gay Studies*, 9 (1–2): 133–147.

White, S. (1998) 'Examining the artfulness of risk talk', in A. Jokinen, K. Juhila and T. Pösö (eds), *Constructing Social Work Practices*. Aldershot: Ashgate.

White, S. (2002) 'Accomplishing the case in paediatrics and child health: Medicine and morality in inter-professional talk', *Sociology of Health and Illness*, 24 (4): 409–35.

White, S. (2003) 'The social worker as moral judge: Blame, responsibility and case formulation', in C. Hall, K. Juhila, N. Parton and T. Pösö (eds), *Constructing Clienthood in Social Work and Human Services*. London: Jessica Kingsley.

White, S. (2006) 'Unsettling reflections: The reflexive practitioner as "trickster" in inter-professional work', in S. White, J. Fook and T. Gardner (eds), *Critical Reflection in Health and Social Care*. Buckingham: Open University Press.

White, S., Fook J. and Gardner F. (eds) (2006) *Critical Reflection in Health and Social Care*. Buckingham: Open University Press.

White, S. and Stancombe, J. (2003) *Clinical Judgement in the Health and Welfare Professions: Extending the evidence base*. Buckingham: Open University Press.

White, V. (1995) 'Commonality and diversity in feminist social work', *British Journal of Social Work*, 25: 143–56.

White, V. (2006) *The State of Feminist Social Work*. London: Routledge.

Whitebook, J. (2005) 'Against interiority: Foucault's struggle with psychoanalysis', in G. Gutting (ed.), *The Cambridge Companion to Foucault* (2nd edn). New York: Cambridge University Press. pp. 312–47.

Wiles, P. (1957) 'Property and equality', in G. Watson (ed.), *The Unservile State: Essays in liberty and welfare*. London: George Allen & Unwin.

Williams, C. (2006) 'The epistemology of cultural competence', *Families in Society*, 87 (2): 209–20.

Williams, F. (1996) 'Postmodernism, feminism and the question of difference', in N. Parton (ed.), *Social Theory, Social Change and Social Work*. London: Routledge.

Willumsen, E. and Skivenes, M. (2005) 'Collaboration between service users and professionals: Legitimate decisions in child protection: A Norwegian Model', *Child and Family Social Work*, 19: 197–206.

Wilson, A. and Beresford, P. (2002) 'Madness, distress and postmodernity: Putting the record straight', in M. Corker and T. Shakespeare (eds), *Disability/Postmodernism: Embodying disability theory*. London: Continuum.

Wilson, E. (1977) *Women and the Welfare State*. London: Tavistock.

Wise, S. (1990) 'Becoming a feminist social worker', in L. Stanley and S. Wise (eds), *Feminist Praxis: Research, theory and epistemology*. London: Routledge.

Witkin, S. (1991) 'Empirical clinical practice: A critical analysis', *Social Work*, 36 (2): 158–63.

Witkin, S. (1996) 'If empirical practice is the answer, then what is the question?', *Social Work Research*, 20 (2): 69–75.

Wittgenstein, L. (1961) *Tractatus Logico-philosophicus*. London: Routledge.

Wolcott, H. (2001) *The Art of Fieldwork*. Walnut Creek, CA: AltaMira.

Wolf, N. (1999) *Fire with Fire: The new female power and how it will change the 21st century*. London: Chatto & Windus.

Wolfreys, J. (2000) 'In perspective: Pierre Bourdieu', *International Socialism Journal*, 87, at: http://pubs.socialistreviewindex.org.uk/isj87/wolfreys.htm

Wolfreys, J. (2002) 'Pierre Bourdieu: Voice of resistance', *International Socialism Journal*, 94, at: http://pubs.socialistreviewindex.org.uk/isj94/wolfreys.htm

Wollstonecraft, M. (1975, 1792) *A Vindication of the Rights of Woman*. Harmondsworth: Penguin.

Wood, M. and James, C. (2005) 'Multicultural education in Canada: Opportunities, limitations, and contradictions', in C. James (ed.), *Possibilities and Limitations: Multicultural policies and programs in Canada*. Halfax, NS: Fernwood Publishing. pp. 93–107.

Wooffitt, R. (2005) *Conversation Analysis and Discourse Analysis: A comparative and critical introduction*. London: Sage.

Woolgar, S. (ed.) (1988) *Knowledge and Reflexivity: New frontiers in the sociology of knowledge*. London: Sage.

Woolgar, S. and Pawluch, D. (1985) 'Ontological gerrymandering: The anatomy of social problems explanations', *Social Problems*, 32 (3): 214–27.

Wynn, R. and Wynn, M. (2005) 'Empathy as an interactionally achieved phenomenon in psychotherapy: Characteristics of some conversational resources', *Journal of Pragmatics*, 38: 1385–97.

Yan, M. and Wong, Y. (2005) 'Rethinking self-awareness in cultural competence: Toward a dialogic self in cross-cultural social work', *Families in Society*, 86 (2): 181–8.

Yip, K. (2006) 'Reflectivity in social work practice with clients with mental health illness', *International Social Work*, 49: 245–55.

Young, I.M. (1990) *Justice and the Politics of Difference*. Princeton, NJ: Princeton University Press.

Yuen-Tsang, A.W.K. (1999) 'Chinese communal support networks', *International Social Work*, 42 (3): 359–71.

Zimmerman, D.H. (1976) 'Record-keeping and the intake process in a public welfare agency', in S. Wheeler (ed.), *On Record: Files and dossiers in American life*. New Brunswick, NJ: Transaction Books. pp. 319–54.

Index